Sommaire Rom

Trois rubriques en lien avec chaque unité de ton manuel :

- ***Workshop* :** un atelier avec une règle animée pour comprendre et des activités pour t'entraîner en grammaire.
- ***Storytelling* :** une histoire animée à découvrir pour chaque thème !
- ***Discovery Game* :** un jeu pour mémoriser quelques repères de civilisation anglo-saxonne tout en t'amusant. Sauras-tu battre le chronomètre ?

Unit 1

Workshop: Used to
Storytelling: **Lamb to the slaughter**
Discovery Game: Guess what?

Unit 2

Workshop: *Le double comparatif*
Storytelling: **Pilgrims**
Discovery Game: Guess what?

Unit 3

Workshop: *Le* present perfect *en* be + *BV*-ing
Storytelling: **Dian Fossey's world**
Discovery Game: Crosswords

Unit 4

Workshop: *Le* past perfect
Storytelling: **Rosa Parks**
Discovery Game: Crosswords

Unit 5

Workshop: *Le conditionnel*
Storytelling: **Frankenstein**
Discovery Game: Crosswords

Unit 6

Workshop: Reported speech
Storytelling: **Memories of a prom night**
Discovery Game: Guess what?

Et aussi : Un jeu pour réviser 100 **verbes irréguliers**.
Une activité pour découvrir 16 **expressions utiles**.

Let's Step in 3e

PALIER 2 NIVEAUX A2/B1

Evelyne GERMAIN
Coordinatrice
Lycée Jules-Ferry, Coulommiers

Sylvie BASSO
Collège François-Mitterrand, Créon

Nathalie HOLLINKA-ROUSSELLE
Collège Beau-Soleil, Chelles

Nathalie VEZON
Collège Gérard-Philippe, Bagnols-sur-Cèze

Sandy LOCKHART
Formatrice au Greta Tertiaire Nord 77

Nicolas KASPRZYK
Collège et lycée Notre-Dame-de-Sion, Paris
Chargé de cours à l'Université Paris IV

HATIER

Conception graphique : L'Ovale Design, Dany Mourain

Mise en page : Dany Mourain, L'Ovale Design

Illustrations : Alteau (p. 175), Matthew Broersma (p. 116), Johanna Crainmark (p. 131), Didier Crombez (pp. 124-125, 130, 132), Mathieu Maillefer (pp. 63, 134-137), Philippe Mouche (pp. 12-13, 15-17, 24, 37-41, 47-54, 68-89, 102-105), Clémence Paldacci (pp. 117-120), Benoît Springer (pp. 14, 21, 29-36, 44, 60-62, 92-93).

Iconographie : Brigitte Célérier / Hatier Illustrations

Cartographie : Légendes Cartographie

Relecture : Martine Solsonna, Collège Saint-Exupéry, Perpignan

Corrections : Valérie Sper-Benet

CD-Rom :

Studio son : Vincent Bund

Illustrations : Benjamin Bécue, Mathieu Maillefer.

PRÉFACE

***Let's Step in* 3e** permet à tous les élèves de consolider leurs connaissances et de progresser à leur rythme tout en marquant nettement son positionnement de passerelle vers la classe de seconde.

Présentation de la méthode

***Let's Step in* 3e** a pour visée de favoriser l'expression sous toutes ses formes, écrite ou orale, en plaçant tous les élèves au cœur de situations de communication.
Pour cela, la méthode met à disposition des enseignants des **supports authentiques** variés : photos, gravures, articles de presse, extraits de fiction, dépliants, interviews... dans l'esprit du **Cadre Européen Commun de Référence pour les Langues**. Elle est accompagnée d'un **CD classe**, d'un **DVD** et de **transparents**, en lien étroit avec les activités de classe.

Structure du manuel

Le manuel s'ouvre sur un ***Welcome Back*** : l'élève réactive ses connaissances du Palier 1 et de la classe de 4e. Suivent six ***Units***, chacune centrée sur un thème culturel conforme au programme et à l'esprit d'ouverture du Palier 2.

● Les *Units* ont été construites pour permettre au professeur de choisir différents parcours de consolidation ou d'approfondissement, en s'appuyant sur les propositions du *Fichier pédagogique* :
- La double page d'**ouverture** permet à l'élève d'entrer dans la *Unit* de façon active.
- Le ***Step 1*** permet de réactiver des connaissances indispensables pour la validation de A2 pour le Brevet des collèges.
- Le ***Step 2*** vise spécifiquement les apports fondamentaux du programme de 3e.
- Le ***Step 3*** permet de réinvestir ces acquis et introduit des apports langagiers complémentaires.
Chaque *Step* se conclut par une tâche appelant l'élève à réactiver l'essentiel.
- Dans les deux ***Projects***, proposés en fin d'unité, l'élève réinvestit les objectifs communicationnels de la *Unit* dans une réalisation concrète pouvant servir à valider des compétences du B2i.

● Différents outils sont à disposition dans le manuel pour construire l'autonomie de l'élève.
- ***Focus on*** permet, avec les rubriques *Scanning* et *Webquest*, un approfondissement actif du contenu culturel de la *Unit*, et l'élève y développe des compétences de lecture rapide et sélective.
- ***Remember and Practise*** propose une explication claire des objectifs grammaticaux des *Steps*, et des exercices d'entraînement contextualisés.
- La rubrique ***Words*** lui permet de travailler la dérivation et l'inférence, et d'acquérir des compétences transférables.
- La **Méthodologie**, activée dans les ***Steps*** et développée en fin de manuel, aide l'élève dans la réalisation des tâches (écrire un e-mail, téléphoner...).
- Les activités du ***Workbook***, dont la rubrique ***To make it short***, encouragent l'élève à sélectionner et hiérarchiser les informations recueillies. L'élève réfléchit systématiquement sur les faits de langue grâce à la PRL et peut évaluer ses acquis linguistiques avec *Let's Recap*.

● Le CD Audio-Rom élève intégré au manuel est divisé en deux parties.
La **partie audio** contient les compréhensions de l'oral centrales des ***Steps*** et les ***Sounds*** du *Textbook*.
La **partie rom** propose des récits animés pour un entraînement à la compréhension de l'oral, des règles illustrées pour les principaux points de grammaire, accompagnées d'exercices de difficulté graduée, et des activités de découverte culturelle.

● Des outils d'évaluation sont mis à la disposition du professeur et de l'élève :
- Dans le manuel, le ***Checkpoint*** permet un point en fin de *Unit* sur les cinq activités langagières.
- ***My Passport*** permet d'évaluer chacune des compétences communicationnelles (A2- B1), en lien avec le manuel. L'apport culturel de chaque *Unit* est également clairement évalué.
- Le **Fichier pédagogique** propose un ***Extra-Checkpoint*** évaluant les cinq activités langagières aux niveaux A2 et B1 à la fin de chaque *Unit*.

Nous espérons que ***Let's Step in* 3e** vous aidera à accompagner efficacement vos élèves dans leur apprentissage de l'anglais !

Les auteurs.

Déroulement d'une unité

Les 3 Steps

Step 1 • Consolider tes acquis.

Objectif de la page
Deux pages pour **revoir** les structures essentielles.

Sounds
Pour t'entraîner à la prononciation, avec des exercices dans ton *Workbook* et sur ton CD.

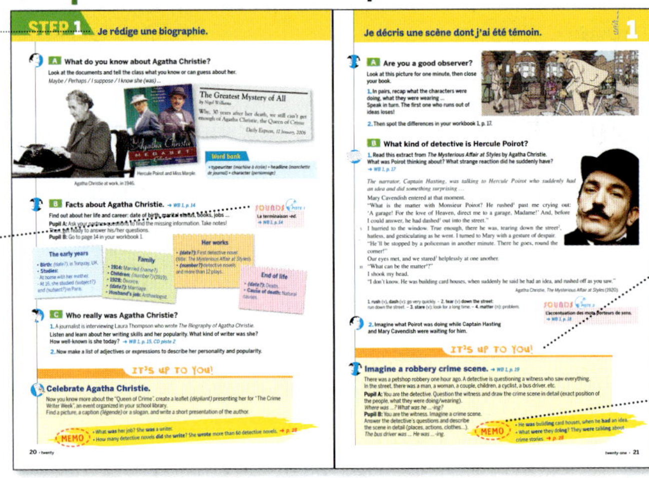

It's up to you!
Une activité communicative pour réutiliser ce que tu as appris sur la page.

MEMO
Pour te rappeler les points à réactiver.

Step 2 • Apprendre de nouvelles structures au programme.

Objectif de la double page

Get ready!
Pour découvrir un thème et une structure nécessaires pour avancer dans le *Step*.

Step forward!
Pour apprendre les structures nouvelles à partir d'un document écrit ou sonore.

Enregistré sur ton CD.

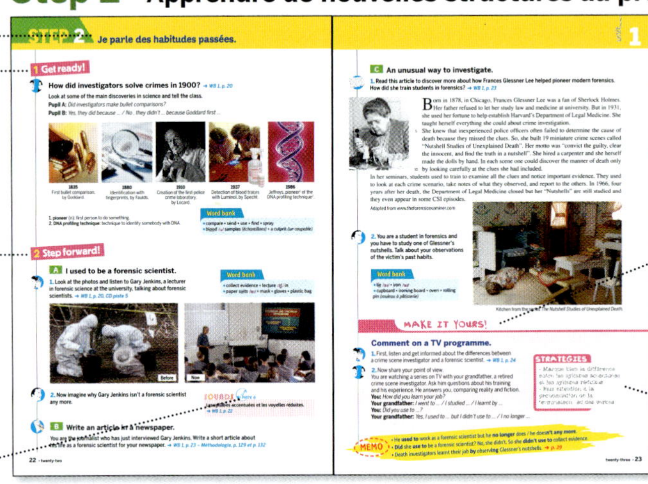

Make it yours!
Pour réutiliser ce que tu as appris dans une tâche concrète.

Strategies
Des astuces pour t'aider à réussir l'activité proposée.

Step 3 • Approfondir les objectifs des *Steps 1* et *2*.

Objectif de la double page

Step forward!
Des documents, écrits ou sonores, pour te préparer progressivement à la seconde.

Word bank
Des mots-clés pour prendre la parole.

Quelques aides lexicales pour comprendre le vocabulaire difficile.

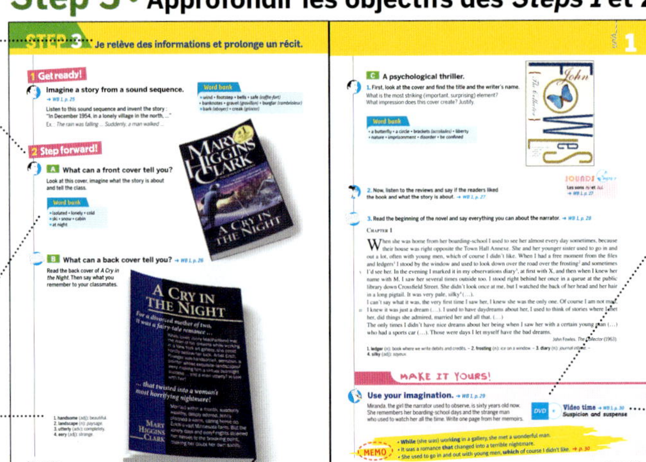

Video time
Des extraits vidéo, accompagnés d'une fiche d'exploitation dans ton *Workbook*.

Des renvois à la **méthodologie** pour trouver des conseils utiles.

Comprendre les pictogrammes.

- Production orale en continu
- Compréhension de l'écrit
- Compréhension de l'oral
- Production orale en interaction
- Production écrite

Focus on

Découvrir des points culturels ou de civilisation.

Pour élargir tes connaissances culturelles et civilisationnelles sur des pays anglophones vus dans la *Unit*.

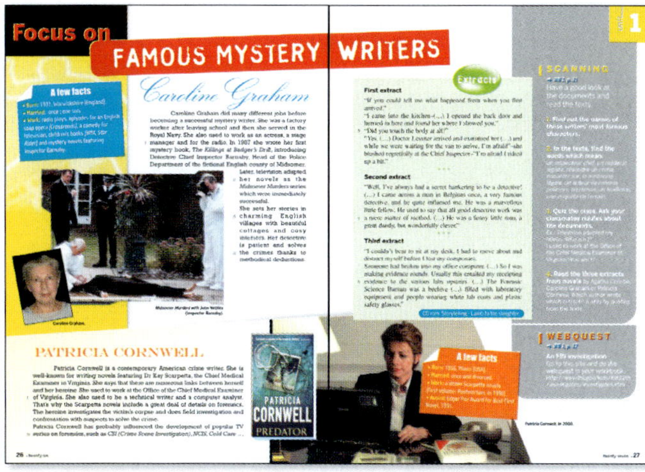

Scanning

Pour t'entraîner à comprendre l'essentiel d'un texte.

Webquest

Pour prolonger le travail de la *Unit* sur internet avec une fiche guide dans ton *Workbook*.

Remember and practise

T'entraîner.

3 pages pour réviser les structures vues dans chaque *Step*.

Des explications simples et des exercices en contexte.

Des renvois au **Mémento**, pour trouver plus d'explications et d'exercices.

D'autre activités dans la partie **Rom** de ton CD.

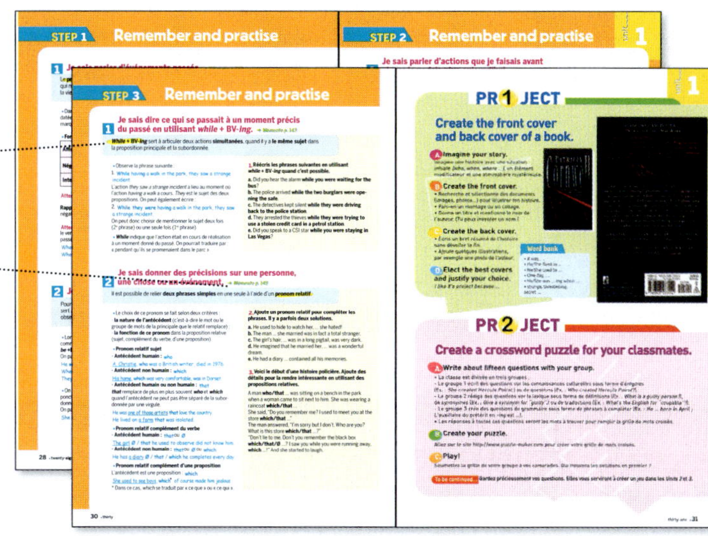

Projects

Pour réinvestir tout ce que tu as appris dans la *Unit*.

Le ***Project 1*** porte spécifiquement sur la *Unit*.

Le ***Project 2*** peut être fait de façon indépendante, ou se construire sur trois *Units* pour réaliser un projet final de plus grande envergure.

Words

Words

Pour revoir et mémoriser le vocabulaire du thème de la *Unit*.

Play on words

Pour apprendre à construire des mots et acquérir plus de vocabulaire de manière autonome.

Checkpoint

Faire le point pour avancer.

Pour faire le point sur les cinq activités langagières et te préparer à valider le niveau A2 et B1.

Workbook

Les activités du *workbook* accompagnent celles du manuel. Ton professeur t'indiquera celles qui sont à faire en classe ou à la maison.

Pour comprendre et t'entraîner

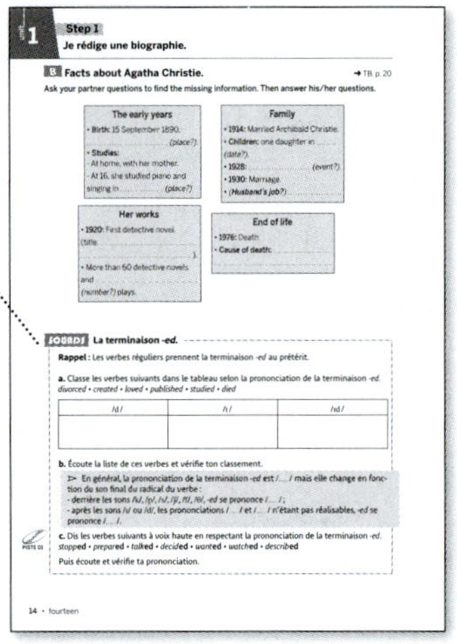

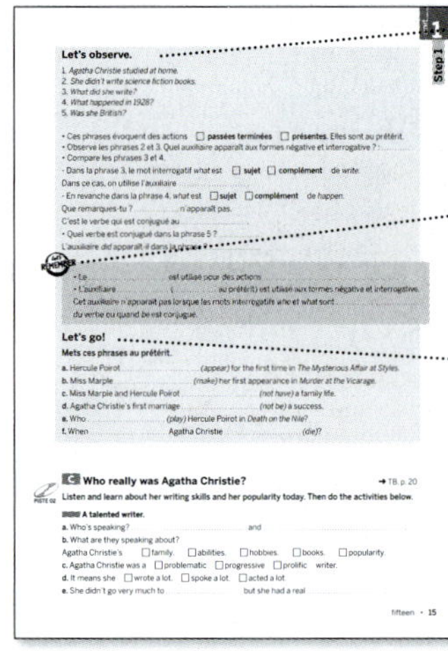

Sounds
Pour travailler ta prononciation grâce à ton CD.

Let's observe
Pour réfléchir sur la langue et comprendre les structures étudiées.

Let's remember
Pour bien mémoriser ces structures.

Let's go!
Pour utiliser la structure étudiée dans un exercice.

Pour guider ton travail

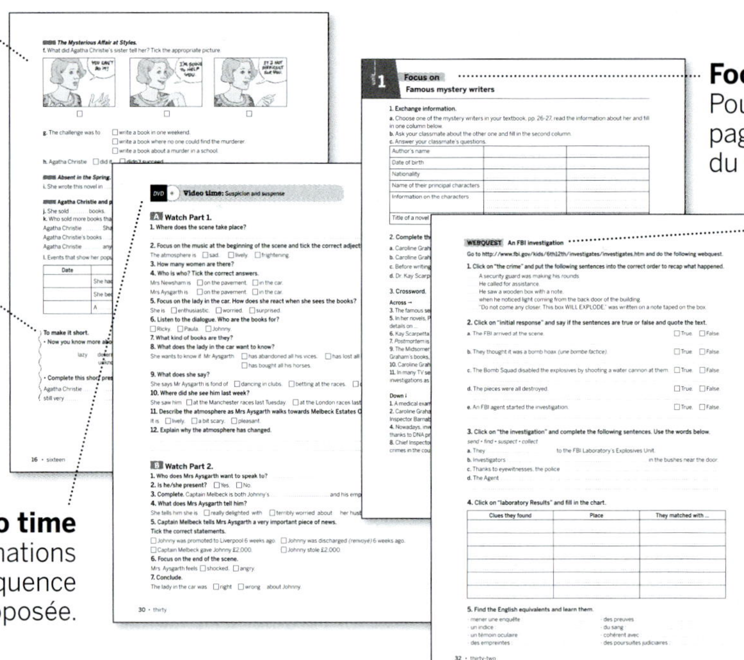

Des **exploitations** pour guider ta compréhension des documents audio ou écrits.

To make it short
Pour synthétiser les informations essentielles du document étudié et les retenir.

Video time
Pour repérer les informations essentielles de la séquence vidéo proposée.

Focus on
Pour guider ta lecture des pages *Focus on* du manuel.

Webquest
Pour t'accompagner dans la recherche d'informations sur les sites internet proposés.

Pour t'auto-évaluer

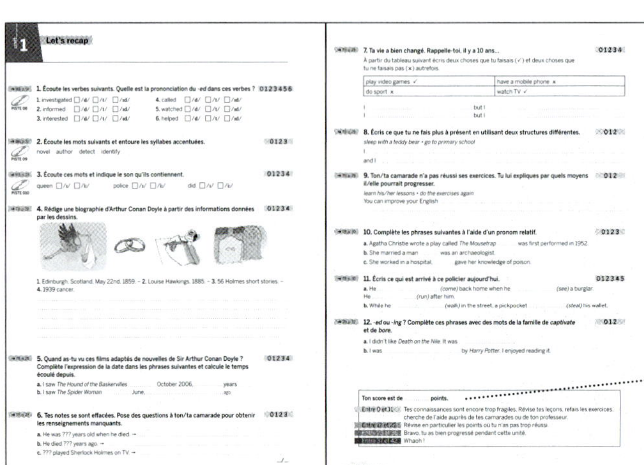

Let's recap
Pour vérifier l'acquisition de tes connaissances à la fin de chaque *Unit*.

Tu peux mesurer tes progrès en fonction du score que tu obtiens et guider ainsi tes révisions.

My Passport

Pour faire le point sur tes acquis de l'année.

Une partie **Civilisation** que tu pourras remplir au fur et à mesure de l'année pour rassembler les informations sur les pays, les villes, les personnes ou les événements abordés dans le manuel.

Des pages **Test** où tu répondras à des questionnaires ludiques pour réfléchir à tes habitudes d'écoute, de parole, d'expression écrite ou orale.

Des grilles d'**auto-évaluation** pour faire le point régulièrement sur ton niveau A2 ou B1 dans les différentes compétences travaillées.

CD Audio-Rom

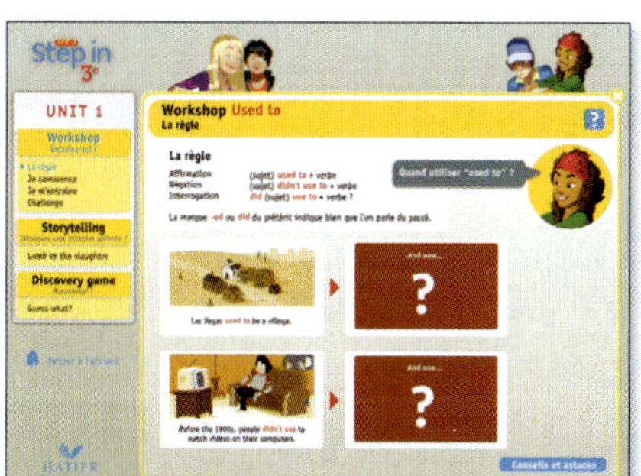

Workshop
Des règles animées et des exercices simples pour revoir les points de grammaire tout en t'amusant !

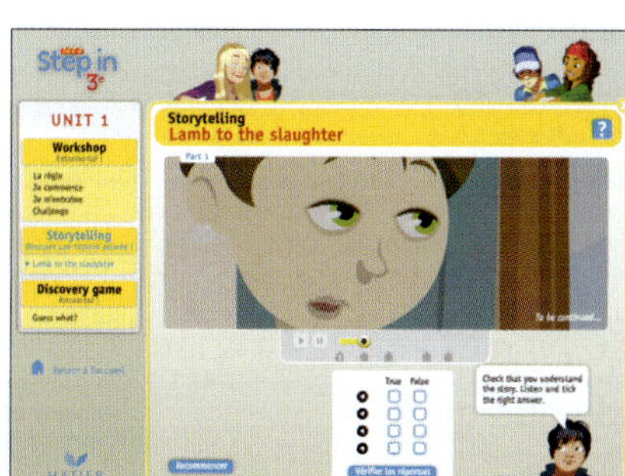

Storytelling
Des histoires enregistrées et animées pour t'entraîner à la compréhension de l'oral.

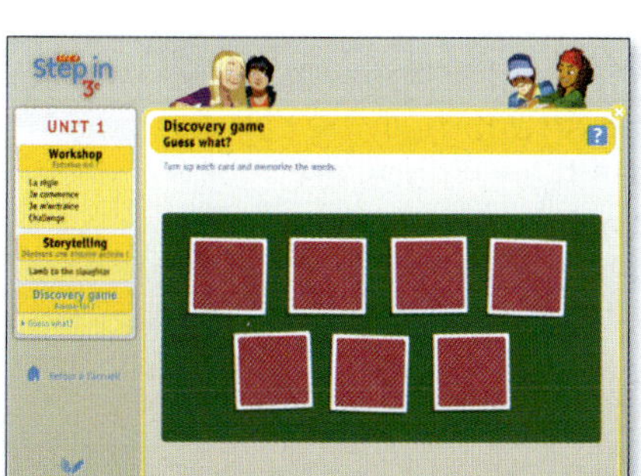

Discovery Game
Des jeux chronométrés pour t'aider à mémoriser des éléments culturels et linguistiques.

En plus : des activités pour réviser les **verbes irréguliers** et découvrir des **expressions utiles**.

Sommaire

OUTILS FONCTIONNELS	OUTILS LINGUISTIQUES	OUTILS PHONOLOGIQUES
• Décrire quelqu'un. • Exprimer une probabilité. • Décrire une action en cours. • Décrire une maison. • Parler d'habitudes. • Exprimer des interdictions et des permissions. • Donner des directions. • Faire des suggestions. • Parler de ses intentions.	• Les adjectifs composés • La probabilité *(must / may / can)* • Le présent *be* + BV-*ing* • *There is / are* • Le présent simple • L'obligation et la permission *(must / have to / can)* • L'interdiction et la permission *(be forbidden to / be allowed to)* • *What about...? / Why don't you...?* • *be going to* + BV	
• Se renseigner sur la vie et la personnalité d'un auteur. • Évoquer le passé d'un personnage. • Décrire une scène et ce qui s'y passait. • Parler de l'évolution d'un métier. • Faire référence à des actions simultanées.	• Le prétérit simple • Le prétérit *be* + BV-*ing* • *Used to* + BV Rom • *Not any more / no longer* • *By* + BV-*ing* (expression du moyen) • *While* • Les propositions relatives	• La terminaison -*ed* • Accentuation des mots porteurs de sens • Syllabes accentuées et voyelles réduites • Les sons /ɪ/ et /iː/
• Décrire comment une société est organisée. • Évoquer ce que quelqu'un a subi. • Évoquer des motivations. • Parler de progression.	• Le passif présent • Le passif au prétérit • L'expression du but (*to* + BV) • Le double comparatif (*more and more*) Rom • Les quantifieurs *many / few / much ...* • Le gérondif • Le passif à deux compléments	• Le suffixe –*tion* • La diphtongue /ɪə/ • Les accents américain et britannique
• Évoquer des expériences. • Donner des détails sur des expériences. • Évoquer l'investissement de quelqu'un dans un projet. • Évoquer des contraintes exercées.	• Le *present perfect* • Le superlatif • Le *present perfect* vs le prétérit • *for / since* • Le *present perfect* en *be* + BV-*ing* Rom • *Want someone to* + BV • Les composés de *some / any / no* • *Make someone do something* • Le *present perfect* passif	• La prononciation du *th* • Les liaisons • Les sons /ɔː/ et /əʊ/

Sommaire

OBJECTIFS DE COMMUNICATION ET TÂCHES	CONTENUS CULTURELS

unit 4 Living together p. 66-81

unit 5 Another place, another time ... p. 82-97

unit 6 Celebrations p. 98-113

ANNEXES

Story time

OUTILS FONCTIONNELS	OUTILS LINGUISTIQUES	OUTILS PHONOLOGIQUES
• Parler d'obligations et d'interdictions passées. • Évoquer ce qui était possible ou non. • Parler de ce qui était permis. • Évoquer une situation antérieure à une autre. • Organiser des idées pour débattre. • Évoquer le contexte d'une situation antérieure à une autre.	• *Have to* + BV / *be allowed to* + BV au passé • *Be able to* + BV au passé • Les déterminants *(a, the, Ø)* • *Let somebody do something* • Le *past perfect* Rom • Les mots de liaison *(although, however, whereas, that's why)* • Le *past perfect* en *be* + BV-*ing*	• Les sons /æ/ et /ɑː/ • Les sons /ʌ/ et /ɜː/ • La prononciation de *the*
• Expliquer ce que l'on fera, pourra ou devra faire. • Donner des conseils. • Évoquer une situation imaginaire. • Mettre quelqu'un en garde. • Faire des suppositions sur ce qui est arrivé.	• Le futur (*will* + BV) • Les subordonnées de temps *(when, as soon as ...)* • L'obligation et la capacité au futur *(will have to / will be able to)* • *Should* • Le conditionnel : *If I were..., I would* Rom • *Had better* • La probabilité passée (*must have* + participe passé) • Les pronoms réfléchis	• La prononciation de *ou* • Les lettres muettes • La prononciation de *of*
• Rapporter ce que quelqu'un est en train de dire. • Rapporter ce que quelqu'un a dit. • Rapporter ce qui s'est passé. • Émettre des souhaits. • Mettre en valeur certaines informations.	• Le discours indirect (verbes introducteurs au présent) • Le discours indirect (verbes introducteurs au passé • 1) Rom • Le discours indirect (verbes introducteurs au passé • 2 : concordance des temps) Rom • *I wish I could ...* • La forme emphatique	• La prononciation du *u* • L'accent tonique avec les suffixes -*ese* et -*ian* • L'accentuation des mots composés

Welcome back!

A Meeting the host family.

1. Kyle, a young teenager from Binger, a very small town in Oklahoma (USA), is going to spend a few weeks with a host family in London. Read the e-mail his host family sent him. → *WB 1, p. 3*

What do they look like? Who will come and pick him up? When? Where?

Print | Answer | Ans. to all | Resend | Delete

From: ASAD PATEL
Object: Heathrow

Our_Family.jgp | See attachment | Download attachment

Dear Kyle,
As agreed, I'm going to pick you up at Heathrow airport tomorrow at 9:45 a.m. with my wife, our fifteen-year-old daughter and our six-year-old son.
I have attached a photo to help you recognize us at the airport. In this photo I'm on the right next to my daughter Sharmila, who is the dark-haired girl in the back. My father's holding our son Jawad and you can see Neelam, my wife, on the left. The black-haired girl in front is Sharmila's cousin, Niral! She might come with us tomorrow.
Looking forward to seeing you. Have a good flight.
Asad Patel

2. Use the information in the e-mail to find out the identity of the people in the photo.

Word bank

- sari (traditional dress for Hindu women)
- pigtails *(couettes)*
- cross her arms • smile

B Arrival at the airport.

→ *WB 1, p. 3*

When Kyle arrives, he phones his mother. Listen to their conversation. What is Kyle's problem? Who came to the airport to pick him up?

IT'S YOUR TURN!

Describe a friend or someone in your family.
Tom is a dark-haired boy ... / He is a blue-eyed teenager ...

C Discovering Brick Lane.

1. This is where the Patels live. Look at the photographs for one minute, shut your book and say everything you can remember. → Méthodologie, p. 128

There are ... on the left.
In the foreground, there is ...
A man is wearing/carrying ...

Word bank

- crowded • busy
- walk • talk • shop • have lunch
- shop signs

2. Mr Patel loves his neighbourhood. Listen to his conversation with Kyle. What kind of restaurants are there in Brick Lane? Why? → *WB 1, p. 4*

DVD **Video time**
Discover more about Brick Lane.

D A curry restaurant. → *WB 1, p. 4*

1. Read this advert for a curry restaurant. What are its strong points?

2. Listen to this conversation between Mr Patel, his cousin Kalim, and Kyle. What is Kalim's daily routine?

Eating Indian food is a delicate matter for many. A lot of the food is high in calories and can be very greasy.
Try our restaurant. The food tastes really good, even better than in other restaurants. Our chef cooks his curries in the oven* and keeps oil to a minimum because he uses the natural fat of the meat.

*oven (n): *four.*

IT'S YOUR TURN!

Describing a typical day.

What do you do on a typical Wednesday? Ask five questions to your classmate and answer his/her questions. Then report about your classmate's habits.

Pupil A: *What time ...? / When ...? / Do you ...? How ...?*
Pupil B: *I ... from ... to ... / Before ...*
Pupil A: *He/She gets up at ... / He/She doesn't ... after ...*

Word bank

- wake up • have breakfast / lunch / dinner • go out • practise / do sport • do your homework • cook

Welcome back!

E A description of Kyle's house.

Listen to Kyle describing his house.
Then look at these photographs.
Which one is Kyle's house? → *WB 1, p. 6*

Word bank

- detached • semi-detached
- floors • front garden • back garden • flat
- quiet • noisy

IT'S YOUR TURN!

Renting a place.

Your family wants to rent a house. Ask the real estate agent *(agent immobilier)* about what is important for you.
How many ... are there? / Is there a ...? / Are there any ...?
Your classmate answers your questions.

F Helping with the housework.

Listen to Sharmila explaining who does what at home. → *WB 1, p. 6*

IT'S YOUR TURN!

Helping with the housework. → *WB 1, p. 7*

Ask your classmate what he/she does to help his/her parents at home.
Do you often ...? / Do you sometimes ...?

Then recap to the class.
Anna/Tom never ... / He/she ... twice a week / every day.
His/her mother often ...

Word bank

- tidy your room • dust *(dépoussiérer)* • wash the car • do the cooking • clean the windows • make your bed • go shopping

G Discovering some English school rules. → WB 1, p. 7

1. Look at the note Sharmila's school gave her and say what is allowed or forbidden to do. Imagine what is forbidden to wear.

Word bank
- a watch • earrings • flip-flops *(tongs)* • bandanas • gloves • winter scarves

Our school is a place for learning and students must be dressed appropriately.

- **Remember that all pupils must wear the school uniform:**
  - a blazer, white shirt, school tie, black trousers and black shoes for boys;
  - a skirt, a school tie, white long-sleeved blouses*, navy V-necked sweaters with school logo, black leather shoes for girls.
- **Pupils are forbidden to use electronic devices** (including mobile phones and iPod/MP3 players, etc.) during the school day.
  All pupils must turn off their electronic devices from the time they enter the building in the morning until 1:55 p.m.
  Please do not call or text message your child during the school day.

***blouse** (n): *chemisier.*

2. Listen to Kyle and Sharmila speaking about the dress codes in their schools. What is Kyle allowed to wear in his school?

IT'S YOUR TURN!

Talking about dress codes.

You are in a host family in England. Your correspondent is telling you what you are allowed or are forbidden to wear and do in his/her school. Tell him/her about the dress code in your school in France.

Pupil A: You are the English correspondent.
Pupil B: You are the French correspondent.

Welcome back!

H Taking the tube in London.

1. What is an Oyster card? Why is it a good idea to get one?

Why should I have one?

Faster: Oyster saves you time–no more queuing for tickets as you can pay in advance.
Easier: Your Oyster card is reusable–just top it up with cash or renew your Travelcard/Bus Pass when needed.
Cheaper: Oyster single fares are always cheaper than cash.

2. Sharmila and a friend of hers are talking to Kyle about this card. What do they like about it? Where can you get one? → *WB 1, p. 8*

I Meeting someone at a tube station.

1. Kyle's host family lives near Shoreditch tube station. It's Saturday afternoon, he has to meet Sharmila at London Bridge station. Use the map and say how he can get there.

He has to take the ... line. / He can get off at the ... stop.

* **DLR:** Docklands Light Railway.

2. Sharmila is phoning Kyle to tell him how to get to London Bridge. What lines does he have to take? → *WB 1, p. 9*

IT'S YOUR TURN!

Giving directions.

Your friend is at Farringdon station and wants to meet you at Bermondsey station. He's phoning you. Tell him/her what lines to take.

Welcome back!

J Visiting the best places around London.

1. **You're preparing a trip to London. What do you know about the places on the photos? What are you interested in and why? Suggest places to visit during your next trip.**

What/How about going to York? We can ... and I am keen on ...
Could we go / Why don't we go to Leicester? We can ... there.

Word bank

- be keen on / be fond of / be crazy about
- can't stand / can't bear / hate

Warwick Castle

The Houses of Parliament

Brighton Pavilion

Shakespeare Museum

2. **Read the message Mr Patel sent on the Internet and the answers he received. What places do people suggest he visits with Kyle?** → *WB 1, p. 9*

Answer Classify Quote Print

From: Asad Patel — We are receiving an American teenager for a few months. Of course we are planning to show him the well-known monuments in London but have you got any suggestions on places to visit with a 15-year-old teenager, outside London?

From: Amar — How about spending a day in Brighton? The Pavilion is worth a visit. Or you can try the orb-run: you go down the hills in a sort of giant balloon. Big thrills for sure!

From: Peter White — How about spending a day in Stratford-upon-Avon and visiting the Shakespeare Museum? Warwick Castle is not far and is worth visiting too. Teenagers are usually fond of castles and knights.
Peter

3. **Listen to Kyle and Sharmila talking about their plans for tomorrow. What are they going to do?** → *WB 1, p. 9*

IT'S YOUR TURN!

Informing tourists. → *WB 1, p. 10*

You are working at the tourist office in London. Visitors ask you for information about places to visit in and around London. Suggest the best places to visit with their kids. Then, they tell you what they are going to do.

CASINO
UP TO 98%
PAYBACK ON DOLLAR SLOTS
SINGLE DECK "21"
10¢ ROULETTE

unit 1

From detective stories to thrillers

STEP 1

Je rédige une biographie.
Je décris une scène dont j'ai été témoin.

STEP 2

Je parle des habitudes passées.

STEP 3

Je relève des informations et prolonge un récit.

Focus on: FAMOUS MYSTERY WRITERS

PROJECTS

1. Create the front cover and back cover of a book.
2. Create a crossword puzzle for your classmates.

CHECKPOINT

Starter

Play the detective: solve this murder mystery.

A rich man was found murdered one Sunday morning. His wife immediately called the police. The police questioned the wife and staff in the hall. The following alibis were given:

- The wife declared she was in bed reading a book.
- The cook said she was cooking breakfast.
- The gardener claimed he was planting seeds.
- The daughter said she was getting the mail.
- The maid explained she was cleaning the windows.

The police instantly arrested the murderer.

Who did it? And how did the police know?

STEP 1 Je rédige une biographie.

A What do you know about Agatha Christie?

Look at the documents and tell the class what you know or can guess about her.

Maybe / Perhaps / I suppose / I know she (was) ...

Agatha Christie at work, in 1946.

Hercule Poirot and Miss Marple.

The Greatest Mystery of All
by Nigel Williams

Why, 30 years after her death, we still can't get enough of Agatha Christie, the Queen of Crime?

Daily Express, 12 January, 2006

Word bank

- **typewriter** *(machine à écrire)* • **headline** *(manchette de journal)* • **character** *(personnage)*

B Facts about Agatha Christie. → WB 1, p. 14

Find out about her life and career: date of birth, marital status, books, jobs ...

Pupil A: Ask your partner questions to find the missing information. Take notes! Then, get ready to answer his/her questions.
Pupil B: Go to page 14 in your workbook 1.

SOUNDS PISTE 1
La terminaison *-ed.*
→ WB 1, p. 14

The early years
- **Birth:** *(date?)*, in Torquay, UK.
- **Studies:**
  - At home with her mother.
  - At 16, she studied *(subject?)* and *(subject?)* in Paris.

Family
- **1914:** Married *(name?)*.
- **Children:** *(number?)* (1919).
- **1928:** Divorce.
- ***(date?)*:** Marriage.
- **Husband's job:** Archaelogist.

Her works
- ***(date?)*:** First detective novel (title: *The Mysterious Affair at Styles*).
- ***(number?)*** detective novels and more than 12 plays.

End of life
- ***(date?)*:** Death.
- **Cause of death:** Natural causes.

C Who really was Agatha Christie?

1. A journalist is interviewing Laura Thompson who wrote *The Biography of Agatha Christie.*
Listen and learn about her writing skills and her popularity. What kind of writer was she? How well-known is she today? → WB 1, p. 15, CD piste 2

2. **Now make a list of adjectives or expressions to describe her personality and popularity.**

IT'S UP TO YOU!

Celebrate Agatha Christie.

Now you know more about the "Queen of Crime", create a leaflet *(dépliant)* presenting her for "The Crime Writer Week", an event organized in your school library.
Find a picture, a caption *(légende)* or a slogan, and write a short presentation of the author.

MEMO
- What **was** her job? She **was** a writer.
- How many detective novels **did** she **write**? She **wrote** more than 60 detective novels. → p. 28

Je décris une scène dont j'ai été témoin.

A Are you a good observer?

Look at this picture for one minute, then close your book.

1. **In pairs, recap what the characters were doing, what they were wearing ...**
Speak in turn. The first one who runs out of ideas loses!

2. **Then spot the differences in your workbook 1, p. 17.**

B What kind of detective is Hercule Poirot?

1. **Read this extract from *The Mysterious Affair at Styles* by Agatha Christie.**
What was Poirot thinking about? What strange reaction did he suddenly have?
→ *WB 1, p. 17*

The narrator, Captain Hasting, was talking to Hercule Poirot who suddenly had an idea and did something surprising ...

Mary Cavendish entered at that moment.
"What is the matter with Monsieur Poirot? He rushed[1] past me crying out: 'A garage! For the love of Heaven, direct me to a garage, Madame!' And, before I could answer, he had dashed[1] out into the street."
I hurried to the window. True enough, there he was, tearing down the street[2], hatless, and gesticulating as he went. I turned to Mary with a gesture of despair.
"He'll be stopped by a policeman in another minute. There he goes, round the corner!"
Our eyes met, and we stared[3] helplessly at one another.
"What can be the matter[4]?"
I shook my head.
"I don't know. He was building card houses, when suddenly he said he had an idea, and rushed off as you saw."

Agatha Christie, *The Mysterious Affair at Styles* (1920).

1. **rush** (v), **dash** (v): go very quickly. – 2. **tear** (v) **down the street**: run down the street. – 3. **stare** (v): look for a long time. – 4. **matter** (n): problem.

SOUNDS *PISTE 3*
L'accentuation des mots porteurs de sens.
→ *WB 1, p. 18*

2. **Imagine what Poirot was doing while Captain Hasting and Mary Cavendish were waiting for him.**

IT'S UP TO YOU!

Imagine a robbery crime scene. → *WB 1, p. 19*

There was a petshop robbery one hour ago. A detective is questioning a witness who saw everything.
In the street, there was a man, a woman, a couple, children, a cyclist, a bus driver, etc.

Pupil A: You are the detective. Question the witness and draw the crime scene in detail (exact position of the people, what they were doing/wearing).
Where was ...? What was he ...-ing?

Pupil B: You are the witness. Imagine a crime scene.
Answer the detective's questions and describe the scene in detail (places, actions, clothes...).
The bus driver was ... He was ...-ing.

MEMO
- He **was** build**ing** card houses, when he **had** an idea.
- What **were** they do**ing**? They **were** talk**ing** about crime stories. → *p. 28*

STEP 2 Je parle des habitudes passées.

1 Get ready!

How did investigators solve crimes in 1900? ➜ *WB 1, p. 20*

Look at some of the main discoveries in science and tell the class.

Pupil A: *Did investigators make bullet comparisons?*

Pupil B: *Yes, they did because ... / No , they didn't ... because Goddard first ...*

1835
First bullet comparison, by Goddard.

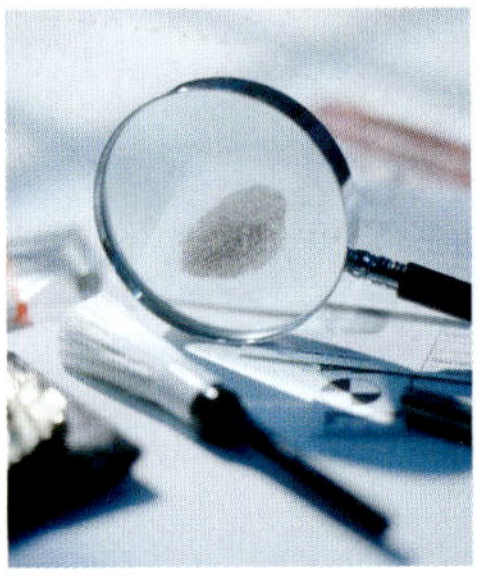

1880
Identification with fingerprints, by Faulds.

1910
Creation of the first police crime laboratory, by Locard.

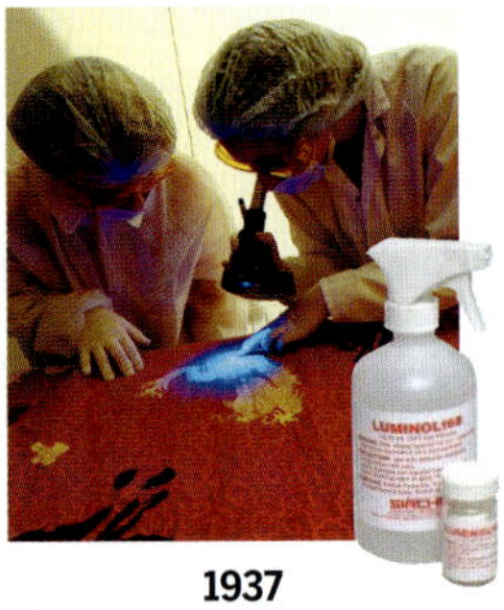

1937
Detection of blood traces with Luminol, by Specht.

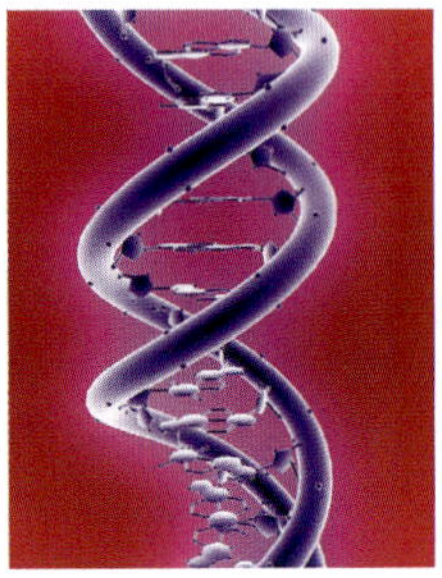

1986
Jeffreys, pioneer[1] of the DNA profiling technique[2].

1. **pioneer** (n): first person to do something.
2. **DNA profiling technique:** technique to identify somebody with DNA.

Word bank

- compare • send • use • find • spray
- bl<u>oo</u>d /ʌ/ samples *(échantillons)* • a culprit *(un coupable)*

2 Step forward!

A I used to be a forensic scientist.

1. Look at the photos and listen to Gary Jenkins, a lecturer in forensic science at the university, talking about forensic scientists. ➜ *WB 1, p. 20, CD piste 5*

Word bank

- collect evidence • lec<u>t</u>ure /tʃ/ in
- paper s<u>ui</u>ts /uː/ • mask • gloves • plastic bag

Before

Now

2. Now imagine why Gary Jenkins isn't a forensic scientist any more.

SOUNDS PISTE 6

Les syllabes accentuées et les voyelles réduites.
➜ *WB 1, p. 22*

B Write an article in a newspaper.

You are the journalist who has just interviewed Gary Jenkins. Write a short article about his life as a forensic scientist for your newspaper. ➜ *WB 1, p. 23 – Méthodologie, p. 129 et p. 132*

C An unusual way to investigate.

1. **Read this article to discover more about how Frances Glessner Lee helped pioneer modern forensics. How did she train students in forensics?** → *WB 1, p. 23*

Born in 1878, in Chicago, Frances Glessner Lee was a fan of Sherlock Holmes. Her father refused to let her study law and medicine at university. But in 1931, she used her fortune to help establish Harvard's Department of Legal Medicine. She taught herself everything she could about crime investigation.
She knew that inexperienced police officers often failed to determine the cause of death because they missed the clues. So, she built 19 miniature crime scenes called "Nutshell Studies of Unexplained Death". Her motto was "convict the guilty, clear the innocent, and find the truth in a nutshell". She hired a carpenter and she herself made the dolls by hand. In each scene one could discover the manner of death only by looking carefully at the clues she had included.
In her seminars, students used to train to examine all the clues and notice important evidence. They used to look at each crime scenario, take notes of what they observed, and report to the others. In 1966, four years after her death, the Department of Legal Medicine closed but her "Nutshells" are still studied and they even appear in some CSI episodes.

Adapted from www.theforensicexaminer.com

2. **You are a student in forensics and you have to study one of Glessner's nutshells. Talk about your observations of the victim's past habits.**

Word bank

- lie /aɪ/ • iron /aɪ/
- cupboard • ironing board • oven • rolling pin *(rouleau à pâtisserie)*

Kitchen from the series *The Nutshell Studies of Unexplained Death.*

MAKE IT YOURS!

Comment on a TV programme.

1. First, listen and get informed about the differences between a crime scene investigator and a forensic scientist. → *WB 1, p. 24*

2. Now share your point of view.
You are watching a series on TV with your grandfather, a retired crime scene investigator. Ask him questions about his training and his experience. He answers you, comparing reality and fiction.
You: *How did you learn your job?*
Your grandfather: *I went to ... / I studied ... / I learnt by ...*
You: *Did you use to ...?*
Your grandfather: *Yes, I used to ... but I didn't use to ... / I no longer ...*

STRATEGIES

- Marque bien la différence entre les syllabes accentuées et les syllabes réduites.
- Fais attention à la prononciation de la terminaison *-ed* des verbes.

MEMO

- He **used to** work as a forensic scientist but he **no longer** does / he does**n't any more**.
- **Did** she **use to** be a forensic scientist? No, she didn't. So she **didn't use to** collect evidence.
- Death investigators learnt their job **by** observ**ing** Glessner's nutshells. → *p. 29*

STEP 3 Je relève des informations et prolonge un récit.

1 Get ready!

Imagine a story from a sound sequence.

→ *WB 1, p. 25*

Listen to this sound sequence and invent the story :
"In December 1954, in a lonely village in the north, ..."
Ex. : *The rain was falling ... Suddenly, a man walked ...*

Word bank

- wind • footstep • bells • safe *(coffre-fort)*
- banknotes • gravel *(gravillon)* • burglar *(cambrioleur)*
- bark *(aboyer)* • creak *(grincer)*

2 Step forward!

A What can a front cover tell you?

Look at this cover, imagine what the story is about and tell the class.

Word bank

- isolated • lonely • cold
- ski • snow • cabin
- at night

B What can a back cover tell you? → *WB 1, p. 26*

Read the back cover of *A Cry in the Night*. Then say what you remember to your classmates.

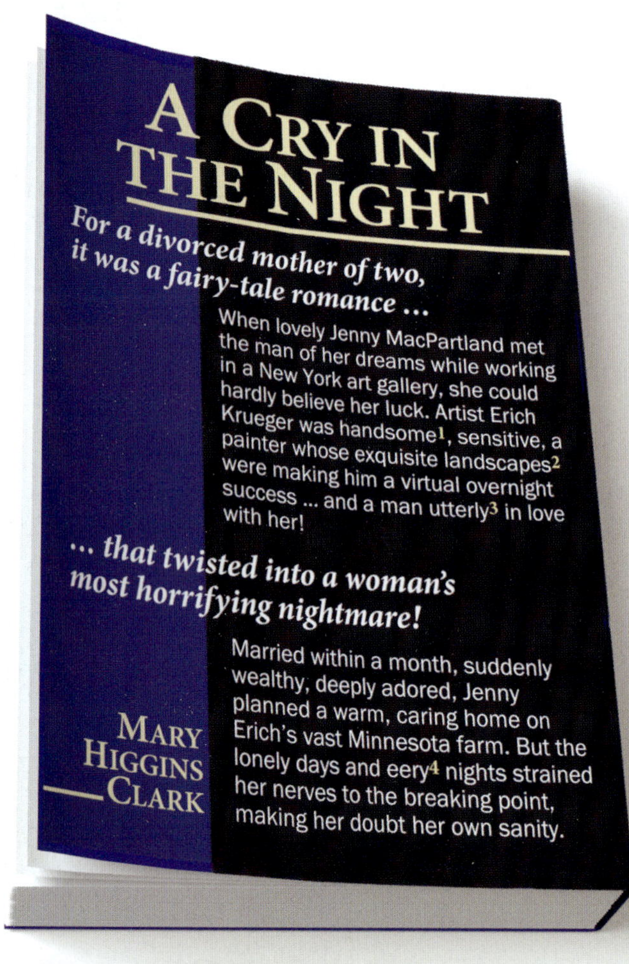

1. **handsome** (adj): beautiful.
2. **landscape** (n): *paysage*.
3. **utterly** (adv): completely.
4. **eery** (adj): strange.

C A psychological thriller.

1. First, look at the cover and find the title and the writer's name.
What is the most striking (important, surprising) element?
What impression does this cover create? Justify.

Word bank

• a butterfly • a circle • brackets *(accolades)* • liberty
• nature • imprisonment • disorder • be confined

SOUNDS PISTE 7
Les sons /ɪ/ et /iː/.
→ *WB 1, p. 27*

2. Now, listen to the reviews and say if the readers liked the book and what the story is about. → *WB 1, p. 27*

3. Read the beginning of the novel and say everything you can about the narrator. → *WB 1, p. 28*

Chapter 1

When she was home from her boarding-school I used to see her almost every day sometimes, because their house was right opposite the Town Hall Annexe. She and her younger sister used to go in and out a lot, often with young men, which of course I didn't like. When I had a free moment from the files and ledgers[1] I stood by the window and used to look down over the road over the frosting[2] and sometimes I'd see her. In the evening I marked it in my observations diary[3], at first with X, and then when I knew her name with M. I saw her several times outside too. I stood right behind her once in a queue at the public library down Crossfield Street. She didn't look once at me, but I watched the back of her head and her hair in a long pigtail. It was very pale, silky[4] (…).

I can't say what it was, the very first time I saw her, I knew she was the only one. Of course I am not mad, I knew it was just a dream (…). I used to have daydreams about her, I used to think of stories where I met her, did things she admired, married her and all that. (…)

The only times I didn't have nice dreams about her being when I saw her with a certain young man (…) who had a sports car (…). Those were days I let myself have the bad dreams.

John Fowles, *The Collector* (1963).

1. **ledger** (n): book where we write debits and credits. – 2. **frosting** (n): ice on a window. – 3. **diary** (n): *journal intime.* – 4. **silky** (adj): *soyeux.*

MAKE IT YOURS!

Use your imagination. → *WB 1, p. 29*

Miranda, the girl the narrator used to observe, is sixty years old now. She remembers her boarding-school days and the strange man who used to watch her all the time. Write one page from her memoirs.

DVD **Video time** → *WB 1, p. 30*
Suspicion and suspense

MEMO
• **While** (she was) work**ing** in a gallery, she met a wonderful man.
• It was a romance **that** changed into a terrible nightmare.
• She used to go in and out with young men, **which** of course I didn't like. → *p. 30*

Focus on FAMOUS MYSTERY

Caroline Graham

A few facts

- **Born:** 1931, Warwickshire (England).
- **Married:** once ; one son.
- **Work:** radio plays, episodes for an English soap opera *(Crossroads)*, a comedy for television, children's books *(BMX, Star Rider)* and mystery novels featuring Inspector Barnaby.

Caroline Graham did many different jobs before becoming a successful mystery writer. She was a factory worker after leaving school and then she served in the Royal Navy. She also used to work as an actress, a stage manager and for the radio. In 1987 she wrote her first mystery book, *The Killings at Badger's Drift*, introducing Detective Chief Inspector Barnaby, Head of the Police Department of the fictional English county of Midsomer. Later, television adapted her novels as the *Midsomer Murders* series which were immediately successful.

She sets her stories in charming English villages with beautiful cottages and cosy interiors. Her detective is patient and solves the crimes thanks to methodical deductions.

Midsomer Murders with John Nettles (Inspector Barnaby).

Caroline Graham.

PATRICIA CORNWELL

Patricia Cornwell is a contemporary American crime writer. She is well-known for writing novels featuring Dr Kay Scarpetta, the Chief Medical Examiner in Virginia. She says that there are numerous links between herself and her heroine. She used to work at the Office of the Chief Medical Examiner of Virginia. She also used to be a technical writer and a computer analyst. That's why the Scarpetta novels include a great deal of details on forensics. The heroine investigates the victim's corpse and does field investigation and confrontation with suspects to solve the crime.

Patricia Cornwell has probably influenced the development of popular TV series on forensics, such as *CSI (Crime Scene Investigation)*, *NCIS*, *Cold Case* …

WRITERS

Extracts

First extract

"If you could tell me what happened from when you first arrived."
"I came into the kitchen–(…) I opened the back door and hurried in here and found her where I showed you."
"Did you touch the body at all?"
"Yes. (…) Doctor Lessiter arrived and examined her (…) and while we were waiting for the van to arrive, I'm afraid"–she blushed regretfully at the Chief Inspector–"I'm afraid I tidied up a bit."

* * *

Second extract

"Well, I've always had a secret hankering to be a detective! (…) I came across a man in Belgium once, a very famous detective, and he quite inflamed me. He was a marvellous little fellow. He used to say that all good detective work was a mere matter of method. (…) He was a funny little man, a great dandy, but wonderfully clever."

* * *

Third extract

"I couldn't bear to sit at my desk. I had to move about and distract myself before I lost my composure.
Someone had broken into my office computer. (…) So I was making evidence rounds. Usually this entailed my receipting evidence to the various labs upstairs. (…) The Forensic Science Bureau was a beehive (…) filled with laboratory equipment and people wearing white lab coats and plastic safety glasses."

CD rom: Storytelling - Lamb to the slaughter.

SCANNING

➜ *WB 1, p. 31*

Have a good look at the documents and read the texts.

1. **Find out the names of these writers' most famous characters.**

2. **In the texts, find the words which mean:** *un inspecteur chef, un médecin légiste, résoudre un crime, enquêter sur, la médecine légale, un auteur de romans policiers, un roman, un feuilleton, une enquête de terrain.*

3. **Quiz the class. Ask your classmates riddles about the documents.**
Ex.: Television adapted my novels. Who am I?
I used to work at the Office of the Chief Medical Examiner of Virginia. Who am I?

4. **Read the three extracts from novels** by Agatha Christie, Caroline Graham or Patricia Cornwell. Which author wrote which extract? Justify by quoting from the texts.

WEBQUEST

➜ *WB 1, p. 32*

An FBI investigation
Go to this site and do the webquest in your workbook.
http://www.fbi.gov/kids/6th12th/investigates/investigates.htm

A few facts

- **Born:** 1956, Miami (USA).
- **Married:** once and divorced.
- **Work:** a dozen Scarpetta novels (First volume: *Postmortem*, in 1990).
- **Award:** Edgar Poe Award for Best First Novel, 1991.

Patricia Cornwell, in 2000.

STEP 1 Remember and practise

1 Je sais parler d'événements passés. → *Mémento p. 142*

Le **prétérit simple** permet de donner des informations sur **un temps révolu**, sur des événements qui n'ont **plus de lien avec le présent**. On l'utilise par exemple pour la biographie, pour parler de la vie et de la carrière d'un personnage. C'est aussi le temps du récit.

- Dans une biographie, on a souvent des informations datées mais l'événement peut être associé à un autre marqueur temporel (*ten years ago, last year, when ...*).

- **Formation du prétérit simple**

Affirmation	She **married** Archibald Christie and **had** one daughter.
Négation	Agatha Christie **didn't study** at school.
Interrogation	How many novels **did** she **write**?

Attention à la prononciation du *-ed*. → *WB 1, p. 14*

Rappel : On utilise l'auxiliaire *did/didn't* aux formes négative et interrogative.

Attention aux questions qui portent sur le sujet : le verbe est conjugué, c'est lui qui porte la marque du passé. On ne doit donc pas utiliser l'auxiliaire *did/didn't*.
What happened?
Who killed him?

1. Complète la biographie suivante en conjuguant au prétérit les verbes indiqués entre parenthèses.

Patricia Highsmith *(be)* an American novelist who *(be)* born in Texas on 19 January 1921. In 1942 she *(graduate)* from college where she *(study)* literature. First, she *(write)* comic books.
She *(become)* famous thanks to Hitchcock because he *(adapt) Strangers on a Train* for television in 1951.
She never *(marry)* and *(not have)* any children. She *(die)* of leukaemia on 4 February 1995.

2. Tu dois interviewer Patricia Cornwell. Imagine les questions portant sur les informations suivantes et rédige l'interview.

Date and place of birth: 6 June 1956, Miami (Florida).
Studies: English.
Marital status: marriage: Charles Cornwell
divorce: 1989.
Publication of the first crime story: *Postmortem*, 1991.
Name of the main character: Dr Kay Scarpetta / forensics examiner.
Number of books written between 1990 and 2008: 16 in the Kay Scarpetta series.

2 Je sais décrire ce qui se passait à un moment précis. → *Mémento p. 143*

Pour décrire ce qui se passait à un moment donné, on utilise le **prétérit *be* + BV-*ing***. Ce temps sert à poser **le cadre d'une action**, à faire **une description** ou à parler d'**une action** que l'on observe **dans son déroulement**.

- Lorsque l'on considère l'action **dans son déroulement**, comme un **arrêt sur image**, on utilise le **prétérit *be* +BV-*ing***.
On parle de ce qui était en train de se passer...
He **was** gesticulat**ing**.
Where **was** he go**ing**?
They **weren't** look**ing** at him.

- On utilise le **prétérit simple** pour parler d'événements ponctuels qui sont arrivés dans le passé ou dans le cadre donné par le prétérit *be* +BV-*ing*.
On parle de ce qui s'est passé...
She was rushing out when I **met** her.

3. Tu as été témoin d'un incident dans la rue. Raconte ce que tu as vu.

I *(walk)* in the street when I *(see)* a man. He *(wear)* a long coat and a hood*. Suddenly, he *(start)* running towards another man who *(sit)* on a bench. He *(grab)* his bag and *(run)* away.
***hood:** *cagoule*.

4. Tu es enquêteur et tu dois interroger un témoin. Pose les questions pour savoir :

- ce que le suspect portait.
- où allait le témoin que tu interroges.
- ce que la victime faisait.
- ce que le témoin a fait après le vol.

1 Je sais parler d'actions que je faisais avant et que je ne fais plus aujourd'hui. → Mémento p. 145

En anglais, on fait la différence entre des actions passées ponctuelles (on emploie alors le prétérit) et des **actions passées répétitives** (on utilise alors l'expression ***used to*** suivie de la base verbale).

• Pour parler d'actions ou de situations passées en insistant sur le fait qu'elles n'ont plus lieu à présent, on utilise l'expression ***used to*** + base verbale.
Used to s'emploie avec l'auxiliaire *did/didn't* aux formes interrogative et négative.

Affirmation	Sujet + ***used to*** + base verbale My mother **used to** read me stories.
Négation	Sujet + ***didn't use to*** + base verbale She **didn't use to** read me thrillers.
Interrogation	***Did*** + sujet + ***use to*** + base verbale **Did** you **use to** be interested in detective stories?

Attention à la prononciation de *used to* /ˈjuːstʊ/.

• Pour parler de ce que l'on ne fait plus ou de faits qui ne sont plus vrais à présent, on utilise l'expression ***not ... any more*** ou ***no longer***.

Remarques :
- ***any more*** se place toujours à la fin de la proposition.
I am **not** afraid of thrillers **any more**.
- ***no longer*** se place avant un verbe mais après le verbe *be*.
I **no longer** read detective stories.
I am **no longer** interested in them.
Quand le groupe verbal est composé, ***no longer*** se place après l'auxiliaire.
She is **no longer** writing plays.

1. La vie a bien changé en deux générations. Ta grand-mère te parle de ses habitudes lorsqu'elle était adolescente.

2. Tu veux en savoir plus. Imagine votre dialogue.

Tu veux savoir si...	Elle te répond que...
elle avait un ordinateur	non, ils n'existaient pas
ses parents avaient une voiture	non, elle allait à l'école à pied
ses parents étaient stricts	oui, ses parents étaient plus stricts que les tiens

3. Ta vie a également bien changé depuis l'école maternelle. Dis de deux façons ce que tu ne fais plus.

Ex. : *sleep in the afternoon at school, have a teddy bear, cry at night, be afraid of the dark ...*

Plus d'exercices sur ton CD audio-rom

2 Je sais exprimer le moyen d'obtenir un résultat. → Mémento p. 140

Pour demander **comment** on peut parvenir à un résultat, on utilise le mot interrogatif ***How ... ?***
Pour exprimer **le moyen** de parvenir à un résultat, on utilise l'expression ***by* + BV-*ing***.

Rappel : Il existe 3 catégories de verbes quand on ajoute la terminaison ***-ing*** :
- ceux auxquels on ajoute directement la terminaison ***-ing*** :
listen → listening • call → calling
- ceux qui perdent le *-e* final :
come → coming • phone → phoning
- ceux qui doublent leur consonne finale :
sit → sitting • run → running

4. Complète les phrases suivantes de façon logique.

a. Investigators can detect blood by ...
b. Police officers can have their evidence analysed by ...
c. They can identify a culprit by ...
d. They can clear an innocent person by ...

STEP 3 Remember and practise

1 Je sais dire ce qui se passait à un moment précis du passé en utilisant *while* + BV-*ing*. → *Mémento p. 143*

While* + BV-*ing sert à articuler deux actions **simultanées**, quand il y a **le même sujet** dans la proposition principale et la subordonnée.

• Observe la phrase suivante :

1. **While** having a walk in the park, they saw a strange incident.

L'action *they saw a strange incident* a lieu au moment où l'action *having a walk* a cours. *They* est le sujet des deux propositions. On peut également écrire :

2. **While they were** having a walk in the park, they saw a strange incident.

On peut donc choisir de mentionner le sujet deux fois (2e phrase) ou une seule fois (1re phrase).

• ***While*** indique que l'action était en cours de réalisation à un moment donné du passé. On pourrait traduire par : « pendant qu'ils se promenaient dans le parc ».

1. Réécris les phrases suivantes en utilisant *while* + BV-*ing* quand c'est possible.

a. Did you hear the alarm **while you were waiting for the bus**?
b. The police arrived **while the two burglars were opening the safe**.
c. The detectives kept silent **while they were driving back to the police station**.
d. They arrested the thieves **while they were trying to use a stolen credit card in a petrol station**.
e. Did you speak to a CSI star **while you were staying in Las Vegas**?

2 Je sais donner des précisions sur une personne, une chose ou un événement. → *Mémento p. 149*

Il est possible de relier **deux phrases simples** en une seule à l'aide d'un **pronom relatif**.

• Le choix de ce pronom se fait selon deux critères :
- **la nature de l'antécédent** (c'est-à-dire le mot ou le groupe de mots de la principale que le relatif remplace) ;
- **la fonction de ce pronom** dans la proposition relative (sujet, complément du verbe, d'une proposition).

• **Pronom relatif sujet**

- **Antécédent humain : who**

A. Christie, **who** was a British writer, died in 1976.

- **Antécédent non humain : which**

His home, **which** was very comfortable, was in Dorset.

- **Antécédent humain ou non humain : that**

that remplace de plus en plus souvent ***who*** et ***which*** quand l'antécédent ne peut pas être séparé de la subordonnée par une virgule.

He was one of those artists **that** love the country.
He lived on a farm **that** was isolated.

• **Pronom relatif complément du verbe**

- **Antécédent humain : that** ou **Ø**

The girl **Ø** / **that** he used to observe did not know him.

- **Antécédent non humain : that** ou **Ø** ou **which**

He has a diary **Ø** / **that** / **which** he completes every day.

• **Pronom relatif complément d'une proposition**

L'antécédent est une proposition : **which**

She used to see boys, **which*** of course made him jealous.

* Dans ce cas, *which* se traduit par « ce que » ou « ce qui ».

2. Ajoute un pronom relatif pour compléter les phrases. Il y a parfois deux solutions.

a. He used to hide to watch her, ... she hated!
b. The man ... she married was in fact a total stranger.
c. The girl's hair, ... was in a long pigtail, was very dark.
d. He imagined that he married her, ... was a wonderful dream.
e. He had a diary ... contained all his memories.

3. Voici le début d'une histoire policière. Ajoute des détails pour la rendre intéressante en utilisant des propositions relatives.

A man **who/that** ... was sitting on a bench in the park when a woman came to sit next to him. She was wearing a raincoat **which/that** ...
She said, "Do you remember me? I used to meet you at the store **which/that** ..."
The man answered, "I'm sorry but I don't. Who are you? What is this store **which/that** ...?"
"Don't lie to me. Don't you remember the black box **which/that/Ø** ...? I saw you while you were running away, **which** ...!" And she started to laugh.

PR1JECT

Create the front cover and back cover of a book.

A. Imagine your story.

Imagine une histoire avec une situation initiale *(who, when, where ...)*, un élément modificateur et une atmosphère mystérieuse.

B. Create the front cover.

- Recherche et sélectionne des documents (images, photos...) pour illustrer ton histoire.
- Fais-en un montage ou un collage.
- Donne un titre et mentionne le nom de l'auteur. (Tu peux inventer un nom.)

C. Create the back cover.

- Écris un bref résumé de l'histoire sans dévoiler la fin.
- Ajoute quelques illustrations, par exemple une photo de l'auteur.

D. Elect the best covers and justify your choice.

I like X's project because ...

Word bank

- X was....
- He/She lived in ...
- He/She used to ...
- One day, ...
- He/She was ...ing when ...
- strange, threatening, secret ...

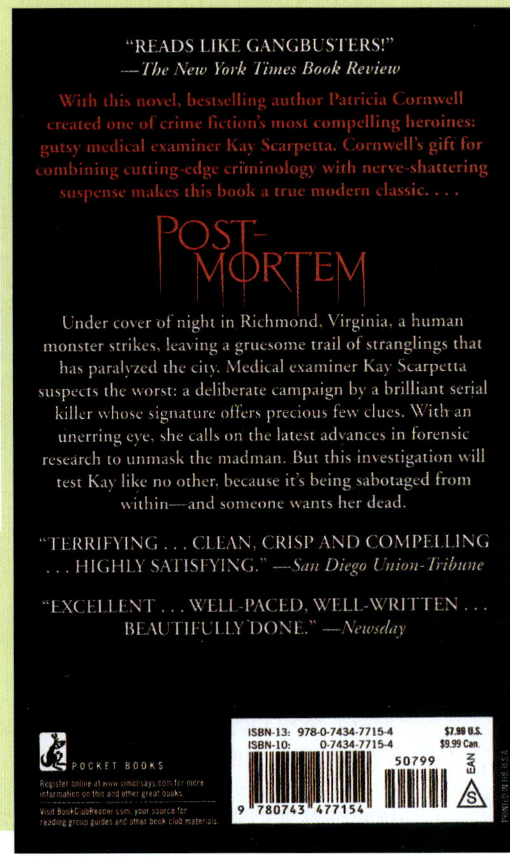

PR2JECT

Create a crossword puzzle for your classmates.

A. Write about fifteen questions with your group.

- La classe est divisée en trois groupes :

  - Le groupe 1 écrit des questions sur les connaissances culturelles sous forme d'énigmes (Ex. : *She created Hercule Poirot.*) ou de questions (Ex. : *Who created Hercule Poirot?*).
  - Le groupe 2 rédige des questions sur le lexique sous forme de définitions (Ex. : *What is a guilty person?*), de synonymes (Ex. : *Give a synonym for "guilty".*) ou de traductions (Ex. : *What's the English for "*coupable*"?*).
  - Le groupe 3 crée des questions de grammaire sous forme de phrases à compléter (Ex. : *He ... born in April* ; L'auxiliaire du prétérit en *-ing* est ...).
- Les réponses à toutes ces questions seront les mots à trouver pour remplir la grille de mots croisés.

B. Create your puzzle.

Allez sur le site http://www.puzzle-maker.com pour créer votre grille de mots croisés.

C. Play!

Soumettez la grille de votre groupe à vos camarades. Qui trouvera les solutions en premier ?

To be continued... **Gardez précieusement vos questions. Elles vous serviront à créer un jeu dans les *Units 2* et *3*.**

Words

1 **Look at this series of words. Which one does not refer to a person?**

investigator • character • witness • murder • killer • burglar

2 **Remember and write the word for:**

a. the opposite of "innocent" (adj).
b. elements at a crime scene that help the investigator find the truth.

3 **Solve the following riddles.**

a. She is her father's girl. Her first letter is a D but for her brother, the first letter is an S!
b. He is a man who has a wife.

4 **Look at the examples below, then complete the sentences with the correct form of the adjective (*-ing* or *-ed*).**

*I saw a terrify**ing** scene.*
*She was terrifi**ed**.*
to terrify (v) → *terrify**ing*** (terrifi**ant**)
→ *terrifi**ed*** (terrifi**é**)

a. The man with the bloody face was really … . *(frighten)*
b. I have never felt so bad in my life! Rob has not even called me: it is so …! *(disappoint)*
c. Jenny felt she had a very … husband. *(love)*
d. My little brother is easily … at night. *(scare)*

5 PLAY WITH WORDS!

a. Observe la phrase suivante.

*Caroline Graham did many different jobs before becoming a **successful** mystery writer.*

b. Réfléchis.

• Quelle est la classe grammaticale de *successful* ? (adjectif, adverbe, verbe).
• Repère la racine de ce mot. Quel est le sens du suffixe *-ful* ?
• Propose une traduction pour l'expression *a successful mystery writer*.

c. À ton tour !

• Propose une traduction pour les mots en gras dans les phrases suivantes.
1. *She is very **resourceful**: she always finds solutions.*
2. *This is a very **useful** book, thanks a lot.*
• Propose un mot en anglais pour compléter la traduction.
3. Ce mur est très **coloré** : *This wall is very …*
4. Ces étudiants ont une attitude **respectueuse**. *These students have a … attitude.*

CD rom : Discovery Game

CHECKPOINT

Read the text.

Skating Rink Robbery

Dr Quicksolve entered the skating rink building. (…) In the main room where the skaters skated around and around, you could hardly carry on a conversation because of the loud music.

The manager, Mr Blade, came over to the detective and signaled for him to come through a nearby door marked "Office". When they went in and closed the door you couldn't hear the music, and you could talk. Two men were sitting in the office. One was holding an ice pack to his head.

"I had the room made soundproof to keep out the loud music the teenagers like so much. The problem is, we've been robbed. I just got here myself, so I'll let my employees, Franck and Joe, tell you what happened. Joe, you go first."

The one with the ice pack spoke up. "I was in here counting the money. I was sitting here my back to the door and someone came in behind me and hit me over the head. When I came to, the money was gone."

"What can you tell us?" Dr Quicksolve asked, turning towards Franck.

"I was out in the main room watching the skaters. I heard a crash from the office here, and I turned around just in time to see a tall man slip out of the office and run out of the building. I came in and found Joe unconscious. I woke him and called the police."

Jim Sukach, *Baffling Whodunit Puzzles: Dr Quicksolve Mini-Mysteries* (1997).

Now do the activities and solve the mystery.

a. Read aloud the following verbs: "entered", "skated", "marked", "robbed", "turned" and "called".
b. Read the text and find out the names of the characters, who and where they are, and what the problem is.
c. Find out if the skating rink and the office are noisy or quiet.
d. Find out what the employees were doing when the robbery happened.
e. Who stole the money? Give your opinion and quote from the text.

Can you speak about one of these subjects for a few minutes? Don't forget to speak clearly and in a loud voice.

Subject 1
Present a mystery writer to the class (Conan Doyle, Caroline Graham, Agatha Christie, Patricia Cornwell ...).
- Make an identity card or write notes to be prepared to talk about one of these authors: name, date of birth and death, nationality, work, characters ...
- Don't write complete sentences.

Subject 2
Last year you didn't focus on your studies enough. Say what you used or didn't use to do instead of working. Compare with this year.
watch TV a lot • play video games • do my exercises but not learn the lessons ...
But this year ... (no longer / any more)

Pairwork.

During a school trip to England someone stole your teacher's bag.
Pupil A, you're a policeman. Pupil B, you answer the policeman's questions and say what you saw.
Don't forget the greetings.

Pupil A
- Demande à B ce qu'il faisait quand le vol a eu lieu.
- Demande ce que B a vu.
- Demande comment ils étaient.
- Demande comment B a réagi.

Pupil B
- Dis ce que vous étiez en train de faire et où (pique-nique, visite...).
- Réponds que tu as vu trois hommes. Dis ce qu'ils étaient en train de faire, puis ce qu'ils ont fait après le vol.
- Réponds en les décrivant.
- Réponds.

Now write the report.

You are the policeman. Write a few lines to report what happened and what Pupil B saw. Use the simple past and the preterite *be* + BV-*ing*.

Listen and find out who the characters are and why one is phoning.

a. Find out what the girl thinks of programmes about forensic scientists.
b. What did the girl's mother use to do?
c. Find out what the boy thinks of forensic investigators.
d. Find out the girl's suggestion.

unit 2

Going West!

STEP 1

Je suis des instructions.
Je raconte une visite.

STEP 2

Je me renseigne sur l'évolution d'un métier.

STEP 3

Je prépare une visite touristique.

Focus on: THE WILD WEST

PROJECTS

1. Create the totem of your group.
2. Play snakes and ladders.

CHECKPOINT

Starter

1. What country is represented?
Say all the words that come to your mind when you look at these pictures.

2. Some pictures show the past and others the present. Can you spot them?

3. From what you see, imagine how Indians and cowboys used to live in the past.

4. What can you say about the changes between the past and today?

STEP 1 Je suis des instructions.

A What is an Indian? → WB 1, p. 37

1. Look at the pictures of these two teenagers. Where do you think they're from?

2. Now listen to them. What is their nationality?

3. Look at the drawing. Where does the confusion about the term "Indian" come from?

Christopher Columbus discovered …
but he thought … so …

CD rom : Storytelling - The Pilgrims

B What are the original inhabitants of North America called? → WB 1, p. 37

Read the text and give another reason for rejecting the term "Indian".

The original inhabitants of North America are referred to as "Native Americans", "Natives", or "American Indians", but according to Christina Berry, a Cherokee writer and producer, there is another way: "The recommended method is to refer to a person by their tribe, if that information is known. The reason is that the Native peoples* of North America are incredibly diverse. It would be like referring to both a Romanian and an Irishman as European. […] The terms 'Indian', 'American Indian', and 'Native American' are an over-simplification of a diverse ethnicity."

*__peoples__ (n): *peuples.*

http://www.infoplease.com

C What is life like on a Navajo reservation today?

1. Listen to this interview. How is a Navajo reservation organized today? How important are the Navajo culture and its traditions? → WB 1, p. 37

2. How could you characterize the Navajo nation today?

SOUNDS PISTE 12
Le suffixe *-tion*.
→ WB 1, p. 38

IT'S UP TO YOU!

Create a medicine wheel. → WB 1, p. 39

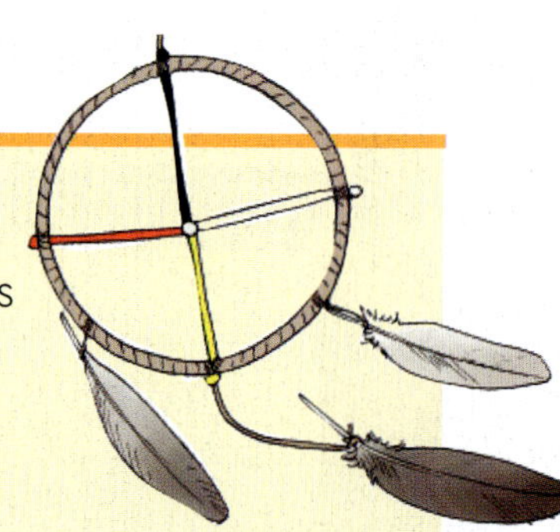

The medicine wheel is representative of American Indian spirituality. It symbolizes the individual journey *(voyage)* we must take to find our own path.

1. Listen to a teenager describing a four-direction wheel, and draw it on a piece of paper.

2. Create your own medicine wheel. Choose the meaning associated with the directions and what the colours symbolize (your present life, your future, your hopes, your fears …).

3. Explain to the class what is represented on your wheel.

DVD **Video time** → WB 1, p. 41
A dreamcatcher

MEMO
- The Navajo nation **is organized** like a small country.
- How **are** Indians **called** today? → p. 44

Je raconte une visite.

A What does the land mean to Native Americans? → WB 1, p. 42

Read the quotes. What do they teach you about the relationship between Native Americans and the land? What is impossible for them to do?

1

"One does not sell the land people walk on."
(Crazy Horse, Sept. 23, 1875)

2

"We did not think we owned* the land. The land was part of us. We didn't even know about owning the land. It's like talking about owning your grandmother. You can't own your grandmother!"
(Kent Nerburn)

*own (v): possess.

3

"The ground on which we stand is sacred ground. It is the blood of our ancestors."
(Chief Plenty Coups)

B What happened to the Navajo in the past?

1. Look at the young man in the photo. Describe him and imagine his feelings.

2. Now, read the text. Why was the land so important for the Navajo? → WB 1, p. 42

In the 1860s, American settlers[1] decided they needed more land. Many treaties were signed with the Navajo but as they weren't respected, raids were organized and atrocities were committed by both the army and the Navajo. A campaign against the Navajo was launched in 1863. They were attacked in Canyon de Chelly, (…) their hogans (…) were (…) burnt, (…) their sheep and cattle were slaughtered, and about two million pounds of corn burnt. Families attempted to hide in caves in the canyon walls, but were hunted and put under armed guard. (…) After many months of imprisonment, about 8,000 men, women and children were forced to make a 300-mile march, remembered as "the Long Walk", across New Mexico to a dry desolate strip of land known as Bosque Redondo. (…) Without their land and their corn, the people were in a state of desperation, made worse by disease[2] and starvation[3]. They were wasting away[4]. (…) During their imprisonment, the Navajo lost about 25% of their people.

www.mondovista.com

1. **settler** (n): a person who came to live in a new country. – 2. **disease** /iː/ (n): illness (n). – 3. **starvation** (n): severe lack of food. – 4. **waste** /eɪ/ **away** (v): die slowly.

IT'S UP TO YOU!

Send an e-mail about your visit to a reservation. → WB 1, p. 43

You visited a Navajo reservation in Arizona. Send an e-mail to a friend and explain what you learnt, what surprised you …
I thought … but …
In the past, they were … so now …

STRATEGIES
→ *Méthodologie, p. 130 :*
Écrire un e-mail.

MEMO
- Hogans **were burnt**.
- A campaign **was** launch**ed**. → p. 44

1 Get ready!

Why did pioneers move west? → WB 1, p. 44

1. Look at the pictures. Why did pioneers move west?

*acres (n): *arpents.*

Word bank

- fur *(fourrure)* • advertisement
- trade *(faire du commerce)* • hunt • dig for gold *(chercher de l'or)* • promote • incite = encourage • settle
- cheap • free

SOUNDS PISTE 13
La diphtongue /ɪə/.
→ WB 1, p. 44

2. Listen to the recording. What were their other motivations?

2 Step forward!

A What difficulties did pioneers meet on their journey? → WB 1, p. 45

Read Elizabeth's story. How difficult was her journey? Did it become easier and easier?

From nearby Liberty, Missouri, in early April 1846, about fifty families prepared to make the journey to the far away Oregon Territory (…). I was then ten years old (…).

After we left Missouri, we went through a wilderness[1] and over a trackless[2] plain. And the journey became harder and harder.

Of those long weary[3] months I cannot clearly tell. I know it was April when we started and October when we reached (…) Salem in Oregon. Sometimes we stopped several days in camp where we found a lot of water and good grazing[4]. (…) Then there were days we toiled[5] over the arid plains till far into the night to reach the life-giving water that was a necessity to us and to our trains. The children of the company walked many many miles ... sometimes I think I walked half of the way to Oregon! (…)

But after all, we had but few difficulties compared with some of the emigrant trains. Some years, you know, cholera wiped out[6] entire families and trains were raided by Indians. (…) Yes, we were very lucky!

http://freepages.history.roots.ancestry.com

1. **wilderness** /ɪ/ (n): uncultivated and uninhabited region. – 2. **trackless** (adj): sans chemins. – 3. **weary** /ɪə/ (adj): tiring and boring. – 4. **grazing** /eɪ/ (n): food for the cattle. – 5. **toil** (v): have hard times. – 6. **wipe out** /aɪ/ (v): *(ici)* kill.

DVD **Video time** → WB 1, p. 47
The Oregon Trail

B What is a modern cowboy? → WB 1, p. 48

1. Read this page from a website. What is the life of a modern cowboy like?

WELCOME TO COWBOY'S CYBER RANCH!!

I'm Ronnie. I am a cowboy from Texas who loves the outdoors: I ride horses and 4-wheelers, I like shooting pool and meeting new people. I am very proud to say that I finally graduated college! I'm finally back in my hometown in Eastern Texas. I can be described as an easy-going country boy. I don't mind helpin' out other people. Honesty is a big thing with me. My favorite type of food is steak. Second choice would be some barbecue.

http://uses.ixpres.com/~txcowboy

2. Listen to Rob talking to young tourists.
What do working cowboys choose that job for?
What's the difference between them and rhinestone cowboys?
→ CD piste 14

A rhinestone cowboy.

Word bank

- pearl buttons • rhinestone /aɪ/ *(strass)*
- lasso /uː/ • rope *(corde)*
- embroidered • dusty • well-worn • beat-up *(usé)*

MAKE IT YOURS!

Chat on line with a modern cowboy. → WB 1, p. 49

You have contacted Ronnie to know more about his ancestors, their job as cowboys in the past and his job now.
He is comparing working cowboys and the growing number of rhinestone cowboys.
Imagine your conversation with him.

You: *What ....for?*
Ronnie: *My ancestors moved west to ...*
I became a cowboy to ...
Rhinestone cowboys are ... I think ...

MEMO
- As **more and more** people came, game became **less and less** plentiful.
- We walked **many** miles but we had **few** difficulties.
- They practise their skills of roping **not to** work with cattle, but **to** compete in rodeos. → p. 45

1 Get ready!

Which tourist attractions are offered in the American West? → WB 1, p. 50

Look at this leaflet and at your map at the end of your textbook.
Where is Cody? What activities and attractions are offered to tourists?

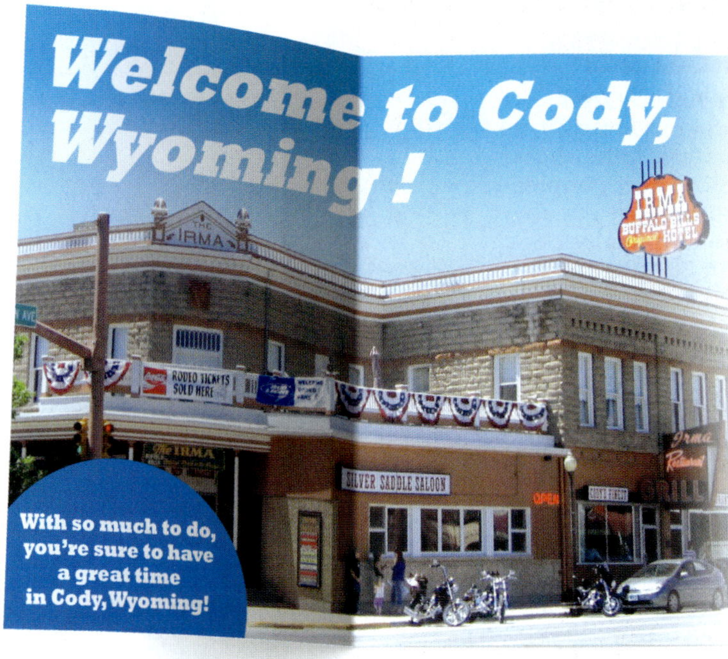

Cody is one of the best places in America to experience the True West. Exploring **Yellowstone**, fishing, hiking*, biking, horse-back riding, rafting trips, and rodeos are all exciting ways to experience this town.
A **Cody Trolley tour** is the best and fastest way of discovering all that Cody, Wyoming has to offer.
In the evening, just stop at **Buffalo Bill's Irma Hotel** to taste their famous Buffalo Burger or go to a bar to listen to country music. And if you have the time, don't miss **Dan Miller's Cowboy Music Revue**.

CD rom : Discovery Game

*hike /aɪ/ (v): go for long walks.

2 Step forward!

A How can a tourist information centre help you?

Listen to this conversation between Randy, a visitor, and a tourist officer.
Which activities does she suggest him? → WB 1, p. 50, CD piste 15

SOUNDS PISTE 16
L'accent anglais
et l'accent américain.
→ WB 1, p. 51

B Booking tickets for Rodeo Night!

→ WB 1, p. 52

Randy wants to book tickets to see a rodeo on 6 July.
What does he have to do?
How much does he have to pay?

Cody Nite[1] RODEO

Price Per Ticket
Adult: $17.00 each
Child (7-12): $8.00 each

June to August at 8:00 p.m.
Gates open at 7:00 p.m.
Rodeo time: 8:00-10:00 p.m.

Each Cody Nite Rodeo ticket is good for any one night from June to August, excluding July 1-5.
All tickets purchased[2] through this website are held at the ticket office. Tickets for the Cody Nite Rodeo can be purchased by calling 1-800-207-0744.
Office Hours: Monday through Friday, 9:00 a.m. - 4:00 p.m.

If you are traveling[3] in a group of 10 people or more, please contact the office.

1. **nite** (n) (US): informal spelling for "night". – 2. **purchase** (v): buy. – 3. **traveling** (US): travelling (GB).

C Find the link between Cody—the town—and Buffalo Bill.

1. What is the short form of William: Walt, Bill or Terence?

2. Read this illustrated biography of Buffalo Bill (1846-1917). What is the link between him and Cody?
→ *WB 1, p. 52*

Buffalo Bill

Sitting Bull and Buffalo Bill in 1886.

Early years

William Cody was born in Iowa, in 1846.
In 1861, he was given a job at the Pony Express to deliver the mail between Montana and California. He completed the distance of 322 miles over one of the most dangerous portions of the entire trail in 21 hours and 40 minutes using 21 horses.

36

William Cody becomes Buffalo Bill

In 1867, Cody began working with the Kansas Pacific railroad and was offered a contract to supply the railroad workers with buffalo meat! He was given his nickname at this time, after he killed 4,280 buffalo in eighteen months (1867-68)!

Buffalo Bill's Wild West

In 1883, he created "Buffalo Bill's Wild West", with 600 actors and 500 animals, and began touring Europe.
The show began with a parade on horseback, with performers from all over the world in their best costumes. For example Sitting Bull (a very famous Sioux chief) and a band of twenty braves appeared.
In 1895, Buffalo Bill participated in founding the town of Cody, Wyoming!

Buffalo Bill's Wild West.

37

MAKE IT YOURS!

Asking and giving information about a tourist attraction. → *WB 1, p. 53*

Pupil A: You are in Cody and you want to visit the Buffalo Bill Museum with your family. Phone the museum to get the information you need (admission, attraction...).

Pupil B: You work at the Museum. Answer your caller's questions about this attraction and admission price.
Then promote "Cowboy Songs and Ballads".

STRATEGIES
→ *Méthodologie, p. 127 :*
Parler au téléphone.

MEMO
- Horse-rid**ing**, raft**ing** and watch**ing** rodeos are typical Western attractions.
- He **was given** a job at the Pony Express. → *p. 46*

Focus on THE WILD

The Gold Rush

Gold diggers in California, in the 19th century.

During the first half of the 19th century, explorers like Lewis and Clark and a lot of pioneers opened the way west to discover new territories or have a better life. In 1848 gold was discovered in California. From then on, thousands of "Forty-Niners" (year 1849) rushed west, hoping to get rich and boosting the population from about 14,000 to over 200,000 in 1852. But prospecting for gold was very hard and a matter of chance. The effects of the Gold Rush were significant. Roads, churches, schools and other towns were built throughout California. "The Golden State" even became California's nickname. However, the Gold Rush also had negative effects: Native Americans who were attacked and pushed off traditional lands responded by attacking the miners.

COMMUNICATIONS

In the Wild West, mail was delivered by stagecoach. But it took a long time. So, in 1860, the Pony Express, a relay of horse riders from Missouri to California, was founded and reduced the delivery to eight days. William Cody and Calamity Jane, two famous figures of the Old West, worked for the Pony Express. However this service only lasted one year: it was replaced by the telegraph system. Eight years later the eastern and western railways were joined and the transcontinental line was completed. Railroads had a profound social effect as more and more women and children migrated, developing a real family life out west.

The Pony Express.

WEST

The cowboys

The cowboy is a famous figure of the Wild West with the outlaw (like Billy the Kid) or the bison hunter (like Buffalo Bill). At that time, his work included riding around the ranch and taking care of the cattle. He also had to drive the cows for several days to cow towns and the nearest railway stations to sell them. Before leaving, the cowboys used to organize roundups: they brought together the scattered[1] cattle, sorted[2], roped[3] and marked the young calves[4].

The 'Stetson' hat and blue jeans are also associated with cowboys. During the Gold Rush, American gold miners and western emigrants wanted clothes which were strong and did not tear easily. Levi Strauss who was a merchant of German origin, started a business supplying denim trousers. The word "denim" was said to come from the name of a French material from the city of Nîmes. According to many people the word "jeans" came from *bleu de Gênes*.

Advert for Levi Strauss jeans, around 1900.

1. . **scattered** (adj): *dispersé* - 2. **sort** (v): *trier.* - 3. **rope** (v): *attacher avec une corde*
4. **calves** (n): *veaux.*

SCANNING

→ WB 1, p. 55

Have a good look at the documents and read the texts.

1. **Find out who these characters were:**
Lewis and Clark, Billy the Kid, Levi Strauss, Buffalo Bill.

2. **In the texts, find the words which mean:**
la ruée vers l'or, le bétail, les explorateurs, un chasseur, la diligence, le courrier.

3. **Are the following statements true or false? Quiz the class.**
a. In California gold was discovered in the sea.
b. People moved west to get a better life.
c. "Stetson" is the name of a famous cowboy.
d. Calamity Jane founded the Pony Express.
e. California's nickname was "The Last Frontier".

WEBQUEST

→ WB 1, p. 55

Lewis and Clark
Go to these sites and do the webquest in your workbook.

1. **Discover the expedition.**
http://www.enchantedlearning.com/explorers/page/l/lewisandclark.shtml

2. **Find out about some members of the expedition.**
http://montanakids.com/history_and_prehistory/lewis_and_clark/

3. **Find out what they discovered.**
http://www.esa.org/portland/

STEP 1 Remember and practise

Je sais utiliser la voix passive. → *Mémento p. 144*

Lorsque l'on choisit de ne pas **mettre en valeur** l'auteur de l'action mais **la personne ou l'objet sur laquelle ou lequel cette action porte**, on utilise **la voix passive**.
La voix passive se forme avec l'auxiliaire ***be*** au temps choisi, suivi du **participe passé** du verbe.

• **Voix active et voix passive.**

The Navajo **elect** a president for the reservation.
On s'intéresse aux auteurs de l'action, à ce que les Navajos font.
→ C'est la **voix active**.

A president **is elected** for the reservation.
On s'intéresse au président. On ne s'intéresse pas aux auteurs de l'action mais au statut de la personne élue.
→ C'est la **voix passive**.

C'est l'auxiliaire *be* qui donne le temps de la phrase.
Their sheep **were** killed. Their land **was** stolen.

• **La voix passive et le complément d'agent.**

On ne mentionne le complément d'agent (c'est-à-dire celui qui fait l'action) que lorsqu'il apporte une information utile. Il est introduit par la préposition ***by***.
The Navajo nation **is led** by a president.

Attention : Les participes passés des verbes irréguliers sont à apprendre par cœur (pp. 172-173), pour les verbes réguliers on ajoute la terminaison *-ed*.

• **Auxiliaires modaux et autres temps à la voix passive.**

Voix active	Voix passive
Présent simple	***am*** / ***is*** / ***are*** + p.p.
They **clean** the house every day. → The house **is** cleaned every day.	
Prétérit	***was*** / ***were*** + p.p.
Scott **repaired** the car. → The car **was** repaired by Scott.	
Futur	***will be*** + p.p.
Someone **will finish** the work later. → The work **will be** finished later.	
Présent *be* + V-*ing*	***is being*** / ***are being*** + p.p.
Ally **is writing** the letter. → The letter **is being** written by Ally.	
Present perfect	***has been*** / ***have been*** + p.p.
Many tourists **have visited** this place. → This place **has been** visited by many tourists.	
Auxiliaire modal	***can be*** / ***must be*** / ***may be*** + p.p.
You **can complete** it later. → It **can be** completed later.	

1. **Décris une *medicine wheel* en utilisant les mots et les expressions ci-dessous.**

the four directions	divide into	around a circle
the circle	indicate	four equal parts
the heat	associate with	symbols
the colours	represent	red

2. **Tu regardes un western avec des amis et tu leur parles des préjudices qu'ont subis les Indiens. Utilise les verbes suivants et leurs compléments.**

- *their spirituality • the buffaloes • their lands*
- *take • kill • (not) respect*

3. **Tu rencontres un *Native American* et tu veux savoir ce qui est arrivé à sa tribu. Demande... :**

a. quand ils ont été chassés *(chase away)*,
b. où leur nation a été envoyée *(send)*,
c. pourquoi leur nation a été envoyée dans des réserves,
d. combien d'Indiens ont été tués,
e. comment ils étaient traités *(treat)*.

4. **Mets les phrases suivantes à la voix passive. (Observe bien le temps de la voix active.)**

a. They are building a new road.
b. Someone has bought all the postcards.
c. They will close the shop during the interseason.
d. Lots of tourists visit the reservation.
e. They closed the museum during the renovation.

5. **L'employé d'un musée explique aux visiteurs ce qui peut ou doit être fait dans le musée.**

a. Postcards / buy / souvenir shop
b. Bags / leave / lockers *(casiers)*
c. Photos / take / outside YES / inside NO
d. Children / accompany / at all times

1 Je sais dire dans quel but je fais une action. → *Mémento p. 140*

Pour **exprimer le but**, on utilise ***to* + base verbale**. Pour poser la question, on utilise : ***What ... for?***

Attention : Il y a deux façons de traduire « pour » en anglais :

- La structure ***to*** + base verbale qui exprime le but :

They moved west **to** get a better life.
Ils allaient vers l'ouest pour avoir une vie meilleure.

- La structure ***for*** + nom ou pronom qui n'exprime pas toujours le but :

The journey west was very difficult **for** pioneers.
Le voyage vers l'ouest était très difficile pour les pionniers.

1. Certains mots de ton exposé se sont effacés. Reconstitue le message avec *for* ou *to*.

a. They moved to the frontier ... start a new life.
b. Farmers raised animals ... food.
c. They took a camping stove ... cook.
d. They travelled in wagon trains ... escape Indian attacks.
e. Having to walk a long way was tiring ... children.

2 Je sais exprimer une progression. → *Mémento p. 137*

Pour dire **« de plus en plus »** ou **« de moins en moins »**, on utilise **le double comparatif**.
Sa construction dépend du nom ou de l'adjectif qui le suit.

- Pour dire « de plus en plus ... », on utilise :

\- ***more and more*** devant un nom ou un adjectif long (**more and more** pioneers) ;
\- ***-er and -er*** derrière un adjectif court (hard**er and** hard**er**).

- Pour dire « de moins en moins ... », on utilise :

\- ***fewer and fewer*** devant un nom dénombrable (**fewer and fewer** pioneers) ;
\- ***less and less*** dans les autres cas (**less and less** water).

Remarque : Les transformations orthographiques sont les mêmes que pour le comparatif :
lucky → luckier and luckier
big → bigger and bigger

2. Explique à ton camarade quelques aspects de la conquête de l'ouest en utilisant un double comparatif.

a. Over the years, the journey west became ... *(– dangerous)* for people.
b. The journey became ... *(+ short)*.
c. As ... *(+ people)* arrived, there was ... *(– food)* on the frontier.
d. ... *(+ pioneers)* went to the frontier during the Gold Rush.
e. Finding land got ... *(+ difficult)*.

Plus d'exercices sur ton CD audio-rom

3 Je sais exprimer une quantité. → *Mémento p. 137*

Un **quantifieur** donne une précision sur la **quantité**.
Il peut être différent si le nom qui le suit est **dénombrable ou indénombrable**.

Quantité \ Nom	**dénombrable** *(pioneers)*	**indénombrable** *(water)*
nulle	no / not any	
petite	(a) few	(a) little
indéfinie	some / any	
suffisante	enough	
grande	a lot of / lots of / many	a lot of / lots of / much
totale	all (the)	

3. Ton camarade a été absent au cours précédent. Fais-lui un résumé des difficultés rencontrées par les pionniers.

a. De nombreux pionniers émigrèrent *(move)* à l'ouest après 1848.
b. Quelques familles eurent des problèmes avec les Indiens.
c. Il y eut assez de terre *(land)* au début.
d. Parfois, ils ne trouvaient pas d'eau.
e. Tous les émigrants cherchaient *(look for)* une vie meilleure.
f. Ils avaient souvent peu d'argent.

STEP 3 Remember and practise

1 Je sais quand utiliser un gérondif. → Mémento p. 138

Le **gérondif**, ou **nom verbal**, se forme en ajoutant ***-ing*** à la base verbale. Il permet de parler d'**activités**. Il peut être **sujet** ou **complément** et s'emploie généralement **après les prépositions** : *of, after, before, by, with, without...*

• Le **gérondif** peut avoir toutes les fonctions d'**un nom commun**. Observe les phrases suivantes.

Singing cowboy ballads is part of western culture.
Le gérondif est sujet du verbe.

They saw western **dancing** at the hotel.
Le gérondif est complément du verbe. Il peut, comme un nom, être qualifié par un adjectif *(western)*.

Before visiting the museum, go to the tourist centre.
Le gérondif suit une préposition.

Les activités (chanter, danser ou visiter) sont mises en valeur.

• **Remarque :** Le gérondif peut avoir un sens général :
Speaking English is easy.
ou plus précis :
Driving fast on a wet road is dangerous.

1. Tu travailles dans un office du tourisme du Wyoming. Propose diverses activités aux touristes en mettant la base verbale qui convient au gérondif.

see • fish • hike • visit • snowboard

a. You can go ... in Yellowstone National Park.
b. ... a buffalo in the wild is a wonderful experience.
c. Are you fond of ...? We have a lot of snow in Cody in winter.
d. Why don't you visit the museum after... in the river?
e. ... the town in a trolley bus is great fun!

2 Je sais mettre en valeur une information en utilisant la voix passive. → Mémento p. 149

Le passif est très utilisé en anglais. Avec certains **verbes à double complément** comme *give, tell, show, offer, ask, send, teach...* **deux formes passives** sont possibles, en fonction de l'information que l'on veut mettre en valeur.

• **Phrase à la voix active :**
He gave me a leaflet.

• **Transformation passive 1 :**
A leaflet was given **to** me.
↓
Information mise en valeur : le dépliant.

• **Transformation passive 2 :**
I was given a leaflet.
↓
Information mise en valeur : la personne (*ici*, moi) à qui on a donné le dépliant.

Remarques :
- Il est **plus courant** en anglais de **mettre en valeur** la **personne** plutôt que l'objet.
- Lorsque c'est la personne qui est mise en valeur à la voix passive, **on utilise en français le pronom « on »**, dont l'équivalent n'existe pas en anglais. Ici : *On m'a donné un dépliant.*

2. Les billets que tu as achetés pour le rodéo ne sont pas valables. Raconte ce qui s'est passé hier soir en mettant le verbe à la voix passive ou active.

a. My friend and I *(refuse)* admission.
b. I *(ask)* where the tickets came from. I *(say)* they *(come)* from an Internet site.
c. I *(tell)* to sit down and wait while the lady *(speak)* to her boss.
d. I *(give)* new tickets and we *(tell)* to come back the next day.

3. Ta famille et toi êtes mécontents de votre séjour dans un hôtel. Tu souhaites laisser ce message sur un forum. Réécris-le en utilisant la voix passive quand c'est possible.

I am very dissatisfied with our stay at that hotel. Nobody told my parents there was no hot water because the system was out of order and nobody gave us any information when I phoned the front desk! And when we left the next day, the manager didn't offer us any compensation for the discomfort. I will never go back to this hotel!

PR1JECT

Create the totem of your group.

A. Make a survey.

- Divisez la classe en 3 groupes.
- Faites un sondage dans le groupe pour déterminer vos qualités et défauts :
hard-working, jealous, talkative, friendly, shy, kind, patient, aggressive, proud, curious, strong, determined, fast, agile, organized, respectful ...
- Effectuez un bilan du sondage :
Some of us are ..., most/lots of us are ...,
few people in our group are ...

B. Choose what best represents your group.

À partir des résultats du sondage, choisissez les animaux, les couleurs et les symboles qui correspondent le mieux au groupe.

C. Create your totem.

Utilisez un support en carton et cherchez des illustrations pour créer votre totem (peinture, dessin, photo, collage).

D. Report to the class.

Présentez le totem de votre groupe à la classe en justifiant vos choix.
Our totem is made of ...
It is a ... to represent ... because most of us are ...

PR2JECT

Play snakes and ladders.

A. Write down your questions.

Par groupe de 2 ou 3, rédigez une dizaine de questions sur le vocabulaire, sur la grammaire ou sur la culture dans la *Unit 2*.
Exemples :
- Mets la phrase suivante au passif :
White settlers forced Indians to live on reservations.
- Comment dirais-tu « du bétail » ?
- Quel est le vrai nom de Buffalo Bill ?

B. Play!

- Mettez toutes les questions en commun. Mélangez-les.
- Divisez la classe en deux groupes.
- Le professeur vous donne un plateau de jeu, un dé et un paquet de questions.
- Déterminez les règles du jeu.

Exemples :
- Un joueur qui arrive sur une case avec une échelle grimpe, alors que le serpent le fait redescendre.
- Un joueur qui arrive sur une case déjà occupée par un pion fait reculer le pion de son adversaire de trois cases...

- Quelle équipe arrivera la première ?

To be continued... **Gardez précieusement vos questions. Elles vous serviront à créer un jeu dans la *Unit 3*.**

Words

1 **Match a means of transportation with one of the verbs:** *sail • ride • walk*

a. a wagon
b. a horse
c. a raft
d. a bike
e. feet

2 **Find the odd one out!**

a. Which verb is not related to money and property?
sell • purchase • buy • own • trade • starve
b. Which word does not refer to animals?
cattle • pioneer • horses • sheep • alligators
c. Which word is spelled the same in the plural?
sheep • worker • woman • ticket

3 **Find the word corresponding to each definition.**

a. To kill animals for food or for their fur.
b. A synonym of "trip" (it starts with a "j"!).

4 **Solve the riddle.**

He loves the west and ranches but he doesn't like getting dirty or roping cows.

5 PLAY WITH WORDS!

a. Observe les phrases suivantes.

1. *The show began with a parade on* ***horseback.***
2. *He supplied the* ***railroad*** *workers with buffalo meat.*

b. Réfléchis.

• Observe l'exemple.

horse + ***back***
élément 1 — élément 2

• Le mot le plus important est **l'élément 2**. L'**élément 1**, *horse*, est un nom qui précise le sens de *back*. L'expression ainsi composée signifie « à **dos de cheval** ». C'est l'élément 2 qui, en français, est traduit en premier.

• Décompose l'exemple 2, ***railroad***, en suivant la même méthode et propose une traduction.

c. À ton tour !

• Propose une traduction pour les mots en gras dans les phrases suivantes.
1. *The young girl was in a* ***wheelchair.***
2. *Have you seen my new* ***raincoat?***

• Propose un mot en anglais pour les expressions suivantes.
3. une tasse à thé
4. un chauffeur de taxi

CHECKPOINT

Listen to an extract from Calamity Jane's autobiography and do the following activities.

a. Write down the dates you hear. Then find out what happened at these dates and write a short timeline.
b. What skills did Calamity Jane possess?
c. Find out two jobs she did.
d. Say if the following sentences are true or false.
- Calamity Jane hunted a lot with the men when her family emigrated.
- She joined General Grant as a scout.
- She was hurt a lot while being a Pony Express rider.

HELP
a scout: *un éclaireur* • a good shot: *un bon tireur*

Speak about this book cover.

a. Present the book.
It's called ... / written by ...
b. Describe the book cover.
c. Speak about the characters:
Where are they going? What for? ...
(Remember what you learned in the *Steps.*)

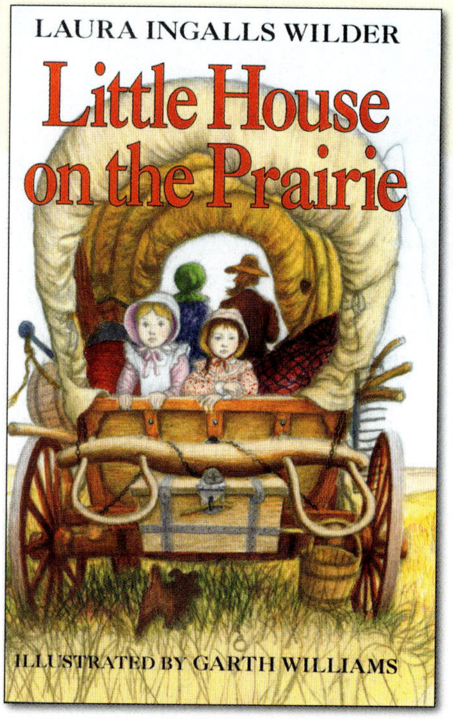

Read this tourist leaflet.

The Little House Today

The official historic site of the Little House on the Prairie as designated by the State of Kansas is located southwest of Independence, Kansas. (...) Today, the Ingalls family's one-room cabin is replicated exactly as Laura described in *The Little House on the Prairie*. (...) All the references to surrounding terrain[1] can be found a short distance from the cabin. (...) Sunnyside School (...) is a one-room school-house that was used from 1872-1947. The school holds authentic desks from the 1870s and 1880s and countless charming country school details. The site also features[2] an original turn-of-the-century Post Office that served the Wayside, Ks., area until the mid 1970s.

Visitors are invited to visit the site from 22 March to 31 October. Monday-Saturday 10:00 a.m. to 5:00 p.m. and Sundays 1:00 p.m. to 5:00 p.m. Admission is by donation.

Adapted from www.littlehouseontheprairie.com

1. **surrounding terrain** (n): *les alentours.* – 2. **feature** (v): *proposer, présenter.*

Now do the following activities.

a. Find out where this little house is located.
b. Say why it is well-known.
c. Speak about the other buildings near this little house (type of buildings, details about the furniture, authentic or not? ...)
d. Can you visit it on 1 November? On a Wednesday in May?
e. You want to visit it on a Sunday. Find out the opening times and the price.

Quiz the class.

Make true or false statements about the American west. Then quiz the class.

Ex.: **Pupil A:** American settlers moved west in order to get a better life.
Pupil B: True.

Pupil A: Indians and American settlers lived together peacefully.
Pupil B: False. The Indians were pushed off their lands.

Write a postcard.

You're on holiday in the American west. Two days ago you attended a rodeo. You're writing a postcard to your best friend and telling her/him about it. → *Méthodologie, p. 130*

- Say if there were a few or a lot of people.
- Describe the costumes of the cowboys (colours, materials ...).
- Give details about the different activities during the rodeo.

WINDOW OF OPPORTUNITIES
PHONE
I am different but I am lovable.
VIOLENCE brings VIOLENCE
Safety brings cheers, accidents bring tears.
NO VIOLENCE KNOW PEACE
I drive You drive He dies! SAVE LIVES!
SHOW RACISM THE RED CARD!
I respect you, do respect me!

unit 3

Better, nicer, safer

STEP 1

Je parle de l'expérience de quelqu'un.
J'interroge quelqu'un sur son expérience.

STEP 2

Je dresse le bilan d'une situation.

STEP 3

Je donne mon opinion et réagis à celle des autres.

Focus on: Wonderful Initiatives in South Africa

PROJECTS

1. Create a comic strip or a film.
2. Test your knowledge.

CHECKPOINT

Starter

1. Look at the photo.
- Where was it taken? Imagine who wrote the speech bubbles.
- Read the speech bubbles. What are they about? Imagine what the people who wrote them want.
- Imagine other slogans and write speech bubbles to create your own wall of opportunities.

2. "My Ideal World" → *WB 1, p. 80*
Listen to the poem, "My Ideal World". Find out how the author of this poem feels and imagine why.

Je parle de l'expérience de quelqu'un.

A Discover some road safety signs.

Have you ever seen these signs? Can you guess what they mean?

The first sign means you ***must*** */* ***mustn't*** */* ***have to*** */* ***can't*** *...*

1

2

3

4

5

6

1. **avoid** (v): try not to.
2. **ticket** (n): *PV, amende.*

B Talk about your behaviour on the road. → *WB 1, p. 59*

You and your friend are both quite serious road users but not perfect!

Pupil A: You go to school by bike.
Pupil B: You drive a motor scooter.

In turn, ask your partner what he/she has already done while cycling/riding and answer his/her questions.

Have you ***ever*** *...? / Yes, I have* ***already*** *... / No, I have* ***never*** *... / I have ...* ***once/a few times****.*

Word bank

- cycle • text / send a text message • go through a red light • ride
- behaviour *(comportement)* • MP3 player • helmet • pavement *(trottoir)*

C Is texting while driving (TWD) dangerous? → *WB 1, p. 60*

Listen to these young American people talking about their TWD experiences. What was the most surprising opinion you heard?

SOUNDS *PISTE 20*
La prononciation du *th*.
→ *WB 1, p. 61*

IT'S UP TO YOU!

Choose a candidate for a job! → *WB 1, p. 61*

Three candidates filled in an application form *(formulaire)* to apply for the job of delivery man *(livreur)*.

1. Make groups of four. Pupil A is the manager, pupils B, C and D are the assistants.
Each assistant has a candidate's application form. The assistants answer the manager's questions.

Manager: *Have they ever ...?*
Assistant: *Mr X has never ... / has ... once.*

2. The manager chooses the best candidate and explains why.

MEMO
- **Have** you **ever texted** while driving?
- **I've done** it **a few times**.
- It's **the** long**est** message I **have ever written**. → *p. 60*

J'interroge quelqu'un sur son expérience.

A Are driving licences different across the Atlantic?

All American and Canadian States have adopted Graduated Driver License* programmes for under-18 drivers. A teenager is asking a driving instructor questions about this specific licence.

***license** (US) (n): licence (UK).

1. **Listen to the dialogue. What are the specificities of the American driving licence?** → *WB 1, p. 62*

2. **What do you think about the American system? How different is it from the French system?**

B What are the restrictions for Graduated Driver Licenses?

→ *WB 1, p. 62*

Look at these tables and compare the Graduated Driver Licenses in these two states.

They both have set (fixer) *...*
Idaho has ... for / since ...
Arizona passed its GDL law in ...

Arizona GDL (updated 07/2008)	
Level 1	Minimum age: 15 ½
Level 2	Minimum age: 16 No driving between midnight and 5 a.m. Maximum: 1 passenger under 18 for the first six months
Level 3	Minimum age: 16

Idaho GDL (updated 2001)	
Level 1	Minimum age: 14 ½
Level 2	Minimum age: 15 No driving between sunset and sunrise Maximum: 1 passenger under 17 for the first six months
Level 3	Minimum age: 18

C How do some parents keep an eye on their teen's driving? → *WB 1, p. 63*

Look at the illustration and read the texts. Discover a parents' solution to reduce risky behaviour.

Track Them or Trust Them?

American Family Insurance introduced a program[1] in August 2007 in Colorado to monitor[2] teen drivers with a car-mounted video camera that records erratic or dangerous driving behavior[3].

http://www.denverpost.com

"In some videos we've seen kids text-messaging, fiddling with the stereo and talking over their shoulders to their friends while they were driving," American Family Insurance's Steve Witmer said.

http://www.timesonline.co.uk

Katie Baldwin, 17, has enrolled[4] in American Family Insurance's teen safe driver program. Katie says Drivecam has made her a safer driver. "I've learned from it, actually being able to see what I did wrong."

http://abclocal.go.com

1. program (US) (n): programme (UK). – **2. monitor** (v): control. – **3. behavior** (US) (n): behaviour (UK). – **4. enrol** (v): join.

IT'S UP TO YOU!

Interview someone on his/her experiences. → *WB 1, p. 63*

An American teenager is asking a young French driver about his/her driving experience.

Pupil A: You are the American teenager. You want information about how long he/she's had his/her licence, his/her parents' attitude and his/her driving at night ... and ask for details! You can make comments.

Pupil B: You are the young French driver. Imagine your answers, give details about the experiences you've had.

MEMO
- Katie Baldwin **has enrolled** in a teen safe driver programme.
- American Family Insurance **introduced** this programme in August 2007. → p. 60

STEP 2 Je dresse le bilan d'une situation.

1 Get ready!

What is bullying?

1. Look at the pictures and try to give a definition.

2. Say if these acts are bullying. Justify your answers. → *WB 1, p. 64*

... is (not) bullying because ...

What other acts of bullying can you think of?

Word bank
- funny • common ≠ occasional
- harmless ≠ harmful *(blessant)*
- game • fun
- push • steal

- Insulting someone. / Calling someone names.
- Spreading rumours about someone.
- Hitting someone who did nothing to you.
- Refusing to talk to someone because he was rude to you.
- Sending death messages on the Internet.
- Playing a trick on April Fools' Day (April 1st).

3. What do bullies want? What do they want others to do?

Word bank
- show respect • frighten • have a good time • give money • be afraid of ...

2 Step forward!

A What has he been doing for some time?

1. Look at the document and imagine what this man's job is and why he is interested in the problem of bullying.

2. Then listen to an interview with Robert Frenette. How and why has he been fighting against bullying?
→ *WB 1, p. 65, CD piste 21*

Word bank
- bully • campaign against • be a victim of • work for • advise • inform

SOUNDS PISTE 22
Les liaisons.
→ *WB 1, p. 66*

B Write an e-mail. → *WB 1, p. 67*

Some young people have been bullying one of your classmates for some time. You are sending an e-mail to Robert Frenette. Tell him what your classmate has been enduring and what the bullies want him/her to do.

Some people have been ... for/since ...
They want him/her to ... / He/She feels ... /
They don't want him/her to ...

STRATEGIES

Comme tu t'adresses à quelqu'un que tu ne connais pas, adopte le bon registre de langue.
→ *Méthodologie, p. 130* : **Écrire un e-mail.**

C What have they been doing against bullying? → WB 1, p. 68

1. Read the text and learn about what two wardens[1] have been doing against bullying in schools.

This year, two street wardens[1] from Tamworth, Staffordshire, are going into schools to promote the message of Anti-bullying. The scheme[2] has been running since 2001 but this is the first time that two of the wardens, James Vanstone and Brian Lees, have decided to get involved with Anti-Bullying Week.

James said, "Brian and myself came to the conclusion that we needed to tackle[3] anti-social behaviour in schools, as well as beyond[4] the school gates. So far, James and Brian have visited 16 of the 30 schools in Tamworth from infant to high schools.

They do a presentation for the pupils and then show them a video clip from last year's campaign, "Make a stand and wear a band".

"I believe the kids have learnt about what to do if they are being bullied as well as why people bully and the different kinds of bullying," said James.

Since they started, James and Brian have also been running an inter-school competition asking pupils to design a poster that makes a stand against cyber-bullying. The winning posters will be published in Tamworth's Talk Back magazine.

Adapted from www.anti-bullyingalliance.org.uk

1. **warden** (n)≈ *gardien de la paix.* 2. **scheme** /ki:/ (n): programme. – 3. **tackle** (v): fight against. – 4. **beyond** (prep): outside.

2. Imagine you are in an English school which is very active against bullying. Tell James and Brian what you and your school have been doing recently.

Word bank

- participate in Anti-Bullying Week • make / display posters • punish • call parents • organize meetings • inform • report • suspend • expel

DVD **Video time** → WB 1, p. 69
An anti-bullying cartoon

An anti-bullying demonstration in London.

D What can you do if someone bullies you?

→ WB 1, p. 70

Listen to this advice in case of bullying.

MAKE IT YOURS!

Imagine a conversation.

A principal is phoning Brian Lees about the violence in his school. He's telling him what has been going on in his school. Brian Lees gives him information about his action in schools and the message to give to bullied pupils.

Pupil A: You play the part of the principal.
Some pupils have been ... / I want/don't want them to ...

Pupil B: You play the part of Brian.
Have you been ...?

STRATEGIES

N'oublie pas l'intonation montante dans les *Yes/No questions.*
→ Méthodologie, p. 127 : **Parler au téléphone.**

MEMO
- They **wanted** me **to buy** cigarettes.
- The scheme **has been running** since 2001.
- You must tell **somebody**. → p. 61

STEP 3 Je donne mon opinion et réagis à celle des autres.

1 Get ready!

A What do you think of graffiti?

Do you like graffiti? Why? Why not?

Word bank

- disgusting • dirty • neglected • beautiful • creative
- wall • district • signature /tʃə/

STRATEGIES

Utilise des expressions comme :
In my opinion … / I dislike … / I am (not) fond of …
→ *Méthodologie, p. 127* :
Formuler son opinion.

B What do they think of graffiti?

→ *WB 1, p. 71, CD piste 23*

Listen to find out what these people think of graffiti. Who do you agree/disagree with? Why?

SOUNDS PISTE 24

Les sons /ɔː/ et /əʊ/.
→ *WB 1, p. 71*

2 Step forward!

A Graffiti in Bristol, England. → *WB 1, p. 71*

Read the article. What does Will think about graffiti in his city?

Julia Thompson talked to Will Briggson, a fifteen-year-old boy, who has decided to fight against graffiti.

Will, how did you get involved in removing graffiti from your neighbourhood?

Well … there're graffiti everywhere on my estate*, and it makes everything look ugly and dirty. Everything's tagged: the halls, the lift, the walls … One day, I saw a group of young people wiping off graffiti from a bus shelter. I talked to them and that's how I started. They're just a bunch of young people like me who're fed up with the estate being spoilt by tagging.

A cleaning squad.

So you work in a team?

That's what we do, we're a sort of cleaning squad but it's a really hard job. Some tags are very hard to get rid of and anyway, as soon as it's clean, the taggers come back, spray paint everywhere and make everything dirty again. I think we should make them clean up their own mess!

Do you think the situation is getting any better?

Well … yes. More and more young people want to be part of the cleaning squad and we're trying to have an art wall set up on our estate so that taggers can express themselves … and we can keep our city clean!

*estate (n): *lotissement.*

Word bank

- ugly • repulsive • dirty
- get rid of / remove (*enlever*) • clean

B Can graffiti be art?

1. Look at this mural by Banksy, a very famous British graffiti artist. What does it represent? How has it been created? Say if you like it or not and why. → *WB 1, p. 73*

A TV aerial has been ...

Word bank

- watering can • TV aerial /eərɪəl/ • stencil
- water • turn into • transform into

Banksy, *The Watercan Girl*.

2. Read these headlines about Banksy. → *WB 1, p. 74*
What do these headlines tell us about Banksy and his murals?
What has a London council* decided?
What do you think about this decision?

*council (n): *municipalité*.

1 Has Banksy's real identity been discovered at last?

The Independent, Monday, 14 July 2008.

2 ➔ COUNCIL PRESERVES BANKSY MURALS

BBC, Wednesday, 7 November 2007.

3 > Artist Banksy "captured in photo"

BBC, Wednesday, 31 October 2007.

Banksy, *Music Rat*.

DVD **Video time** → *WB 1, p. 75*
A mobile "art house"

MAKE IT YOURS!

A radio show.

You are a Londoner. One of Banksy's creations was stencilled on the wall next to your home for days. Today, it has been removed.

1. Listen to your neighbour's reaction, Elizabeth, on "Have Your Say!" on CBC 6. What does she think of graffiti?

2. **Pupil A:** Phone in and say what you think about Elizabeth's reaction.
Pupil B: Phone in and react to your classmate's or Elizabeth's opinion.
Pupil C/D ...: Phone in and react to what the others have said.

I agree with Jenny because ... / I disagree with Tony and Elizabeth ...

STRATEGIES

Réemploie les expressions que tu connais pour exprimer ton opinion.
→ *Méthodologie, p. 127* : **Formuler son opinion.**

MEMO
- We **made** them **clean** the wall.
- **Has** Banksy's real identity **been** discover**ed** at last? → *p. 62*

Focus on Wonderful Initiatives

Zip Zap Circus School

A juggling class at the Zip Zap Circus School.

For decades, millions of black people suffered from poverty and racism in South Africa. Their situation has improved and some organizations are working to make things even better.

In Cape Town, the Zip Zap Circus School (created in 1992) is an organization which helps and educates South African children. It attracts kids and teenagers of all races and social backgrounds: some live in nice suburbs[1], some live in poor areas or on the streets.

At the circus, the children learn the trapeze, the trampoline, juggling … They practise and rehearse[2] their acts for the next show. But they also learn practical skills[3]. They make the costumes, build their props[4], repair the equipment to be able to get a future job outside the school.

Racism is not tolerated in the circus. Zip Zap teaches the children mutual respect, trust[5] and tolerance.

1. suburbs (n): *banlieues.* - **2. rehearse** (v): *répéter.* - **3. skill** (n): *compétence.* - **4. prop** (n): *accessoire.* - **5. trust** (n): *confiance.*

GAPA

In 2001, near Cape Town, a group of grandmothers and a doctor formed a non-profit organization called Grandmothers Against Poverty and AIDS[1]. Since then, GAPA has been providing educational workshops[2] and support to hundreds of grandmothers whose families have been affected by HIV/AIDS.

A knitting workshop at GAPA.

During these workshops, they are given medical information and taught about nursing, gardening, human rights and business skills. The gardening workshops have encouraged many grandmothers to start up vegetable gardens at their homes. GAPA has also started an Aftercare Service for vulnerable children after school. Grandmothers make them do their homework, teach them skills (knitting[3], beadwork[4] …) or tell them traditional stories.

Moreover, GAPA has opened co-operatives in which grandmothers sell their handmade products (blankets, cushions, clothes, beadwork …). GAPA has been very successful in helping South African grandmothers to cope better with their daily lives.

1. AIDS (n): *SIDA.* - **2. workshop** (n): *atelier.* - **3. knitting** /nɪtɪŋ/ (n): *tricot.* - **4. beadwork** (n): *objets fabriqués avec des perles.*

in South Africa

The Wall of Peace, site of the old jail in Durban.

Community murals

Colourful paintings on walls can be seen everywhere in South Africa. These murals, which have been more and more popular since the mid-90s, bring people together. While painting, professional artists work side by side with children or adults from different cultures and backgrounds.
These murals not only focus on the diversity of the South African people, they are also a means[1] to inform. Democracy, freedom, traditional stories and images of daily life are very popular topics[2] in murals. Moreover, the paintings decorate the buildings and the streets brightly, making them nicer.

Adapted from www.kabatana.net

1. means: (n): *moyen.* - **2. topic:** (n): *sujet.*

CD rom: Storytelling - Dian Fossey'sworld

SCANNING

→ *WB 1, p. 76*

Have a good look at the documents and read the texts.

1. **Find out who is involved in these initiatives.**

2. **Name three major problems in South Africa.**

3. **Pick out some values that make things better in South Africa.**

4. **Find out three means of educating.**

5. **In the texts, find the words which mean:**
améliorer, partout, se débrouiller, rassembler les gens, une origine sociale, la liberté, des produits faits main.

WEBQUEST

→ *WB 1, p. 77*

Cyberbullying
Go to these sites and do the webquest in your workbook.

1. **Define cyberbullying.**
http://netbullies.com/pages/1/index.htm

2. **Explain the forms cyberbullying can take?**
http://www.direct.gov.uk/en/YoungPeople/HealthAndRelationships/Bullying/DG_070501

3. **Comment on the statistics.**
http://www.isafe.org/channels/sub.php?ch=op&sub_id=media_cyber_bullying

1 Je sais faire un bilan de mes expériences. → Mémento p. 143

Le ***present perfect*** sert à faire **un bilan**, à exprimer **ce que l'on a déjà ou jamais fait**. Il se forme avec l'auxiliaire ***have*** au présent suivi du **participe passé** du verbe.

• Pour se renseigner sur ce que quelqu'un a **déjà** fait, on utilise l'adverbe ***ever*** placé juste avant le participe passé du verbe.

Have you ever **sent** a text message while driving?

• Pour parler de la **fréquence** de ces activités, on place **l'adverbe de fréquence** entre l'auxiliaire et le participe passé.

I **have** never / sometimes **sent** a text message while driving.

Attention : Les expressions indiquant un **nombre de fois** se placent en fin de phrase.

I **have texted** once / twice / several times.

Remarque : *ever* s'utilise aussi avec le superlatif pour souligner le caractère exceptionnel d'une action.

It's **the best** idea I've ever had.

It's **the most dangerous** thing I've ever seen.

Rappel : Le superlatif est utilisé pour dire qu'une chose est unique par rapport à toutes les autres de sa catégorie.

	Adjectifs courts	Adjectifs longs
Superlatif de supériorité (le plus...)	**the** + adjectif + **-est** **the** greatest artist	**the** + **most** + adjectif **the most** dangerous behaviour
Superlatif d'infériorité (le moins...)	**the least** + adjectif **the least** interesting (rarement avec un adjectif court)	

1. Pose trois questions à cette conductrice de scooter pour savoir si elle a déjà fait ces actions.

2. Un conducteur fait le bilan de ses premiers mois de conduite et parle de ce qu'il a déjà fait et de la fréquence à laquelle cela s'est produit. Écris ces phrases.

a. forget seatbelt / a few times
b. drive at night / once
c. use mobile while driving / never
d. drive over the limit / rarely

3. Réagis à ces commentaires que te fait un ami.

Ex. : *"I've decided to stop speeding behind the wheel!*
→ *"It's **the best** decision you've **ever** taken."*

a. Look at my new designer helmet!
b. This article about road safety is great!
c. That TV programme about teens' driving was really stupid!
d. This car is so safe and so comfortable!

2 Je sais faire un bilan et donner des détails sur ce qui est arrivé. → Mémento p. 143

Pour faire un **bilan** ou **parler des conséquences** d'un événement passé sur le présent, on utilise le ***present perfect***.
Mais pour **donner des détails** sur cet événement en le situant **dans le passé**, on emploie le **prétérit**.

• On utilise le ***present perfect*** lorsqu'on s'intéresse aux **conséquences présentes**, au **résultat**, ou lorsque on fait un **bilan**.

I've lost my keys.
(Conséquence : je ne peux pas rentrer chez moi.)

I've had a bad day!
(Bilan de ma journée.)

• On utilise le **prétérit** lorsqu'on situe l'événement dans le temps. On raconte les détails de cet événement passé et on ne s'intéresse pas à ses conséquences sur le présent.

I've had an awful day! This morning, I **arrived** late, I **lost** my keys ...

Le prétérit est souvent associé à un marqueur temporel comme ... *ago / last year / yesterday / in 2008.*

4. Un jeune va prendre une leçon de conduite. Le moniteur fait un bilan avec lui pour vérifier qu'il est en règle. Utilise les informations suggérées pour répondre.

Ex. : *"Have you paid for your registration?"*
"Yes, I have. I paid for it when I came two days ago."

a. bring valid ID* / I *(register)*
b. read your highway code / this summer
c. give a photo / this morning
d. fill in the forms / I first *(come)*

***ID:** identity card.

1 Je sais dire quelle est mon activité depuis un certain temps. → *Mémento p. 143*

Quand on veut mettre en valeur l'**activité** qui est celle du sujet **depuis un certain temps** jusqu'au moment présent, on utilise le ***present perfect* en BV-*ing*** (*has/ have been* + BV-*ing*).

• On emploie le ***present perfect*** en **BV-*ing*** pour des actions qui ont commencé dans le passé et qui durent toujours. La durée est exprimée par :
- ***for*** suivi d'une durée : **for** some years.
- ***since*** suivi du point de départ de l'action : **since** 2006 / **since** I left.
Le mot interrogatif est *How long*.
How long have they been fighting?

• Formation du ***present perfect*** en **BV-*ing***

Affirmation	We **have been** designing posters.
Négation	We **have not been** participating.
Interrogation	**Have** you **been** designing posters?

Remarque : Le *present perfect* en **BV-*ing*** est incompatible avec des verbes dont on n'envisage pas le déroulement (*love, like, know, be* ...) et ne peut être suivi d'un complément indiquant une quantité précise (*I've written two letters*).

1. Ta famille et toi avez été très occupés depuis ce matin. Écris ce que vous avez fait. Conjugue le verbe et complète avec *for* ou *since*.

a. I ... *(read)* comics ... 9 a.m.
b. My parents ... *(do)* the shopping ... one hour.
c. My sister ... *(phone)* her friends ... forty minutes.
d. My twin brother ... *(play)* tennis ... 10:30 a.m.

2. Ton camarade est en retard. Tu l'informes sur l'intervention des deux policiers dans la classe. Choisis la forme simple ou la forme en BV-*ing*.

a. They ... *(answer)* our questions about bullying.
b. They ... *(work)* together for ten years.
c. They ... *(already / visit)* sixteen schools.
d. They ... *(visit)* schools since 2001.
e. They ... *(meet)* more than 500 pupils.

Plus d'exercices sur ton CD audio-rom

2 Je sais exprimer une volonté. → *Mémento p. 147*

Pour dire ce que quelqu'un veut que quelqu'un d'autre fasse, on utilise ***want* suivi d'une proposition infinitive** : *want someone to do something*.

Affirmation	He **wants** me **to** respect others.
Négation	They **don't want** me **to** be violent.
Interrogation	Do they **want** me **to** respect others?

Remarque : Cette structure est également possible avec *expect* (s'attendre à), *tell* (dire), *ask* (demander), *teach* (apprendre, enseigner)...

3. Ces élèves n'ont pas respecté le règlement du collège. Dis ce que le principal veut qu'ils fassent.

3 Je sais parler de personnes, de choses ou de lieux indéfinis. → *Mémento p. 137*

On utilise les **pronoms composés de *some*, *any* et *no*** pour parler de personnes, de lieux ou de choses indéfinis. Leur choix dépend de la nature des phrases (affirmative, négative ou interrogative).

• ***some***, ***any*** et ***no*** sont associés à :
-***body*** ou -***one*** pour parler de personnes indéfinies
somebody / someone / anybody / nobody ...
-***where*** pour parler de lieux indéfinis
somewhere / nowhere ...
-***thing*** pour parler de choses indéfinies
anything / nothing ...

• Les composés de ***some*** sont plutôt utilisés dans des affirmations et les composés de ***any*** dans des questions ou des négations.

4. Ce collégien rentre chez lui enthousiaste. Complète la conversation qu'il a avec sa mère, avec un composé de *some*, de *any* ou de *no*.

"Mum, guess what!"
"Did you do ... special? Did you go ...?"
"Yes, we did ... very interesting."
"Did ... come in your class? "
"Yes, two wardens. They told us about an inter-school competition. That's ... I want to take part in."

STEP 3 Remember and practise

1 Je sais faire le bilan de ce qui a été subi.

Le ***present perfect* passif** permet de faire **un bilan** de ce qui a été fait ou de s'intéresser à **ce qui vient de se passer** (avec *just*), en mettant en valeur **l'objet ou la personne qui subit l'action**.

Le ***present perfect* passif** se forme avec l'auxiliaire ***be*** conjugué au ***present perfect*** *(has/have been)* et le participe passé du verbe.

A group of taggers **has** just **been arrested**.

L'arrestation vient de se dérouler, donc j'emploie le *present perfect*.

Je m'intéresse aux taggers. Ils subissent l'action, donc je choisis la voix passive.

Look! Mr Wilson's bike **has been stolen**.

Je constate le vol (bilan) donc j'emploie le *present perfect*.

Je m'intéresse au vélo de M. Wilson. Le vélo a « subi » l'action, donc je choisis la voix passive.

1. Tu constates que la salle de sport a changé. Explique ces changements.

Ex.: *We can't play basketball any more.* (the baskets / remove)
→ *The baskets have been removed.*

a. It's more comfortable to do the exercises now. *(the old mats / replace)*
b. The room is spick-and-span. *(it / just / clean)*
c. There is new equipment. *(two fitness machines / add)*
d. It's hot in there. *(the heating system / repair)*

2. Tu es chargé(e) de communiquer plusieurs informations à ta classe. Comment dirais-tu que... :

a. trois livres du CDI viennent d'être volés.
b. deux nouvelles salles de cours ont été peintes en jaune.
c. la cantine vient d'être rénovée. *(renovate)*
d. une nouvelle cuisinière a été embauchée. *(hire)*

2 Je sais exprimer une contrainte sur autrui. → *Mémento p. 147*

Pour exprimer **une contrainte sur autrui**, on utilise l'expression ***make somebody* + BV**.

Mr Zidi	makes	**his pupils**	work a lot.
He	makes	**them**	work a lot.
↓	↓	↓	↓
GN ou pronom personnel sujet	V1 : verbe conjugué	GN ou pronom personnel complément	V2 : base verbale

• **Le sujet**, *Mr Zidi*, contraint (*makes* : V1) ses élèves (*his pupils*) à travailler (*work* : V2) ; il n'accomplit pas l'action lui-même.

work est une base verbale, donc il ne se conjugue pas :
Mr Zidi made {Sandra / her} **workØ** a lot.

Remarques : On peut souvent traduire *make somebody do something* par l'expression « faire faire quelque chose à quelqu'un ».

My parents made me tidy up my room.
Mes parents m'ont fait ranger ma chambre.

Lorsque l'expression *make somebody* est suivie d'un adjectif qualificatif, on utilise le verbe « rendre » dans la traduction.

She made him **happy**.
Elle l'a rendu heureux.

3. Ton ami Chris, qui a 18 ans, est allé à une fête hier. Commente les images.

dance • listen • play • stay • sleep at her place • give up driving

Ex.: Chris was tired but Anna made ...
It was late but Tom made ...

PR1JECT

Create a comic strip or a film.

A. Choose a theme and make a survey.

Group 1: Work on relationships between people.
• Votre sondage portera sur les relations entre élèves, avec les adultes...
• Posez vos questions au groupe 2.
Have you ever been bullied / pushed someone / been ...?
Are you satisfied with ...?

Group 2: Work on your school environment.
• Votre sondage devra porter sur les problèmes liés aux bâtiments, aux salles de classe, à la cantine...
• Posez vos questions au groupe 3.
Have you ever written ... / made ... dirty?
What do you suggest to ...? / How could we ...?

Group 3: Work on timetables, school clubs and activities in your school.
• Votre sondage devra porter sur les emplois du temps, les clubs, les activités proposées dans votre établissement.
• Posez vos questions au groupe 1.
Have you ever participated in ...? / Do you sometimes leave at ...? / What do/don't you like in ...?

B. Create a comic strip or film.

• Sélectionnez les réponses les plus intéressantes et représentatives de votre questionnaire.
• Choisissez un slogan, le(s) héros de votre bande dessinée ou allez sur le site http://stripgenerator.com/create/ pour créer une bande dessinée ou http://www.dfilm.com/live/home.html pour créer votre film.

C. Elect the best.

La classe vote pour la meilleure réalisation.

PR2JECT

Test your knowledge.

A. Write questions.

• Par groupe de quatre ou cinq, rédigez des questions sur ce que vous avez vu dans la *Unit 3*.
• Classez-les en 3 catégories: *Grammar*, *Vocabulary*, *General Knowledge*.

B. Write your own rules.

• Apportez un plateau de jeu, des jetons et des dés.
• Attribuez une couleur à chaque catégorie.
• Inventez vos propres règles pour les couleurs restantes.
When you are on a blue square, you answer a question on Grammar ...
When you are on a ... square, you lose your turn / you have to answer two questions / you choose your question ...

C. Now toss the dice and have fun!

PROJET FINAL : Ajoutez les questions que vous avez créées dans les *Projects 2* des *Units 1* et *2*. Amusez-vous bien !

Words

1 **Complete the sentences with the right word.**

ticket • polls • speed • safety • risky

a. If you don't respect the ... limit, the police can give you a ...
b. Parents' associations promote ... on the road.
c. Opinion ... have shown that dangerous driving is still common.
d. Texting while driving is very ... behaviour.

2 **Match some of these words to their definitions.**

threaten • licence • behaviour • frighten • improve • seatbelt

a. Legal document authorizing to hunt, drive, fish.
b. The manner of conducting oneself.
c. Make better (v).

3 **Write three equivalents for "clean" (v).**

4 **Find the odd one out!**

dirty • repulsive • disgusting • safe • ugly

PLAY WITH WORDS!

5 **a. Observe la phrase suivante.**

Perhaps the supporters of graffiti don't realize the impact that graffiti have on the ***neighbourhood****.*

b. Réfléchis.

• Quelle est la classe grammaticale de *neighbourhoods* ? (adj, n, adv, v).

• Décompose ce mot en indiquant la racine et le suffixe.

• La racine de ce mot signifie « voisin ». Propose une traduction pour *neighbourhood*.

c. À ton tour !

• Propose une traduction pour les mots en gras dans les phrases suivantes.
1. ***Motherhood*** *really changed her: she looked very happy and relaxed.*
2. ***Childhood*** *can be the best moment in life.*

• Comment traduirais-tu en anglais le mot « fraternité » ?

CD rom : Discovery Game

CHECKPOINT

Listen to the TV report and do the following activities.

a. Listen to the report and say what it is about.
b. How many children are victims of this problem?
c. Explain what has increased* the problem.
d. Give two reasons why children don't say they are victims of it (at home and at school).
e. What recommendation does the expert give?

***increase** (v) **:** *augmenter, accentuer.*

Make a survey.

Subject 1

Ask your classmates five questions about their use of the Internet. Then collect the results and give statistics.

Ex.: *Have you ever downloaded music or films?*
How long have you been downloading films?

Subject 2

Ask your classmates five questions about graffiti.

Ex.: *Have you ever painted anything on a wall?*
What is the nicest graffiti you have ever seen?

Then collect the results and give statistics.

Ex.: *hardly anyone / one out of five / 50% / nearly everyone / most of the pupils ...*

Comment on a survey.

Recap on all the results you got in making one of the above surveys. Express your opinion.

Ex.: *...% of people in the class have already downloaded ... / done graffiti ...*
In my opinion / I think ...

Read the article.

Bewitching[1] Art of Slowing Traffic

Residents closed their North Oxford Street so they could create their own traffic-calming measures.

Artist Ted Dewan, 46, lives in Beech Croft Road, Summertown, and he has been leading efforts to cut traffic speeds for the past five years.

Last Saturday, the residents of the street creatively painted road surfaces, put up picnic tables, potted[2] trees and toy sheds[3] to narrow the road. (…) They called this new kind of art "roadwitches" and, according to Mr Dewan, a children's author, they have started a global phenomenon : some cities around the world are copying their technique.

The first roadwitch project took place (…) in 2002. Since then they have even built a living room in the street!

Mr Dewan, who lives with his wife Helen Cooper and their daughter Pandora, seven, said: "Ever since a child was hit by a car in 1999, people on our street have been campaigning to calm down the traffic and improve the security of pedestrians[4]. The campaign took a turn when we started (…) building art installations in the street; it distracted car drivers which made them slow down. Pieces such as Living Room proved very successful both at calming traffic and bringing people out into the street."

Adapted from www.oxfordmail.net,
Tuesday, 17 July 2007.

1. **bewitch** (v): *ensorceler*. – 2. **potted** (adj): *en pot*. – 3. **shed** (n): *cabane*. – 4. **pedestrian** (n): *piéton*.

Now do the following activities.

a. Read the text and find out where the event takes place and who had the idea (address, family information, job).
b. Find out what people did in this street Saturday 14 July.
c. Explain what these "roadwitches" are for.
d. Find out examples of "roadwitches".
e. Say if the following statements are true or false and justify by quoting from the text.
- Other cities in the world have copied these traffic-calming measures.
- The residents of this street started the road safety campaign after the death of a child in a car crash.
- They have been campaigning for three years.
- The "Living Room" project wasn't popular.

Write a letter.

You are staying with a British family in Oxford. Driving through Summertown you see a roadwitch. Write a letter to a friend about it.
- Explain to him/her what a roadwitch is and describe it.
- Say why it has been set up.
- Describe the car drivers' and the pedestrians' reactions.

A roadwitch, Beech Croft Road, Oxford, England, July 2003.

FOR
COLORED
ONLY

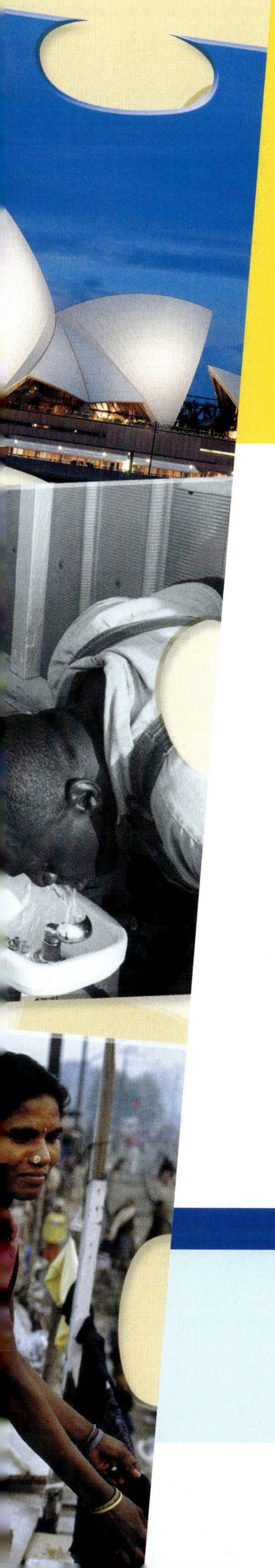

unit 4

Living together

STEP 1

Je me renseigne sur les droits et les devoirs dans le passé.
Je rends compte de l'évolution des droits dans le passé.

STEP 2

J'explique un événement passé.

STEP 3

Je défends une opinion et j'argumente.

Focus on: *Fighting Segregation in the USA*

PROJECTS

1. Create a card against exclusion.
2. Create your own slam.

CHECKPOINT

Starter

1. These photographs show three different countries.
Which ones? Can you match the photos in pairs?

2. Which contrasting aspects of each country does each pair illustrate?

CD Rom: Discovery Game.

STEP 1 Je me renseigne sur les droits et les devoirs dans le passé.

AFRICAN ANCESTRY
TRACE YOUR DNA. FIND YOUR ROOTS.

A African American identity today. ➜ *WB 2, p. 3*

Listen to this commercial about African Ancestry. What are many African Americans interested in today? How can technology help them?

B Talk about how slaves had to live.

1. Match each verb with an element on the right and say whether slaves had to do these actions or weren't allowed to do them. ➜ *WB 2, p. 3*

- sleep
- talk
- read
- be
- wear
- use
- work

- educated
- in small huts on plantations
- their birth name
- old and ill-fitting* clothes
- in their own languages
- from sunrise to sunset
- at all

***ill-fitting** (adj): too big or too small.

2. Can you imagine why some of these things weren't allowed?

Word bank
- communicate • write • rebel against
- identity • culture

C What was life like for African Americans after slavery?

➜ *WB 2, p. 4, CD piste 27*

Slavery was abolished in 1868. Former slaves were free but not considered as American citizens. Until the sixties, the rights of many African Americans were limited.

Listen and say what they had to do or what they weren't allowed to do.

SOUNDS *PISTE 28*
Les sons /æ/ et /ɑː/.
➜ *WB 2, p. 4*

IT'S UP TO YOU!

Prepare a video-conference.

1. Your teacher has organized a video-conference with an African American who grew up in a segregated city of Alabama.

Pupil A: Ask him/her what he/she was or wasn't allowed to do and what he/she had to do at that time.
Where did you have to …? / Did you have to …? / Were you allowed to …?

Pupil B: Answer the questions. ➜ *WB 2, p. 5*

STRATEGIES
Présente-toi et rappelle le but de cette vidéoconférence.

2. Recap on the segregation laws in Alabama and the consequences on African Americans' everyday life.
They were not allowed to … so they had to …

Word bank
- buses • schools • restaurants
- marriage /ɪ/ • trains • voting rights

➜ Go to pages 74-75 to learn more about segregation and the Civil Rights Movement.

MEMO
- Black people **had to** use "Colored-only" drinking fountains.
- They **weren't allowed to** use "White-only" bathrooms. ➜ *p. 76*

Je rends compte de l'évolution des droits dans le passé.

A It was a long way to the voting rights of 1965. → WB 2, p. 6

Look at the documents. What do they tell you about African Americans' voting rights? What did African Americans have to do to vote? When and how did things change?

The VRA* ensures that every American has the right to vote "with no ifs, ands or buts."

But the battle for equal opportunity is not yet over.

***VRA:** Voting Rights Act of 1965.

B 2008, Change they believe in! → WB 2, p. 6

Read the reactions of some black people who voted on 4 November 2008. Why was this election historic for them?

Bakewell, 62, grew up in the segregated city of New Orleans. There, he recalled, his family wasn't allowed to vote because they couldn't pass the infamous literacy test. (…)
Now, 43 years later, Bakewell cast his vote[1] for a fellow[2] African American, Barack Obama, in what he described as one of the most thrilling[3] moments of his life. "It was an absolutely incredible feeling to be able to be a witness to this in my lifetime (…)."
For Iris Hill (…), "This election means a great deal. So much had to change to get to this point," she said. Mrs Hill (…) was thinking of her grandmother, who was born in 1929 and lives in North Carolina. She was part of the Civil Rights Movement in the 1960s, (…) fighting for basic rights. She wasn't able to vote, back in the sixties, but was able to vote in this election for an African American for president.

www.latimes.com

1. **cast a vote** (v): vote. – 2. **fellow** (n): someone who has something in common with you. – 3. **thrilling** (adj): exciting.

IT'S UP TO YOU!

Write an article about a black American centenarian.

Ann Nixon Cooper voted at the age of 106! She witnessed a lot of changes in her lifetime.
You write an article about her experiences.

In the sixties, black Americans weren't allowed to …
They had to … / They weren't able to …
When she was younger, she probably had to …

Ann Nixon Cooper, 106 years old, Atlanta, 2008.

STRATEGIES

→ Méthodologie, p. 129 : **Se préparer à une production écrite.**

MEMO
- She **wasn't able to** vote.
- I **was able to** witness this change. → p. 76

1 Get ready!

Who are the Aborigines? → WB 2, p. 8

Read these texts and discover facts about the Aborigines and their relationship with white settlers. How were Aborigines considered in the past?

▶ Thurs 24 May, 2007

As a young girl, Aborigine[1] Jackie Huggins was not counted as part of the Australian population. (...) On Sunday, Aborigines will celebrate the 40th anniversary of a 1967 vote that extended Australian citizenship to Aborigines. "At 11 years of age I became a citizen[2] of my own country, where my people had lived for 70,000 years," Huggins recalled in an interview with Reuters on Thursday.

Jackie Huggins.

Adapted from www.cwo~lucumi/australia2.html

1. **Aborigine** (n): first inhabitant of Australia. – 2. **citizen** (n): member of a country.

Captain Cook (1728-1779) on *The Endeavour*.

When European people first came to Australia (led by Captain James Cook in 1770), they initially declared Australia *terra nullius*, "a land without owners", because the nomadic Aborigines were considered uncivilized. They used the term *terra nullius* as justification for taking whatever they wanted.
For British settlers, Aborigines did not have the social or political organization to legally qualify as "people."
Then in 1778, Captain Arthur Philip brought the first European settlers using the ships of the "First Fleet".

Adapted from http://www.petra.ac.id

2 Step forward!

A What happened to Aboriginal children in the past?

→ WB 2, p. 9, CD piste 30

Listen to Grace's story. What did the white government do to her? What didn't they let her do?

SOUNDS PISTE 31
Les sons /ʌ/ et /ɜː/.
→ WB 2, p. 9

B Report someone's experience. → WB 2, p. 10

Jackie Huggins has come to your school to inform you about the story of Aboriginal children and to tell you about her mother's experience in an institution.
Imagine your conversation.

Pupil A: You play the part of Jackie Huggins.
When my mother was ... years old, she was with ...
Suddenly ...

Pupil B: You ask her questions.
Did she meet / see ...?
What did they let ...?
What did they make her ...?

Word bank
- see her brothers and sisters
- meet her family • play with children • wake up at any time
- do chores = do the housework
- choose food

C Why was this man famous in Australia?

Who is this man? Why was he given compensation? What had happened to him before? → WB 2, p. 11

Death of an Aboriginal activist of respiratory failure

6 June 2008

Bruce Trevorrow has died. He was 50.

Bruce Trevorrow.

Last year he went down in history when he became the first of the "Stolen Generations" to receive compensation. Bruce was among the 100,000 Aboriginal children who were victims of the ethnic assimilation programme, led by white Australian governments from the early 20th century to the 1970s.

When he was 13 months old, Bruce was admitted to hospital, suffering from gastroenteritis. Soon after, he was given to a white family because the hospital had wrongly recorded he was an orphan and that he was not correctly looked after.

His mother wrote to the authorities to get some news, but she was told he was still in hospital and they didn't let her see Bruce again until he was 10.

Bruce's childhood was far from happy. He was the only black child, growing up among white children. So he not only felt different from his foster parents and fellow pupils, but he also suffered from bullying at school.

So traumatic was his childhood and adolescence, that in 1998 he launched a legal action against the Australian government. He claimed that the fact that he had been "stolen" had ruined his life and was responsible for his difficulties, namely depression and unemployment. He also claimed he had lost his cultural identity.

He finally got A$525,000 in compensation.

D Write a letter to a judge to ask for compensation.

In 1998, Bruce addressed a letter to a judge to ask for compensation.
He explained what he had been through.

Imagine what he wrote. → WB 2, p. 12

The hospital had recorded ...
Before I was sent to a white family, my parents had not ...
That's why I'm asking ...

STRATEGIES
→ Méthodologie, p. 130 : Écrire une lettre.

MAKE IT YOURS!

Comment on the news. → WB 2, p. 13

1. Listen to the news on 13 February 2008. Why was the Prime Minister's speech historic on that day?

2. You attended the Prime Minister's speech and you tell your family what happened.

This afternoon, Prime Minister Rudd apologized for ...
Before him no government had ...
He addressed the Stolen Generations that the white government had ...

DVD **Video time** → WB 2, p. 14
A long-awaited moment

MEMO
- They did not **let** us **kiss** our father goodbye.
- Bruce **had become** one of the 100,000 victims of the Stolen Generations. → p. 77

STEP 3 Je défends une opinion et j'argumente.

1 Get ready!

India today.

1. Look at the map at the end of your textbook and say what you know about India (capital, famous cities or places, climate, size).

2. Read this information about India.
What do these figures show?
Why is English one of the official languages in India?

Population:	over 1 billion inhabitants
Religions:	Hinduism (83%), Islam (13%), Christianity (2.3%), Buddhism, Sikhism (2%)
Official languages:	Hindi and English + 14 other national languages.

Word bank

- poverty • spicy food • saris • temples
- different religions / customs • the British Empire
- large • densely populated • mixed

2 Step forward!

A Who are the Dalits? → WB 2, p. 15, CD pistes 32-34

What place do the Dalits have in Indian society? Why?

SOUNDS PISTE 35
La prononciation de *the*.
→ WB 2, p. 16

B Dalits in modern India.

Look at these documents. Explain what they show about contemporary India, using the link words below. → WB 2, p. 16

Whereas ... / Although ... / However ... / That is why ...

A few facts about India and Dalits

• Although the country celebrates itself as the world's biggest democracy, India's 170 million Dalits (17% of the population) must endure segregation, economic exclusion and routine violence ...

• The traditional taboos are the same for Dalit men and Dalit women. However, Dalit women suffer from them more often. Men are dominant in Dalit communities. That's why Dalit women are discriminated against not only by people of higher castes, but also within their own communities.

• Only 10% of Dalit girls are literate, whereas 30% of Dalit boys are literate.

These Dalit women earn a living cleaning sewage*.

A Dalit woman is sweeping the street.

Word bank

- broom *(balai)* • dirt *(saleté)* • rubbish *(détritus)* • equal rights
- suffer from • be oppressed by • be excluded from
- dirty • disgusting • literate ≠ illiterate • run-down / neglected

*sewage (n): *égoûts.*

C A changing society?

1. Who is Chandra Bathran? What had he been looking for for years? → *WB 2, p. 18*

24-year-old Chandra Bathran is a young hard-working Indian. However, finding a job was not easy for Chandra as he belongs to one of the most socially disadvantaged classes of Indian society.

Although discrimination was banned by the Protection of Civil Rights Act of 1976, it is still widely practised. That's why Chandra says finding a job as a bus driver has been little short of a miracle.

"I had been looking for a decent job for months, I had been knocking at every door but it always ended up in the same way: the doors were slammed in my face as soon as employers realized I was a Dalit …"

Then Chandra heard of the Indian government's reservation scheme[1] for socially disadvantaged classes. He decided to apply for this job as a bus driver in the busy city of Mumbai and he was hired[2]. He makes $45 a month, which is not much even by Indian standards. But thanks to this job, Chandra has broken out of India's old caste system.

"I am very proud", Chandra says. "I had been hoping to get such an opportunity for years. My grandparents had been working as street sweepers for fifty years when they died and they didn't have a choice. Now I know my children will be allowed to choose the job they want."

1. reservation scheme (n): *système d'emplois réservés.* – **2. hire** (v): *embaucher.*

2. Now explain what it means to be a Dalit in India today. What has changed? What has not changed?

Dalits used to be excluded …
They didn't use to go to school … / to have …
Nowadays (De nos jours), *although they have the same …*
However, they can …

MAKE IT YOURS!

Free the Dalits! → *WB 2, p. 19*

A meeting is organized by *Free the Dalits*, an international organization fighting against discrimination. Chandra Bathran is invited to talk about his experience at this meeting. He confronts Madhu Kumar, one of the bosses who refused to hire him.

Pupil A: You are the representative from *Free the Dalits.*
Pupil B: You are Chandra Bathran, the Dalit bus driver.
Pupil C: You are Madhu Kumar, the boss who refused to hire Mr Bathran.

Prepare to explain your side of the story. Now act out your part!

MEMO
- Only 10% of Dalit girls can read **whereas** 30% of Dalit boys can.
- **Although** discrimination was banned in 1976, it is still widely practised.
- Chandra **had been looking** for a job for months. **However**, no one wanted to hire him.
- He is a Dalit, **that's why** finding a job was so difficult. → p. 78

Focus on Fighting Segregation

Martin Luther King Jr.
during the Civil Rights March
in Washington D.C., 28 August 1963.

Martin Luther King Jr

"I have a dream that my four little children will one day live in a nation where they will not be judged by the color of their skin but by their character."

Martin Luther King Jr (15 January, 1929 - 4 April 1968) was an American clergyman[1] and an active leader in the American Civil Rights Movement. He wanted to fight racial discrimination and segregation through non-violent means[2]. He organized boycotts, sit-ins and marches. In Birmingham, Alabama, he organized the boycott of discriminatory businesses, sit-ins in "White-only" lunch counters and everyday peaceful demonstrations. These initiatives successfully fought against segregation and for equal employment opportunities in the city.
In 1963, during the March on Washington for Jobs and Freedom, King made his famous "I have a dream" speech. In 1968 he was assassinated. He had received the Nobel Peace Prize four years before.

1. clergyman (n): pastor. - **2. means** (n): methods.

Sit-ins

In the 60s black people were not allowed to attend many segregationist public facilities. However, in February 1960, black students sat down at a "White-only" lunch-counter and ordered food. They didn't move until they had been served, which was forbidden. When they were arrested, a new group took their place. The students always remained non-violent and respectful. This sit-in movement was very successful: within six months, segregation had ended in restaurants in twenty-six southern cities.
This non-violent strategy also developed in public parks, swimming-pools, theatres, churches, libraries, museums and beaches.

A sit-in in a "White-only" restaurant, Greensboro, North Carolina, February 1960.

in the USA

Symbolic Protest

The American athletes Tommie Smith and John Carlos, and the Australian athlete Peter Norman.

In 1968, during the Mexico Olympic Games, two African American athletes made the Black Power salute during their medal ceremony. They had won the gold and bronze medals in the men's 200-metre race. They had stepped up to the podium without their shoes, wearing black socks (symbolizing poverty among African Americans), civil rights buttons and one black glove each. When the American anthem was played, they bowed their heads and each raised a fist in the air, in a gesture of protest against racism in the United States. The Australian 200-metre silver medalist wore a human rights badge on the podium as a sign of solidarity.

Smith and Carlos were suspended from the U.S. team and banned from the Olympic Village. Back home they were subject to abuse* and they and their families received death threats.

* **abuse** (n): *injures, insultes.*

SCANNING

→ *WB 2, p. 20*

Have a good look at the documents and read the texts.

1. Pick out information about the people in the texts and the documents: names, jobs or activities.

2. Find out the different means of fighting segregation.

3. In the texts, find the words which mean:
les droits civiques, la solidarité, l'hymne américain, un rêve, la liberté, le prix Nobel de la paix, l'égalité, la dignité, discriminatoire, pacifique

WEBQUEST

→ *WB 2, p. 21*

South Africa
Go to these sites and do the webquest in your workbook.

1. Learn about Apartheid.
http://encarta.msn.com/encyclopedia_761561373/apartheid.html

2. Find out about Nelson Mandela.
http://news.bbc.co.uk/2/hi/7500615.stm#early

Rosa Parks

Discover "Sister Rosa Parks" by The Neville Brothers to know more about her.
→ *WB 2, p. 20*

Rosa Parks, one of the symbols of fight against segregation. Her arrest started a successful boycott led by Martin Luther King Jr.

CD Rom: Storytelling - A Civil Rights Heroin.

STEP 1 Remember and practise

1 Je sais parler de ce qui était autorisé, interdit ou obligatoire. → *Mémento p. 146*

Pour exprimer **la permission**, **l'interdiction**, **la capacité** ou **l'obligation** au passé, on utilise les expressions équivalentes aux modaux : ***be allowed to*** (permission), ***be able to*** (capacité), ***have to*** (obligation).

- **L'expression d'une permission ou d'une interdiction au passé.**

What **were** you **allowed to** do?

I **was allowed to** take the bus but I **wasn't allowed to** sit at the front.

- **L'expression d'une obligation au passé.**

What **did** you **have to** do?

I **had to** walk to school.

Attention : À la **forme négative**, *have to* exprime une **absence de nécessité ou d'obligation**.

I **didn't have to** walk to school.
(Je n'étais pas obligé de le faire.)

- **L'expression d'une capacité au passé.**

They **were able to** order food at the counter.
(Ils ont pu commander…)

Were you **able to** pass the test?
(As-tu réussi à…)

I **wasn't able to** tell the difference.
(Je n'ai pas réussi à…)

Remarque : Contrairement à ***could*** (***can*** au passé), ***be able to*** fait référence à une situation unique.

I **was able to** see where they were.
(J'ai pu le faire à ce moment précis.)
Mais : When I was six, I **could** swim.
(capacité permanente)

1. Parle de la vie de tes grands-parents dans les années 50. Complète les phrases en utilisant *be able to, have to* ou *be allowed to.*

a. There were no buses at that time so they ... walk to school.
b. They ... wear an apron *(tablier)*.
c. They ... speak Chinese because it wasn't taught at school.
d. Teachers ... use corporal punishment.
e. They ... wear make-up or unconventional clothes.

2. Reformule les phrases suivantes en utilisant *be able to, have to, be allowed to.*

a. It was forbidden for black people to sit at the front of buses. → *Black people …*
b. The law obliged black people to go to segregated schools.
c. The Voting Rights Act made it possible for black people to vote.

3. Un jeune étudiant noir américain a pu retrouver ses ancêtres. Explique ce qu'il a dû faire ou ce qu'il a pu faire.

find his ancestors • do a lot of research • send letters • take time to go to Africa • meet his cousins last summer.

2 Je sais quand utiliser l'article *the* et l'article *Ø*. → *Mémento p. 136*

Quand on parle de **personnes**, de **notions** ou d'**objets précis**, déterminés, on utilise **l'article *the*** devant le nom.
Lorsque l'on parle de **personnes ou de choses en général**, on utilise **l'article *Ø*** devant le nom.

- Ø Slaves had to sleep in Ø small huts on Ø plantations.

On parle des esclaves en général, du type d'habitation qu'ils utilisaient généralement et de plantations, sans préciser lesquelles en particulier.

- After **the** Civil War, most of **the** states in **the** South of **the** USA became segregationist.

Il s'agit d'une guerre bien précise, de certains États en particulier.
On dit ***the*** *South* et ***the*** *United States* car ce sont des entités uniques.

Remarque : *the* se prononce /ðiː/ devant un son voyelle.
The American voters. The English community.

4. Complète le texte avec les articles *the* ou *Ø*.

In ... state of Alabama, ... segregation was ... law.

On ... buses of Montgomery ... black people had to sit at ... back. They weren't allowed to use ... seats at ... front.

... restaurants were also segregated and ... owners of ... cafeterias and ... lunch counters refused to serve ... black people.

In 2008, ... first black American president was elected. It was a historic moment, especially for ... black people who used to live in ... segregated cities.

1 Je sais exprimer l'antériorité au passé. → Mémento p. 144

Quand on veut relater des **faits** qui s'étaient **déjà produits à un moment du passé**, on utilise le ***past perfect*** (***had*** + participe passé).

- On utilise le **prétérit** pour évoquer une action qui s'est déroulée à un moment du passé.

I **moved** to Sydney in 1995.

On utilise le ***past perfect*** pour évoquer une action qui s'est produite avant ce même repère passé.

I **had** (already) **become** a teacher when I **moved** to Sydney in 1995.

- Le *past perfect* simple est aussi utilisé pour des actions qui venaient juste de s'accomplir à un moment donné du passé.

I had just **passed** my exam at that time.

- Le *past perfect* est souvent utilisé avec des repères temporels tels que *by (by 1900)* ou *before (before that, the week before ...)*.

They **had** already **settled** in Australia by 1900.
Ils s'étaient déjà installés en 1900.

He **had come** the week before.
Il était venu la semaine précédente.

- **Formation du *past perfect*.**

Affirmation	Sujet + *had* + participe passé I **had lost** my keys.
Négation	Sujet + *hadn't* + participe passé I **hadn't lost** my keys.
Interrogation	*Had* + sujet + participe passé **Had** you **lost** your keys?

1. Après plusieurs années loin de sa famille, Bruce a retrouvé les siens puis raconté ce qui s'était passé durant son absence. Imagine ce qu'il a pu dire.

a. My brothers and sisters ... *(grow up)* with my parents.
b. My father ... *(lose)* his job.
c. My mother ... *(stay)* at home and ... *(bring up)* my brothers and sisters.
d. My parents ... *(not stop)* looking for me.
e. I ... *(have)* awful experiences at school.
f. I ... *(never keep)* a job for more than one year.

2. Les parents biologiques de Bruce ont raconté les retrouvailles avec leur fils dans un journal. Imagine leurs propos en complétant ces phrases avec des verbes au prétérit ou au *past perfect* selon le cas.

a. When Bruce saw us, he ... *(cry)* because he ... *(not see)* us for ages.
b. He ... *(continue)* visiting his foster family who ... *(bring)* him up for so many years.
c. He ... *(be)* away from us for so long that he ... *(not feel)* at home with us at the beginning.
d. When we first ... *(contact)* him, he ... *(just find)* a job.
e. He ... *(tell)* us he ... *(feel)* uncomfortable with his foster family.

Plus d'exercices sur ton CD audio-rom

2 Je sais exprimer une permission. → Mémento p. 147

Pour exprimer **la permission**, on peut utiliser la structure « sujet + ***let*** + nom (ou pronom personnel complément) + base verbale ».

- **Affirmation**

My parents **let** me **see** my friends last weekend.
Mes parents m'ont laissé voir mes amis le week-end dernier.

- **Négation**

My parents **don't let** me **see** my friends.
Mes parents ne me laissent pas voir mes amis.

- **Interrogation**

Do your parents **let** you **see** your friends during the week?
Tes parents te laissent-ils voir tes amis en semaine ?

Remarque : *allow to* exprime une autorisation donnée alors que *let* exprime une tolérance (on laisse faire sans forcément approuver).

3. Complète les phrases suivantes à l'aide de *let* (forme affirmative ou négative), d'un pronom complément et du verbe donné entre parenthèses.

a. Bruce's foster parents were very strict. They ... *(see)* his friends.
b. Bruce's biological parents had no information. The Aboriginal Protection Board never ... *(know)* what had happened to him.
c. The Australian authorities were very strict with Aboriginal parents. They often ... *(write)* to their children but they ... *(see)* them.
d. The white governments often separated Aboriginal children from their families. They rarely ... *(grow up)* with their brothers and sisters.

STEP 3 Remember and practise

1 Je sais utiliser des mots de liaison pour articuler mes idées. → Mémento p. 140

Pour structurer des arguments ou une explication de façon logique, on utilise des **mots de liaison**. On peut ainsi marquer l'**opposition** (***whereas***), la **concession** (***however, although***) ou la **conséquence** (***so, that's why***).

• ***Whereas*** relie une proposition subordonnée à la proposition principale. Il signifie « alors que », « tandis que » et marque un **contraste**, une **opposition**.

She was poorly-dressed whereas he wore a beautiful suit.
proposition principale — proposition subordonnée

• ***However*** et ***although*** permettent d'exprimer la **concession**, mais ils ne s'emploient pas de la même façon.

- ***However*** s'emploie souvent en début de proposition. Il est généralement suivi d'une virgule et signifie « cependant ».

She was more than 70 years old. **However**, she was still working very hard.

- ***Although*** introduit une subordonnée. Il signifie « bien que ».

Although she was sick, she didn't go to the doctor's.
proposition subordonnée — proposition principale

• ***So*** et ***that's why*** expriment une **conséquence**.

- ***So*** signifie « donc » :

Mrs Singh lost her job, **so** she decided to fight for her rights.

- ***That's why*** signifie « c'est pourquoi » :

Dalits are oppressed, **that's why** many charities defend their rights.

1. Commente cette photo en utilisant un mot de liaison pour lier les phrases entre elles. Attention à la ponctuation.

a. This family is Dalit. They have to live in this poor district.
b. They are separated from the upper castes. They are supposed to have the same rights.
c. The girl looks happy to be photographed. Their neighborhood is poor and run-down.
d. Dalits are outcastes. Caste Hindus have the top jobs.

2. Présente la situation des Dalits en utilisant des mots de liaison pour articuler ton discours.

a. Explique l'histoire des Dalits : quelle conséquence a eu sur eux la légende de Brahma ?
(not create by Brahma / exclude from society)
b. Évoque le contraste avec les autres castes.
(• very poor / uneducated / illiterate / have to work
• higher castes / rich /educated)
c. Dis que les choses, cependant, commencent à changer.
(hope for the Dalits / right to vote/ first Dalit schools)

2 Je sais utiliser le *past perfect* en *be* + BV-*ing*. → Mémento p. 144

On utilise ***had been* + BV-*ing*** pour indiquer que l'action, déjà commencée à un premier moment précis du passé, était toujours en cours à un second moment du passé.

• Observe la phrase suivante.

When Luka arrived in Reno in July 2008, Belinda had already been living there for two years.
Lorsque Luka est arrivé à Reno en juillet 2008, cela faisait déjà deux ans que Belinda y habitait.

Remarques :
- Cette forme est souvent utilisée avec ***for*** (suivi de la durée de l'action : *for 2 weeks*) ou ***since*** (suivi du point de départ de l'action : *since Tuesday*).
- Elle ne peut pas être utilisée avec l'expression d'une quantité précise.

They **had written** five letters when she came in.
(La rédaction des cinq lettres était terminée quand Mary est entrée.)

3. Conjugue le verbe entre parenthèses au *past perfect* en *be* + BV-*ing* ou au prétérit, selon le sens de la phrase.

a. We ... *(not visit)* Mumbai for long when we saw an old Dalit cleaning the sewage.
b. Chandra Bathran ... *(wait)* for an opportunity for months when he was hired.
c. Martin Luther King ... *(make)* his famous speech after black Americans ... *(protest)* for months.
d. Aborigenes ... *(fight)* for their rights for many years when Cathy Freeman ... *(represent)* them at the Olympic Games in Sydney in 2000.

PR1JECT

Create a card against exclusion.

Une association a décidé de lancer une campagne contre l'exclusion. Un concours de création de cartes sur ce thème est organisé et ta classe y participe. Formez des groupes et soyez créatifs !

A. Choose the sort of discrimination you wish to illustrate.

Choisissez la discrimination que vous voulez illustrer (une de celles vues dans les *Steps* de la *Unit* ou une autre...).

B. Create your card.

- Choisissez une illustration (vous pouvez dessiner ou imprimer une image d'Internet).
- Trouvez un slogan et un texte.
- Mettez en page votre carte.

C. Present it to the class.

Répartissez-vous la parole dans le groupe et présentez votre carte à la classe en expliquant vos choix.

D. Elect the best.

Accrochez vos cartes au CDI et organisez un vote pour élire la meilleure carte !

PR2JECT

Create your own slam.

A. Listen to a slam.

- Écoute ce slam!

Segregation
Isolation
Separation
Part of your past
Part of your present
No more tears
No more tension
Stop humiliating
Start uniting
You're my world
I'm your world
This is our world!

- Le slam est une poésie conçue pour être déclamée en public. Il peut être rimé ou pas, métré ou pas.
Slam signifie « claquer » : repère dans ce slam ce qui « claque » l'auditeur (idées et sonorités).

B. Write your own slam.

- Par groupe de quatre ou cinq, écrivez un slam sur une discrimination de votre choix.
- Listez les raisons de votre choix. Vous en aurez besoin pour la question suivante.

C. Show time!

- La classe est votre scène ! Expliquez à votre public pourquoi vous avez choisi ce sujet.
- Récitez votre slam. N'hésitez pas à le faire à plusieurs voix afin de le rendre plus vivant.

D. Elect the best slams.

La classe vote pour les slams qu'elle a préférés.
Vous pouvez ensuite les mettre sur papier et les afficher !

The slam singer Iyeoka Ivie Okoawo.

To be continued... Gardez précieusement les meilleurs slams. Vous les intégrerez dans votre émission de télé de la *Unit 6*.

Words

1 **Complete these sentences with: *from, for, up, as.***

a. The Untouchables were totally excluded … the caste system.
b. He had been looking … a decent job for a long time.
c. They were considered … inferior until the 20th century.
d. They won't give … the fight.

2 **Find the word corresponding to each definition.**

literate • hire (v) • neglected • broom • rights

a. This adjective means you can read and count.
b. Synonymous with "run-down" for buildings.
c. The government guarantees them to its citizens.
d. You use one to sweep.
e. Give a job.

3 **Unscramble them!**
Read the sentences and put the letters in the right order to find the correct word.

TYRID • CLEXINUOS • PAGLOOZIE

a. When you are rejected, you suffer from …
b. When you say sorry, you …
c. When something isn't clean, it is …

4 PLAY WITH WORDS!

a. Observe les phrases suivantes.
1. *With African Ancestry you can* ***finally*** *discover your roots.*
2. *It was an* ***absolutely*** *incredible feeling.*
3. *They reacted* ***angrily****.*

b. Réfléchis.
• Quelle est la classe grammaticale des mots en gras ? (adj, n, adv, v)
• Pour chacun de ces mots, écris le mot racine. Quelle est la classe grammaticale de cette racine ? Déduis-en la règle : « Pour former un …, j'ajoute le suffixe -… à … »
• Que remarques-tu pour les mots dont la racine se termine avec un *-l* ?

c. À ton tour !
• Traduis les trois phrases ci-dessus.
• Traduis en anglais les phrases suivantes.
1. Ils se rencontrent habituellement à Londres.
2. Elle m'a répondu avec gentillesse.
3. Il a fait l'exercice facilement.

CHECKPOINT

Read the text.

Untouchable

In the 1930s India was under British colonial domination.

Bakha, a young man of eighteen (…) had been working in the barracks of a British regiment for some years (…) and had been caught by the glamour of the "white man's" life. The Tommies[1] had treated him as a human being and he had learnt to think of himself as superior to his fellow-outcastes. (…) Bakha was a child of modern India. He had looked at the Tommies (…) with wonder and amazement when he first went to live at the British regimental barracks with his uncle. (…) And he had soon become possessed with an overwhelming desire to live their life. He had been told they were sahibs, superior people. He had felt that to put on their clothes made one a sahib too. He had begged[2] one Tommy for the gift of a pair of trousers. The man had given him a pair of breeches[3] which he had to spare. (…) Then he had had the good luck to come by some money[4] at the British barracks. (…) He had been able to buy the jacket, the overcoat, the blanket he slept under. (…) His father had been angry at his extravagance, and the boys of the outcastes' colony (…) cut jokes with him (…) calling him "Pilpali sahib" (imitation sahib).

Mulk Raj Anand, *Untouchable* (1935).

1. a Tommy (n): a British soldier. – **2. beg** (v): ask. – **3. breeches** (n): short trousers. – **4. to come by some money:** to get some money.

Now do the following activities.

a. Find out the name of the main character, where he lived, his job and his nationality.
b. Find out what caste he belonged to. Justify by quoting from the text.
c. Pick out all the words connected to clothes.
d. Say if the following sentences are true or false and justify by quoting from the text.
- He hated the British.
- A British soldier had sold him trousers.
- His friends had made fun of him.

e. Say how he had managed to buy clothes and why he had wanted them.

Write a diary.

You're a British child and you live at the regimental barracks with your father.
Write about Bakha in your diary.
- Say what he wore, and compare him with the other outcastes.
- Say what he had to do and wasn't allowed to do, and compare with yourself.
- Say what he hoped or wanted (although he was an outcaste).

Use link words like *whereas*, *although*, *however* ...

Listen to the interview and do the following activities.

a. Find out the date of this interview, where it takes place and who the characters are.
b. Say where the main character lived when he was very young.
c. Explain what happened to him when he was four years old.
d. Say if the following sentences are true or false.
- He didn't meet his mother any more.
- His father had died before he was able to see him again.
- He had missed his culture to develop his identity.

Interview someone who is part of the Stolen Generations in Australia.

Pupil A	Pupil B
Salue et présente ton invité. Dis qu'il fait partie des générations volées d'Australie.	Réponds aux salutations.
Demande-lui ce qu'il lui est arrivé.	Réponds : des hommes t'ont enlevé dans ton village et t'ont emmené dans une institution à 2 000 kilomètres.
Demande-lui comment était sa vie dans l'institution.	Réponds : interdiction de parler ta langue / obligation de parler anglais.
Demande-lui s'il a revu sa mère.	Réponds que oui, il y a deux ans. Précise que tu ne l'avais pas vue depuis plus de vingt ans.

Speak about segregation in the United States in the 50s and 60s. These documents can help you.

Although Lincoln ..., Whites and Blacks ...
The Blacks were not allowed to ... / had to ...

A few facts

1868 Abolition of slavery by President Lincoln.
1876-1965 Jim Crow Laws: segregation in all public facilities.
1954 Segregation in public schools is declared unconstitutional.
1955 Bus boycott in Alabama against segregation in transports.

A "colored-only" taxi in Birmingham, Alabama, 1962.

unit 5

Another place, another time ...

STEP 1

Je prépare un voyage à l'étranger.
Je donne des conseils pour un voyage.

STEP 2

J'émets des hypothèses dans une situation imaginaire.

STEP 3

J'imagine les causes d'un événement.

Focus on: TE PAPA TONGAREWA MUSEUM

PROJECTS

1. Create a leaflet to inform and advise people.
2. Present a holiday destination.

CHECKPOINT

Starter

1. What are the people doing? Imagine their life.

2. What are they thinking of? What would they like to do or to have? Why?

CD Rom: Discovery Game.

STEP 1 Je prépare un voyage à l'étranger.

A What will he do when he is in New Zealand?

1. Tyler, a fan of *The Lord of the Rings*, is planning his trip to New Zealand.
Read the package holiday *(voyage organisé)* information below and say what he'll do there, where he'll go ...
Then compare more packages. → *WB 2, p. 24*

This package includes:
- 14 nights accommodation
- Rental cars North and South Islands
- Ferry tickets between North and South Island
- 'The Lord of the Rings Location* Guidebook' by Ian Brodie

Cost: NZ$ 2,074 per person

guestnewzealand.com

***location** (n): *lieux de tournage.*

2. Tyler is talking to his friend Hannah about his trip to New Zealand.
Listen and find out more about the package he has chosen.
→ *WB 2, p. 24, CD piste 39*

SOUNDS *PISTE 40*
La prononciation de *ou*.
→ *WB 2, p. 25*

B Flight and hotel confirmation.

Tyler has received an e-mail confirming his flight and hotel.

1. Look at the document and say when he'll leave, how he'll travel to New Zealand, where and how long he'll stay ... → *WB 2, p. 26*

Word bank
- leave • stay • cost *(coûter)* • fly *(voyager en avion)* • land *(atterrir)*
- 1 NZ$ ≈ 0.50 US$ ≈ 0.40 €

Thank you for booking a package on our site. You'll find your hotel and flight confirmation below.

Kiwi International Queen Street Hotel and Hostel

Located in Auckland's city centre, this hotel is 1 km from Aotea Square and less than 2 kms from Sky City Casino, Auckland, New Zealand. – Single room.
Check in: 13/04/10 Check out: 25/04/10 **Total: NZ$ 2,457.11**

London (LHR) to Auckland (AKL)	Departure: 11/04/09 22:15 - 12:10	British Airways
Auckland (AKL) to London (LHR)	Return: 25/04/09 13:25 - 06:20	Air New Zealand

2. Imagine what he'll do when he gets to the airport and then at the hotel (taxi, phone call, shower, lunch ...).
When he is/gets ..., he'll ...

IT'S UP TO YOU!

Organize your own trip to New Zealand. → *WB 2, p. 26*

You are at the travel agency with a friend to ask for details about your trip. Imagine the conversation.
Ask questions about the time of departure, the transport on arrival, the accommodation, the visits ...
What time will we ...? / What will we ... when we ...?
Pupil A: You are the tourist.
Pupil B: You are the woman/man at the travel agency.

MEMO
- He **will go** to New Zealand but he **won't see** any Maori places.
- **When** we **get** there, we'**ll join** a two-hour guided tour.
- I'**ll send** you some photos **as soon as** I find a cybercafé. → *p. 92*

Je donne des conseils pour un voyage.

A Fast facts about New Zealand.

Look at the illustrations below and say what you'll be able to see or what you'll have to do if you go to New Zealand.

In New Zealand I'll be able to see ... / I'll have to pay ...

Word bank
- kiwis • banknote
- put one's watch forward

LONDON	AUCKLAND
12:00 a.m.	12:00 p.m.

B What you should know before going to New Zealand.

→ *WB 2, p. 27*

Read these pages from a guide for tourists travelling to New Zealand. What should you bring in your suitcase if you go there this summer? If you want to avoid problems, what shouldn't you do?

DVD **Video time** → *WB 2, p. 29*
Discover Maori Culture

BEFORE YOU ARRIVE

When you should come: New Zealand is suitable to visit all year round but we recommend November to April. Skiing is only possible during the winter months.
Passport and visas: You need a valid passport. Visit the New Zealand Immigration website for further information.
What you should bring: If you plan to visit New Zealand during the colder months between May and September, bring warm clothes and a waterproof jacket.

ONCE YOU'RE THERE

Health Risks: There are no major health risks in New Zealand. However you shouldn't drink water from lakes, ponds or rivers.
Driving: Most foreign driving licences are acceptable. New Zealanders drive on the left!

Don't miss "The New Zealand Maori Arts & Crafts Institute" in Te Puia.

www.nzyourway.com

IT'S UP TO YOU!

Giving advice to a tourist. → *WB 2, p. 28*

A New Zealander is planning to come to your town in August. Send him/her an e-mail to give him/her advice about his/her trip to France. Write about clothing, currency, activities, driving, weather ...

STRATEGIES

Le touriste ne connaît pas ta ville ou ta région. Pense aux différences entre les deux pays pour que tes conseils lui soient utiles.
→ *Méthodologie, p. 131* : **Écrire un e-mail.**

MEMO
- You'**ll be able to** see kiwis.
- You'**ll have to** put your watch forward.
- You **shouldn't** drink water from lakes, ponds or rivers.
- You **should** bring warm clothes. → *p. 92*

STEP 2 J'émets des hypothèses dans une situation imaginaire.

1 Get ready!

Discover a classmate's preferences in video games. → WB 2, p. 30

Ask a classmate which video cover he/she prefers and why.

Then ask your classmate about his/her video game habits and preferences and tell him/her about yours.

Have you ever ...? – So have I. / I haven't. / Neither have I.
Do you like ...? – So do I. / I don't. / Neither do I.

→ Mémento, p. 140

Word bank

- knight *(chevalier)* • sword *(épée)*
- magic wand *(baguette magique)*
- fantasy = imagination
- evil *(malveillant)*

CD rom : Discovery Game

2 Step forward!

A What game characters do they like best?

Listen to teenagers speaking about video games. What game character would they like to be? Why? → WB 2, p. 30, CD pistes 41-43

SOUNDS PISTE 44
Silent letters.
→ WB 2, p. 31

B Create the identity cards of role-playing game characters and present one to the class. → WB 2, p. 32

1. Create the identity cards of your favourite character and his/her allies. Who would they be? What powers would they have? Then draw them.

2. Present the card of your favourite character to the class.

If I were a game character, I would be ... I would have ...

C Discover some dangerous characters.

Read the identity cards of these villains and say what you had better do or not do when you meet them. → WB 2, p. 32

Word bank
- avoid • be careful of • be impressed
- irritate • set something on fire • run away

ORCUS

This very old demon looks terrifying. He cares for nothing but himself and only wants to spread[1] misery and evil. His skull-topped wand has the power to kill any living being. You had better not say his name: he can hear you from whenever and wherever you are and gets irritated. He is an expert in fighting with a sword.

THE MUMMY

It is a frightening enemy. If it touched you, you would die within six months. It can't move very fast but it can hit you hard. Charms, immobilization, poison don't affect it. Only fire can destroy it. But be careful! When burning, a mummy gives off toxic fumes[2]. You had better avoid them.

THE WITCH

She possesses incredible intelligence. She may take on the appearance of an old harmless woman. You had better have a magician with you when you meet her! Have you got the Robe of Curses[3] or an amulet? Get them ready, you may need them to protect yourself against her spells.

1. **spread** (v): *répandre.* – 2. **toxic fumes** (n): toxic vapours. – 3. **curse** (n): malediction.

MAKE IT YOURS!

Imagine you are playing a video game with your friend.

Your friend is playing a role-playing game. His/her character has just come into the room in the picture. You don't agree on what the character had better do to escape from this room. What could happen? Imagine your conversation. → WB 2, p. 34

Pupil A: *If I were you, I would ... / I wouldn't ...*
I think you'd better ... / you'd better not ...
Pupil B: *Yes, but if the witch ... she would ...*
That's why I'd better ...

MEMO
- **If** I **were** a game character, I **would be** a Jedi.
- You'**d better be** with a magician. → p. 93

STEP 3 J'imagine les causes d'un événement.

1 Get ready!

What is science fiction?

1. Look at this poster.
Which elements situate it in the world of science fiction?

Word bank
- spaceship • spacesuits
- aliens ≠ human beings
- hurt

2. Sarah, Rahila and Rudy are teenagers.
How do they define science fiction?
→ *WB 2, p. 35, CD pistes 45-46*

SOUNDS *PISTE 47*
La prononciation de *of*.
→ *WB 2, p. 35*

2 Step forward!

A *I, Robot*, the story.

1. The film *I, Robot* is based on Isaac Asimov's short stories.
What does Cutie, the robot, think of human beings? → *WB 2, p. 36*

"I've come to talk to you. I've been thinking for two days about who made me. I can't believe that you two humans made me." Donovan turned angrily towards Cutie. But Powell put out his hand. "Why do you say that, Cutie?"
Cutie laughed[1]. It was an inhuman laugh –sharp and regular. "Look at you! The material you are made of is soft and weak[2]. You depend upon food like that"–he pointed at Donovan's sandwich –"to give you energy. Each day you need to sleep and while you're asleep you can do nothing. And if the temperature varies too much you can't work. You are a very inefficient and short-lived piece of equipment." The robot paused. "I, on the other hand, am a perfect and efficient machine. I use energy directly. I'm made of strong metal. I never sleep. And I can work in any temperature. You can't possibly have made me. Obviously no being can create another one of much higher quality than itself."
Donovan jumped up; "All right, you piece of metal, if we didn't make you, who did?"
"Very good, Donovan," Cutie said seriously. "That was in fact the next question. My creator must be more powerful than myself, and so there was only one possibility."
Donovan and Powell looked puzzled[3].

Isaac Asimov, "Reason" in *I, Robot, Short Stories* (1950).

1. **laugh** /lɑːf/ (v): *rire*. – 2. **weak** (adj) ≠ strong. –3. **puzzled** (adj): *intrigué*.

2. The next day, Powell decides to convince Cutie he needs human beings to survive in this hostile environment. → *WB 2, p. 37*

Pupil A: You are Powell. You think Cutie can't survive by himself.
Pupil B: You are Cutie. You think you can do everything yourself. React to what Powell says.

Word bank
- create oneself • think by oneself • programme oneself
- repair • depend on
- independent • efficient • powerful
- each other • together

B Robots and human beings.

Look at this poster and imagine what may/must have happened between the scene described in the short story and now. ➜ *WB 2, p. 37*

The hero is a detective who must have ...
Human beings may/might have ...
Robots must have ...

Word bank

- fight • feel in danger • lose power • discover
- take control • multiply • form an army • attack
- become independent / dangerous • destroy

C Choose your robot!

Imagine you live in 2035: robots are very common. Which model would you choose and why? What would you still do yourself or what wouldn't you do yourself any more if you had a robot? ➜ *WB 2, p. 39*

I would / wouldn't choose a Doggybot because it would ...
If I had a Smartsbot, it/I ...

DVD **Video time** ➜ *WB 2, p. 40*
A perfect robot?

AVAILABLE NOW!

Doggybot will protect you so you can be by yourself when your parents are not home. **Doggybot** will be your best friend, and talk to you thanks to its 1,000-word language. Plus, it can play basketball on its telescopic legs!

Smartsbot will do your homework so you won't have to do it yourself any more. It is very good at maths and physics. It can also be programmed to tidy up your room and it can play the guitar!

15

MAKE IT YOURS!

Imagine a screenplay! ➜ *WB 2, p. 39*

You are a young screenplay writer. You participate in a contest to get a job in Hollywood. Read the situation and imagine what might/must have happened. Then present your story to the class.

I think that aliens / robots / computers must have ...
They might have ... that's why ...

Situation:
Mr Smith opens his window one morning. There's no traffic, no one in the street. Red flowers have grown everywhere.

MEMO
- You can't create someone stronger than **yourself**.
- Robots **must have formed** an army. ➜ p. 94

CD rom : Storytelling - Frankenstein

Focus on

TE PAPA
Museum of

Te Papa Tongarewa ("The place of treasures of this land" in Maori language) is the national museum of New Zealand located in Wellington. It was opened in 1998 and is one of the largest museums in the world. Its exhibitions, storytelling, cultural shows and interactive technology allow visitors to experience virtual travel through time and space in New Zealand.

The satellite map of New Zealand.

OUR SPACE

Our Space is a multimedia interactive exhibition which uses technology, photos and videos to explore New Zealand's past and present. As soon as visitors walk over a 14-metre-long satellite map of the country, a variety of images are projected onto large screens all around the room, allowing them to visit the whole country in a few minutes. In another attraction, visitors are taken 65 million years back to witness the formation of New Zealand and they are told how the country was created both from Maori and geological perspectives. Going back to the future, people can then fly over Wellington in fifty years' time in a futuristic car.

TONGAREWA
New Zealand

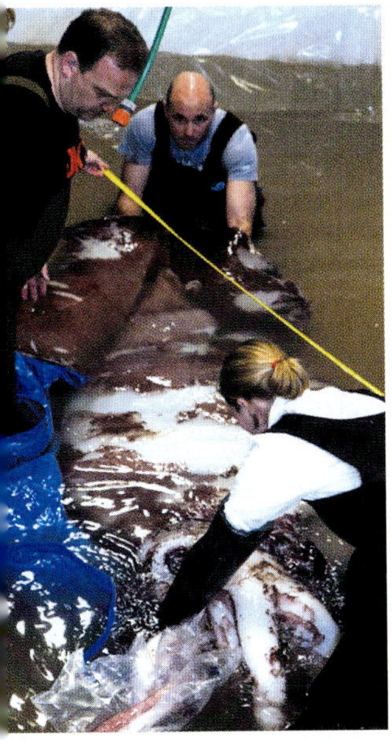

The squid.

The Deep Ride

The Deep Ride makes visitors imagine they come aboard a submarine and start a real-life scientific adventure ride. A deep-sea vehicle simulator allows people to visit a virtual volcano, 2,000 meters under the sea. To complete their journey, people can experience what Captain Nemo must have felt when he faced a giant octopus and have a look at the world's only complete colossal squid* specimen, found in Antarctica in 2007; it weighs 495 kilos.

***squid** (n): octopus.

The Lord of The Rings

***The Lord of the Rings, The Return of the King* (2003) directed by Peter Jackson.**

In this exhibition, visitors will be transported into the world of Middle-Earth. They will discover the amazing secret behind the film. They will be able to enjoy some of its special effects: for example the ones used in the fight scene between Saruman and Gandalf, or the ones used to create the digital armies and the monsters. Visitors will learn how the film-makers made normal actors appear to be the size of a hobbit or a wizard. Interactive technology will demonstrate how live action and miniatures were combined to make the most impressive scenes from the film. Throughout this exhibition, they will be able to see, and even sometimes touch, the props*, costumes, animatronics, miniatures and the famous ring from the films.

***props** (n): accessories.

SCANNING

→ *WB 2, p. 41*

Have a good look at the documents and read the texts.

1. **Find out where this museum is located.**
2. **Look at the pictures and say what visitors are able to see or do in this museum.**
3. **In the texts, find the words which mean:** *une exposition, virtuel, être exposé, un écran, un volcan, une lutte, un trésor sous-marin, des effets spéciaux, un anneau.*
4. **Quiz the class. Ask your classmates about what you can experience in this museum.** *Ex.: Can you discover a deep-sea volcano?*

WEBQUEST

→ *WB 2, p. 42*

New Zealand
Go to these sites and do the webquest in your workbook.

1. **Discover New Zealand.** http://www.worldatlas.com/webimage/countrys/oceania/nzfacts.htm
2. **Discover the Maori.** http://www.virtualoceania.net/newzealand/culture/maori/
3. **Learn about some Maori legends.** http://history-nz.org/maori9.html

STEP 1 Remember and practise

1 Je sais parler de ce que je ferai. → Mémento p. 144

Pour parler d'événements **futurs**, on utilise ***will*** suivi de la **base verbale**.
Pour préciser **quand** on fera une action, on utilise ***when*** ou ***as soon as*** (dès que) suivis d'un verbe **au présent**.

• Pour parler de prévisions ou d'événements planifiés, on utilise ***will***.

I **will** send him a postcard but I **won't** call him!

Remarque : *will* + *not* = *won't*

Will se contracte en ***'ll*** sauf :
- lorsqu'il est dans une question

Will you come tomorrow?
- ou lorsqu'on veut insister

I **will** do it!

• Pour exprimer une **obligation**, une **capacité** ou une **permission** future, on utilise les équivalents de modaux au futur.

I **won't be able to** go to Gareth's party so I **will have to** call him!

She **won't be allowed to** go out next weekend.

• **Contrairement au français**, lorsque la proposition principale est au futur, **la subordonnée de temps** (introduite par ***when***, ***as soon as*** (dès que), ***while***, ***as long as***...) **est au présent**.
Note la différence entre l'anglais et le français dans les exemples suivants.

I **will** call you when I **am** at the hotel.
Je t'appellerai quand je serai à l'hôtel.

As soon as he **comes** back, we**'ll leave**.
Dès qu'il sera de retour, nous partirons.

Remarque : On utilise aussi le présent en ***be* + BV-*ing*** pour parler d'actions à venir. Dans ce cas, on ajoute un marqueur temporel.

I**'m** visit**ing** my uncle next week.

1. **Une famille anglaise a planifié ses vacances d'été en France. Les parents expliquent à leurs enfants ce qu'ils feront et ne feront pas.**

- *Brittany ~~by plane~~ → by car and ferry*
- *~~hotel~~ → at friends'*
- *~~go fishing~~ → go sailing • beach*

2. **Tu es guide pour un groupe de touristes. Explique-leur ce qu'ils pourront ou ne pourront pas faire, et ce qu'ils devront faire.**

a. Try on traditional costumes
b. Use your mobile
c. Listen carefully to me
d. Learn a lot about this period
e. Speak quietly
f. Ask questions

3. **Un groupe de touristes sort de l'aéroport. Dis ce qu'ils feront dès leur arrivée à l'hôtel.**
report to the police • *get changed* (se changer) • *have a shower* ...

As soon as she ... Amber ... / Justin ... when he ...

Amber: "I need a shower ..."
Brooke: "Someone has stolen my mobile!"
Justin: "I'm starving!" *(Je meurs de faim!)*
Nathan: "I can't wait to see the swimming-pool."
Kerry: "We're late. My parents must be worried."
Gary: "I'm so hot!"

2 Je sais donner un conseil. → Mémento p. 146

Pour demander ou donner un **conseil** ou encore exprimer une **quasi-interdiction**, on utilise ***should*** ou ***shouldn't*** suivi d'une base verbale.

• ***Should*** exprime une suggestion, un conseil ou une forte recommandation.

You look tired, you **should** stay at home tonight.
I think you **should** see a doctor!

• ***Shouldn't*** exprime une quasi-interdiction ou un reproche.

You **shouldn't** touch this, it's hot!

• Dans une question, ***should*** sert à demander conseil.

Should I call now?
(Sous-entendu : Penses-tu que c'est une bonne idée?)

4. **Dis ce que ces personnages devraient faire ou ne devraient pas faire.**

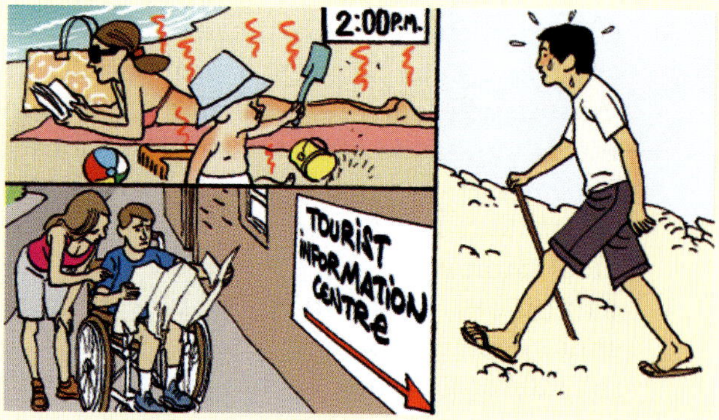

Remember and practise

1 Je sais donner des conseils appuyés. → *Mémento p. 147*

Pour **conseiller vivement** à quelqu'un de faire quelque chose, on utilise l'expression ***had better*** ou ***'d better*** + base verbale.

• Avec ***had better***, la situation évoquée est bien particulière. Alors que ***should*** s'emploie pour donner des conseils « neutres », ***had better*** est utilisé pour donner des conseils de manière plus vive, plus stricte.

You'**d better** react now.

Tu ferais mieux de réagir tout de suite.

You **should** obey your parents.

(Le conseil est valable à tout moment.)

• Avec ***had better***, on sous-entend que si la personne ne respecte pas le conseil, elle s'expose à des conséquences négatives. ***Had better*** a donc parfois une valeur de menace.

You **had better** learn your Maths lesson.

(Sous-entendu : sinon, tu seras puni, tu auras une mauvaise note...)

• Pour conseiller vivement à quelqu'un de ne pas faire quelque chose, on utilise ***had better not***.

You **had better not** tell him what happened.

1. Ces personnes ne font pas ce qu'il faut. Que pourrais-tu vivement leur conseiller de faire dans les situations suivantes ?

tidy • put on warm clothes • swim fast • call the doctor

2 Je sais parler d'une situation imaginaire. → *Mémento p. 145*

Pour évoquer les conséquences possibles d'une **situation imaginaire**, on utilise le conditionnel avec ***would*** + base verbale.

• L'hypothèse est introduite par ***if***. Le verbe de la phrase est conjugué au **prétérit modal**, c'est-à-dire que le prétérit ne renvoie pas à une situation passée mais à une **situation imaginaire**.

If I had a sword ...

• Pour évoquer les conséquences de cette hypothèse, on utilise l'auxiliaire ***would*** + base verbale.

... **I would defy** my enemies.

• **Formation**

Affirmation	I **would play** video games.
Négation	I **wouldn't play** tennis.
Interrogation	**Would** you **play** video games?

Remarque : Au prétérit modal, ***be*** se conjugue avec ***were*** à toutes les personnes *(If I **were**, you **were**, he/she/it **were** ...)*.
Cependant, ***was*** remplace de plus en plus souvent ***were*** à la 1re et à la 3e personne du singulier.

If I **was** at home, I would read on my sofa.

If he **was** ill, he wouldn't work so much.

2. Voici les réponses qu'une jeune fille a données à un questionnaire sur les jeux vidéo. Reconstitue son message.

a. If I .... *(have)* enough pocket money, I .... *(buy)* a RPG.
b. If I ... *(be)* sporty, I ... *(not spend)* so much time on my computer.
c. My friends and I .... *(play)* all day long if our parents .... *(agree)*.
d. If a mummy .... *(attack)* the hero, he .... *(burn)* it.
e. If I .... *(be)* a knight, I .... *(defeat)* all the villains with my sword.

3. Dis à ton ami(e) ce que tu ferais si ta vie était différente.

a. If I ... *(live)* in the USA, I ...
b. If I ... *(win)* the lottery, I ...
c. If I ... *(not have)* so many things to do, I ...
d. If I ... *(have)* a job, I ...
e. And you, what ... you ... *(do)*?

Plus d'exercices sur ton CD audio-rom

STEP 3 Remember and practise

1 Je sais exprimer des hypothèses sur ce qui s'est passé. → Mémento p. 146

Pour parler de **ce qui s'est peut-être** ou **certainement produit** dans le passé, on utilise ***might / may*** ou ***must have* + participe passé**.

- Si l'on est quasiment certain de ce qui s'est produit dans le passé, on utilise ***must have* + participe passé**.

Look at the garden! It **must have** rained in the night.

- Si l'on n'est pas très sûr de ce qui s'est produit, on utilise ***may have* + participe passé**.

I can't find my mobile phone. I **may have** left it at home.

- Si l'on est peu sûr de ce qui s'est produit, on utilise ***might have* + participe passé**.

I can't see Jem. She **might have** missed the bus.

Remarques :

- ***Have*** ne s'accorde pas à la 3e personne car il suit un auxiliaire de modalité (***must*** ou ***may/might***).

It must **have** rained a lot!

- Ces formes verbales sont souvent traduites par des formes impersonnelles en français.

They **may have phoned** yesterday.

Il se peut qu'ils aient téléphoné hier.

1. Imagine ce qui a pu se produire et ce qui est arrivé au personnage. Tu peux utiliser les expressions ci-dessous.

Ex. : *He **must/might have been** here for a long time because ...*

- *aliens • his friend • his car • an old couch • the desert*
- *leave • lose his stuff (bags and papers) • wait • break down • walk for a long time • hitch-hike* (faire de l'auto-stop) *• spend the night • kidnap*

2. Tu as découvert un extraterrestre qui vit sur terre, mais il ne parle pas ta langue. Émets des hypothèses.

a. Il a dû voyager dans un vaisseau spatial.
b. Il se peut qu'il soit venu avec d'autres extraterrestres.
c. Il se pourrait qu'il ait visité d'autres planètes.
d. Il a dû avoir peur *(be afraid of)* des êtres humains.

2 Je sais utiliser les pronoms réfléchis. → Mémento p. 135

On utilise un **pronom réfléchi** (***myself*** / ***ourselves***) comme complément pour faire référence au sujet quand il est identique.

- Observe la différence de sens entre ces deux phrases :

Van Gogh painted **himself**.
*Van Gogh s'est peint **lui-même**.* (Il a fait son autoportrait.)
Van Gogh painted **him**.
*Van Gogh **l'**a peint.* (Il a peint un autre homme que lui).

- La liste des pronoms réfléchis est :

Au singulier : *myself / yourself / himself / herself / itself*
Au pluriel : *ourselves / yourselves / themselves*

- **Remarque :** Il ne faut pas confondre les **pronoms réfléchis** *(myself, yourself, ...)*, qui renvoient au sujet, et les **pronoms réciproques** *(each other, one another)*, qui évoquent un échange entre deux *(each other)* ou plusieurs personnes *(one another)*.

Mary and Pat talked to **each other** for a long time.
Mary et Pat **se** sont parlé pendant longtemps.

3. Tu as vu un film de science-fiction au cinéma avec ton ami Chan. Complète le dialogue avec un pronom réciproque ou réfléchi selon le sens de la phrase.

You: "So Chan, did you have a nice time?"
Chan: "Oh, I enjoyed ... a lot! Did you like the two strange robots with the spiky hair? They were so funny when they spoke to ..."
You: "Oh yes! But I was surprised at the end. It was so moving when they saw ... in the mirror and realized they had become real human beings. I almost cried!"
Chan: "Going to the cinema with you was a really good idea. What else can we do on a rainy night to enjoy ... anyway?"

4. Traduis les phrases suivantes en utilisant un pronom réciproque ou réfléchi.

a. L'extraterrestre a ouvert la porte lui-même.
b. Tous les robots se sont regardés quelques secondes.
c. Les deux jeunes femmes ont construit ce nouveau modèle elles-même.

PROJECT 1

Create a leaflet to inform and advise people.

Créez un dépliant pour mettre en garde les adeptes de jeux vidéo.
Formez des groupes et soyez créatifs !

A. Organize your ideas for the leaflet.

- Parlez des troubles qui peuvent être déjà ressentis (mal aux yeux, mal de dos ou maux de têtes...).
You must have already ... / Your back might have already hurt ...
- Donnez des conseils (durée, lumière, distance de l'écran...).
You should/shouldn't sit ... / play ...
- Vous pouvez citer des témoignages de proches, qui parlent de ce qui changerait si les gens jouaient moins...
If she played less, she would see her friends / go out ... more.

B. Make the leaflet.

- Mettez le dépliant en page.
- Insérez des photos ou des dessins.
- Présentez-le à la classe.

PROJECT 2

Present a holiday destination.

A. Organize your ideas.

- Dans chaque groupe, répartissez-vous les différents thèmes à présenter :
- Informations sur les lieux et les événements (spectacles, marchés...) à ne pas rater.
When you come to ... you'll see / you'll be able to see ...
- Conseils sur la préparation du voyage (météo, vêtements, démarches administratives, argent...) : *You should bring ...*
- Documentez-vous sur chacun de ces thèmes : vous pouvez réutiliser ce que vous avez vu dans la *Unit* et chercher des informations complémentaires au CDI ou sur Internet.

B. Prepare your presentation.

- Répartissez dans chaque groupe les rubriques à aborder (météo, démarches administratives, conseils, lieux à visiter...).
- Attribuez ensuite à chaque membre du groupe l'une des rubriques que vous avez retenues, et répartissez-vous le temps de parole.
- Préparez votre intervention : vous pouvez utiliser le tableau, des images, des extraits audio ou vidéo...

C. Show time!

Présentez votre destination ! Donnez aux téléspectateurs l'envie de s'y rendre. Votre présentation doit être dynamique.

Volcanic crater at Wai-o-Tapu.

D. Elect the best presentation.

La classe vote pour les présentations les plus appréciées.

To be continued... **Gardez précieusement les meilleurs reportages. Vous les intégrerez dans votre émission de télé de la *Unit 6*.**

Words

1 **Find the odd one out and give a title to each series.**
a. lake • pond • cast • river • sea
b. wizard • knight • accommodation • demon • mummy
c. ballooning • hiking • cruising • invading

2 **Match each word to its definition.**
currency • alien • departure • pack
a. The act of leaving.
b. Money of a country.
c. A person from another country or planet.
d. Put your things in a suitcase or in a bag.

3 **Write the opposite of the following words.**
evil • harmless • near • expensive

4 **Select the correct explanation.**
a. If you book your holiday:
- you write your plans in a diary.
- you reserve your holiday in advance.
b. If you buy a package for your holiday:
- you buy a complete travel arrangement.
- you buy a big bag to put your things in.

PLAY WITH WORDS!

5 **a. Observe la phrase suivante.**
*Your **happiness** depends on him.*

b. Réfléchis.
• Quelle est la classe grammaticale de ***happiness*** (n, adj, adv, v)?
• Décompose ce mot en indiquant sa racine et son suffixe.
• Déduis-en la règle :
« Le suffixe *-ness* permet donc de transformer un adjectif en ... »
• Propose une traduction pour ce mot.

c. À ton tour !
• Propose une traduction pour les mots en gras dans les phrases suivantes.
1. ***Kindness** is an important quality.*
2. *I can sense a **coldness** between them.*
• Comment traduirais-tu en anglais les mots « rougeur, « vide » et « paresse » ?

CHECKPOINT

Read the text.

© VUB

Huggy robot for hospitalized children

The Robotics & Multibody Research Group (a research group within Brussels University) is working on Anty, an intelligent robot that will entertain[1] the children at hospital. When developed, the robot will walk, talk and show feelings. Besides[2], Anty will be able to have different personalities, so kids won't get bored with him.

Anty uses sensors for vision, audio and touch to interact with the children. By means of artificial intelligence, Anty will understand the children and express emotions. (...) It will adapt itself to their mood[3].

Anty will be able to look in the direction of a sound. The robot will react if children caress or hug[4] it. As it is meant for kids, the robot will weigh maximum 4 kilos and be 70 cm high.

www.we-make-money-not-art.com

1. **entertain** (v): *amuser.* – 2. **besides** (adv): *en plus, en outre.* – 3. **mood** (n): *humeur.* – 4. **hug** (v): *étreindre, prendre dans ses bras.*

Now do the activities.

a. Read the text and find out who Anty is.
b. Explain what Anty will do.
c. How much will it weigh? How tall will it be?
d. Say if the following sentences are true or false. Justify by quoting from the text.
- Anty won't be able to talk.
- It will understand what the children will say.
- It will react to the children's actions.
- It won't be able to adapt itself to children.

Listen to this survey in an American high school about the procedures in case of fire.

a. Find out if the first person has ever been in a fire.
b. Find out if they would know what to do.
c. Take notes to explain what people would or should do in case of fire.

Make a poster.

Make a poster to explain the procedures in case of a fire in your school.
- Say what people should or shouldn't do.
- Illustrate it.

Talk about your future summer camp.

- Say where you'll go.
- Explain what you'll have to do (chores ...) / be able to do (activities).
- Say what you would like to do.
- Say what you will take or won't be able to take with you when you go there.

A summercamp in Oregon.

Pairwork.

Two pupils are talking during the break. Pupil A has got a problem and doesn't know what to do. He's asking Pupil B's opinion.

Pupil A	Pupil B
Dis à B que tu as mal à la cheville.	
	Demande à A ce qui s'est passé.
Réponds à B (chute en rollers ou à vélo, dans les escaliers...).	
	Dis que cela a dû être effrayant / douloureux...
Dis à B que tu as un match de foot demain et demande-lui ce qu'il ferait à ta place.	
	Dis-lui ce qu'il ferait mieux de faire (aller à l'infirmerie ou chez le docteur, appeler son entraîneur, se reposer...)
Réponds-lui qu'il a raison et promets de faire quelque chose aussitôt que tu finiras les cours.	
	Dis-lui que tu lui téléphoneras ce soir quand tu rentreras et dis au revoir.
Réponds.	

GLAND

unit 6

Celebrations

STEP 1

Je rapporte les propos de quelqu'un.
Je restitue l'ensemble d'un message tronqué.

STEP 2

Je rapporte une expérience passée.

STEP 3

J'exprime mes souhaits.

Focus on: THE HIGHLAND GAMES

PROJECTS

1. Create your yearbook.
2. Make a TV review.

CHECKPOINT

Starter

1. Think of important days and celebrations in your life and name three of them. Then classify them into categories: national days • family celebrations • religious celebrations • other.

2. Why are these celebrations so important to you?

3. Look at the photos. Can you guess what event is celebrated in each document?

CD Rom: Discovery Game.

A Discover the Notting Hill carnival.

Look at the photos and imagine what time of year this takes place and where it comes from. What can people see, hear or do at the carnival?

Word bank
- costumes • drums • parades

Pan (Steel band)

Mas (Masquerade)

A food stall

B What is this carnival about? → WB 2, p. 47

A tourist is phoning an organizer to ask questions about the carnival.
What does she want to know about the Notting Hill carnival?

C A lunch break during the carnival.
→ WB 2, p. 49

You're buying food for your family. Your sister loves chicken, your father and brother both like spicy food, your mother's a vegetarian.
You don't understand the seller's accent. A customer is helping you. Act out the dialogue.

Pupil A: You ask questions and order the food.
I'd like some chicken for ...

Pupil B: You are the customer who's helping.
He says ... is spicy. / He suggests you try ... / He wants to know if she likes ...

CaribAraMa
136 - 138 Kingsland High Street
Dalston, London E8 2NS

Lunch & Dinner Menu

(chilli) spicy

Meat and fish
- Curried Goat[1] £ 5.99
- Stewed[2] Beef £ 4.99
- Jerk[3] Chicken £ 3.99
- Creole Fried Chicken £ 1.00 each
- Steamed[4] Fish £ 4.99

Veggies and sides
- Rice & Peas £ 2.00
- Saffron Yellow Rice £ 2.00
- Boiled Potato £ 1.50

Desserts and drinks
- Choice of Jamaican Patties[5] £ 1.50
- Choice of Homemade Drinks £ 1.80
- Can Drinks £ 0.60
- Pumpkin & Banana Fritters[6] £ 2.99

1. **goat** (n): *chèvre.* – 2. **stew** (n): *ragoût.* – 3. **jerk** (n): spice marinade. – 4. **steam** (n): *vapeur.* – 5. **patties** (n): small pies. – 6. **fritter** (n): *beignet.*

DVD **Video time** → WB 2, p. 50
A colourful carnival

IT'S UP TO YOU!

At the tourist information centre. → WB 2, p. 49

You ask a trainee *(stagiaire)* information about the carnival but his/her answers are sometimes incorrect. The manager corrects them.

Pupil A: You are the tourist and you ask questions about: dates / what to see / how to get there / food / day for the kids ...
I would like to know when ...

Pupil B: You are the trainee and you answer your partner's questions.

Pupil C: You are the manager. Spot the mistakes and get ready to correct.
Excuse me, actually ... / You say the carnival ... but in fact ...

MEMO
- He **asks** him if it is suitable for kids to go there **both** days.
- He **says** the information officer doesn't advise **his** kids to attend the Monday Parade. → p. 108

Je restitue l'ensemble d'un message tronqué.

A Prepare your trip to London.

1. Read this e-mail Sandy received yesterday. Why did Sam send her this e-mail? *→ WB 2, p. 51*

Hi Sandy,
I'm going to book my ticket to London at the travel agency tomorrow. Do you want me to get your ticket at the same time? Let me know, I'm home tomorrow morning because I'm looking after my sister. Is your cousin Sally still joining us there?
I still don't believe we're leaving next Saturday! Do you? Mum keeps giving me all sorts of advice, she's driving me crazy!
Do your parents have a map of London? We really need one. My parents are lending us their camera, so you don't need to take your sister's. We still need to buy an adaptor for our cell phones, have you got one? The plugs in England are not the same as the ones we have in the States.
Bye for now, Sam.
By the way, how much money are you taking with you? Are you changing it before leaving?

2. Sandy tells her parents about what Sam said or asked yesterday in his e-mail.

Sam said he ...
He asked if ...

B Carnival travel information.

1. Listen to this radio travel news flash about how to get to the carnival during this bank holiday weekend. What is the best way? Why?

→ WB 2, p. 51, CD piste 50

2. Sandy and Sam are staying in the south of London and want to go to the carnival on Sunday and go back by tube.

What is the best way to get there?

They should ... because on the radio, they said ...

SOUNDS *PISTE 51*
La prononciation du *u*.
→ WB 2, p. 52

IT'S UP TO YOU!

A very noisy message on your mobile! *→ WB 2, p. 53*

1. A friend of yours, Gareth, was supposed to join you at the carnival. He left you a message but some words are covered by the noises around. Listen to his message and try to guess what he said and asked...
I think he said he was ... / I think he asked where ...

2. Then listen to the message Gareth left on Greg's mobile and check if you were right.

MEMO
- He **said** he **was going** to the travel agency the next day.
- He **asked** me if you **had** a map of London. *→ p. 108*

1 Get ready!

Discover Canada Day.

Look at the leaflet and guess what Canada Day is about. When and how do Canadian people celebrate it?

→ WB 2, p. 54

I suppose Canadian people celebrate the day when …
Canadian people organize …

Word bank

- parade • national day • a day off
- set off fireworks • organize • wave flags

1. **bellydancing** (n): *danse du ventre.* – 2. **awesome** (adj): *impressionnant.*

2 Step forward!

A Celebrations on Canada Day. → WB 2, p. 54

Read this article and find out more about Canada Day. How did people feel that year? Why?

Tens of thousands of people converged on Parliament Hill on Tuesday to wish Canada a happy 141st birthday, (...) many of them wearing red and white and waving Canadian flags.
"Every day, (...) we are working together to achieve the greatness our country deserves. That's why on this Canada Day, we are prouder than ever to call ourselves Canadians (...). Together, we are rich in opportunity and diversity, French and English, Aboriginal and multicultural, native-born and newcomers," Prime Minister Stephen Harper said.
Tyler Koverko, 21, of Toronto, said he had been excited about celebrating Canada Day in the capital for weeks.
He said it was nice to see people from all different cultures and backgrounds coming together to celebrate Canada.
Michelle Bozynski said she had come from Calgary three days before, with her family for a wedding, and had decided to stay for Canada Day. "Everybody is coming from all over, and everyone is celebrating so many different things here today," she said.

Tuesday, 1st July 2008.

B Make your own report on that day. → WB 2, p. 56

1. You are a journalist and you collect a newcomer's reactions on Canada Day. Imagine the short interview you make.

Pupil A: You are the journalist. Ask him/her questions about where he/she comes from, his/her feelings, reasons for coming …
Where … from? / What do you think of …? / How do you feel about …? / Why …?
Pupil B: You are the newcomer. Answer the journalist's questions.
I'm from … / I'm here because … / I want to …

Word bank

- excited • surprised • disappointed
- see the fireworks • gather
- • see the diversity …

2. You've interviewed other newcomers. Now write a short article for the *Ottawa Citizen* newspaper.

I interviewed some newcomers and a woman / a man from … told me that he/she …
Her husband / his wife added …

C Becoming a Canadian citizen.

1. Who can become a Canadian citizen?
What must you do? Read the information from the Citizenship and Immigration Canada website and tell the class. → WB 2, p. 56

Word bank
- booklet *(brochure)*
- apply = ask

Home > Applying for citizenship > Becoming a citizen > How to apply

- You must be at least 18 years old to apply for Canadian citizenship.
- You must have permanent resident status.
- Adults must have lived in Canada for at least three years (1,095 days) in the past four years before applying.
- You must know enough English or French to understand other people and for them to understand you.
- You must know the rights and responsibilities of citizens, such as the right and responsibility to vote. You must also know some things about Canada's history and geography, and about its political system.
- You must take the citizenship test if you are between the ages of 18 and 54. The information you need to know is in the free booklet, *A Look at Canada*, available from Citizenship and Immigration Canada.
- You cannot become a citizen if you are in prison, on parole, or on probation.

Adapted from www.cic.gc.ca, Minister of Public Works and Government Services Canada, 2009.

New Canadian citizens after the ceremony.

2. Listen to Felicitas who remembers the day she became a citizen. What did the judge tell her? What was she asked to do? → WB 2, p. 57, CD piste 52

SOUNDS PISTE 53
L'accent tonique avec les suffixes *-ese* et *-ian*.
→ WB 2, p. 57

MAKE IT YOURS!

Tell your friends about your trip to Canada. → WB 2, p. 58

You are an American boy/girl back from a trip to Canada. You stayed with a host family who had just been given Canadian citizenship.
Explain to your friends what you saw on Canada Day and what your host family told you about the day they became Canadian citizens.

On Canada Day, we went to … / We saw …
My host family told me they had arrived … / They added they had become …
During the ceremony, they were asked / told to …

MEMO
- Michelle **said** she **had come** three days before.
- The judge **asked** us **to raise** our hands.
- The judge **said** he **would read** the oath of citizenship. → p. 109

1 Get ready!

Discover graduation day in the US. → WB 2, p. 60

1. Look at the photos. Which elements show it is a special day? Why is it so special?
Imagine how the people (parents, students, teachers) feel.

Word bank
- happy • proud
- a degree = a diploma • a mortarboard (a kind of hat) • a gown (a long robe) • a suit and tie
- dress formally • wait for • look forward to

1

2

2. Listen to what Alexia says to the school magazine's reporter just after the graduation ceremony. How does she feel? What does she wish? Why?

2 Step forward!

A A graduation poem. → WB 2, p. 61

1. Traditionally, American teenagers say a poem or a short speech at their graduation ceremony.
Read the poem Chris Gallatin wrote for his graduation. Who is he addressing? What does he wish?

Word bank
- grateful = thankful

PISTE 54

What does "thank you" really mean?

"Thank you" is one of those wonderful phrases
people use to express a special gratitude.
But there's often a lot more to it
than those two words can say.
When it comes from the heart, from deep inside,
"Thank you" means so much.
It means thank you for taking the time to show
that you care.
It means you make me feel so nice,
and I wish I could do the same for you ...
just by letting you know how much you mean to me.

2. Imagine you've just graduated. Make a short speech just after your graduation to show your gratitude to your parents, your teachers and your friends. Then tell it to the class.

I am here today to tell you ...
I wish I could say / tell you ... / If only I could show you ...

B What is a prom? → WB 2, p. 62

1. **Look at the documents and guess what a "prom" is. Where do you think the young people in document 2 are going? Imagine the atmosphere and what young people do at proms.**

In the photo on the right, there are ... So ...
Although they are very young ...

Word bank

- a date • evening dress • hairstyle
- tuxedo = dinner jacket • buttonhole *(boutonnière)*
- corsage *(for girls)*

1

2

3

2. **Listen to Lisa, Meg and Ian to learn about prom traditions in their hometowns. Which details show proms are really significant for young people and schools?**

At the prom, she did feel like ...
They do imagine ...

SOUNDS PISTE 55

L'accentuation des mots composés.
→ WB 2, p. 63

CD rom : Storytelling - A Prom Night

MAKE IT YOURS!

A graduation day in your school. → WB 2, p. 64

Pupil A: You are a student. A graduation ceremony and prom were organized in your school. You had a good time but you wish some things could improve next time. Discuss your ideas with the principal.
Next year, we wish we could have more... / If only we could use ... / We think it would be ...

Pupil B: You are the principal and you'd like to know exactly what the students wish. React or insist when you agree or don't agree with the students' requests. Ask for more details.
Where would the prom ...? / Do you wish you could have/use ...? / On the contrary, I do think that ...

MEMO

- **I wish I could stay** in high school one last day.
- I **did feel** like a star! → p. 110

Focus on

THE HIGHLAND

The Highland Games are events which are organized in Scotland and in other countries to celebrate Scottish and Celtic culture and heritage.

Highland Games opening ceremony, Inverness.

Origins

The games go back to contests of strength among the clans in ancient times. It was a way for the chiefs to choose the strongest men to serve as their warriors. In the 19th century old Scottish traditions were revived by Queen Victoria and famous writers like Sir Walter Scott, and the Highland Games became more and more popular. Nowadays, the members of the Royal Family traditionally attend the Braemar Gathering in the north-east in the late summer.

Caber tossing.

Nowadays

Where?

They are held in and around the Scottish Highlands during the summer. They are mostly centred around competitions in piping and drumming, dancing and Scottish heavy athletics. The Cowal Highland Gathering, held in Dunoon, in the South West of Scotland every August, is the largest Highland Games in the country, attracting around 3,500 competitors and about 15,000-20,000 spectators from around the globe.

But Highland Games are also organized anywhere where there are Scottish communities in exile throughout the Commonwealth. For example there are more than 200 different annual games and gatherings across the USA and Canada, each year, not to mention New Zealand, or Australia. In 2007 Japan celebrated the 26th Japan Scottish Highland Games!

GAMES

Heavy events

Some of the athletic and sports competitions symbolize the Highland Games. All the athletes wear a kilt during these competitions.

- Caber tossing: The competitors have to carry a long wooden pole[1] upright. Then they run and try to toss[2] it in such a way that it turns end over end.
- Hammer throwing: A round metal ball is attached to the end of a shaft[3]. The competitors' feet are fixed and the hammer is thrown for distance over the shoulder.
- Weight over the bar: The athletes try to throw a 56-pound[4] weight over a horizontal bar with only one hand.
- Tug of war: It is also known as "rope pulling". It is a sports event in which two teams test their strength by pulling against each other on opposite ends of a rope.

1. pole (n): *poteau.* - **2. toss** (v): throw. - **3. shaft** (v): *manche (de marteau...).*
4. 1 pound (n) ≈ 0,45 kg.

Hammer throwing.

SCANNING

➜ *WB 2, p. 65*

Have a good look at the documents and read the texts.

1. Find out in which countries the Highland games are organized. Explain why.

2. In the texts, find the words which mean:
un événement, la force, des concurrents, un marteau, une corde, des guerriers, un poids, un rassemblement.

3. Quiz the class. Ask your classmates riddles about the documents.
Ex.: What colour is the Scottish flag? Give another word for "throw" ...

WEBQUEST

➜ *WB 2, p. 67*

Tartan Day
Go to these sites and do the webquest in your workbook.

1. Find out about Tartan Day.
http://www.scotlandstartanday.com/tartan-day/tartan-day.asp

2. Find out where Tartan Day celebrated it.
http://www.scotland.org/scotland-week/about/tartan-day-events.html

3. Find out how it is celebrated.
http://www.rampantscotland.com/features/tartanday.htm

Remember and practise

1 Je sais rapporter les propos de quelqu'un au présent. → Mémento p. 148

Pour rapporter des propos au moment où ils sont dits, on utilise le **discours indirect**. Avec un **verbe introducteur au présent**, des changements dans l'**ordre des mots**, des **pronoms personnels** et des **déterminants possessifs** peuvent avoir lieu.

- **Rapporter des propos au présent.**
Le **verbe** reste **conjugué au même temps** mais les **pronoms personnels** et les **déterminants possessifs** sont **modifiés** quand la personne qui rapporte les propos n'en est pas l'auteur.
Emily: "**We** often **play** with **my** sister."
→ She says **they** often **play** with **her** sister.

- **Rapporter une question au présent.**
Lorsqu'une question est rapportée au discours indirect, **on rétablit la forme affirmative**. Une *Yes/No question* est introduite par *if* au style indirect. Pour les *Wh- questions*, on reprend le mot interrogatif du style direct.
Tom: "Where **are you**? **Are you** ready?"
→ Tom wonders where **they are** and if **they are** ready.
Lily: "Where **is it**?"
→ Lily asks where **it is**.

1. Tu entends derrière une porte une conversation entre deux camarades. Shanti est à côté de toi. Tu lui rapportes ce qui est dit.

Sarah is asking ... / He's telling her ...

Sarah: "Ryan, are you coming to Shanti's party?"
Ryan: "Did she invite us?"
Sarah: "She gave you an invitation yesterday!"
Ryan: "I forgot. Are you coming? I don't know her very well and I don't want to be alone."
Sarah: "Of course I'm coming. She's nice and her brother's cute *(mignon)*."

2. Que disent-ils ? Retrouve la phrase au style direct.

a. He wants to know if I know his friend.
b. She says she's staying at her cousin's.
c. They wonder when you will come back.
d. He asks where they are going.

2 Je sais rapporter les propos de quelqu'un au passé. → Mémento p. 148

Pour rapporter des propos au passé, on utilise le **discours indirect** avec un **verbe introducteur au passé**. Des changements dans l'ordre des mots des pronoms personnels et des déterminants sont possibles. Les **temps des verbes** et les **marqueurs spatio-temporels** sont modifiés.

- **Rapporter des propos au passé.**
Avec un verbe introducteur au passé, il faut « décaler » d'un cran dans le passé le verbe de la phrase au style direct.
- Présent simple → Prétérit simple
Jack: "**I am** at home **today**."
→ He said **he was** at home **that day**.
- Présent *be* + BV-*ing* → Prétérit *be* + BV-*ing*
Jack: "**I'm going** to the cinema **tomorrow**."
→ He said **he was going** to the cinema **the next day**."

- **Attention :** Les **marqueurs spatio-temporels** changent.

today → that day
tomorrow → the next day
now → then
this afternoon → that afternoon
next year → the following year
here → there

He said he was leaving **today**. (Si je parle aujourd'hui.)
He said he was leaving **that day**. (Si je parle à un autre moment.)

Remarques :
- Le choix du verbe introducteur permet de retranscrire certaines nuances.
He **shouted** he was fed up. *Il cria...*
She **whispered** she loved him. *Elle murmura...*
- Lorsque l'on précise à qui l'on parle, on préférera *tell* à *say*.
She **told me** the film started at 8 p.m.

3. Tu as eu une conversation téléphonique avec Patty qui t'a invité(e) à son anniversaire. Récapitule cette conversation à ton ami Joe.

Patty wanted to know if ... / She told me ...

You: "Hello, I just wanted to know: what time is your party on Saturday? Is it at your place?"
Patty: "It's here, at my place, from 7 to 10."
You: "And do you want me to bring some food?"
Patty: "John is bringing a cake, and I'm going shopping today, so there's enough food."
You: "By the way I'm coming with my friend Joe, is that ok with you?"
Patty: "Yes, of course I don't mind!"
You: "Ok. We're going to the swimming-pool this afternoon! Do you want to come?"
Patty: "Sorry I'm babysitting this afternoon. Maybe next time!"

4. Ton ami et toi êtes fans d'une émission de téléréalité. Mais la télévision de ton ami est en panne. Le lendemain, tu lui racontes ce qu'a dit l'un des professeurs de l'émission.

"Ian, what you're doing is not singing! Do you understand what we're telling you? We're giving you one last chance today! We really hope you're going to work harder now!"

1 Je sais rapporter les paroles de quelqu'un qui fait référence au passé. → Mémento p. 148

Quand une personne s'est exprimée au passé ou au *present perfect*, ses paroles sont souvent rapportées au ***past perfect***.

• Avec un verbe introducteur au passé, les temps doivent être « décalés » d'un cran.

Discours direct	Discours indirect
Prétérit "I **moved** to Canada four years ago."	*Past perfect* He said he **had moved** to Canada four years before.
Present perfect "I **have** already **been** to Canada."	*Past perfect* He said he **had** already **been** to Canada.

Rappel : Les marqueurs du passé peuvent subir des modifications.
"I arrived **a month ago**."
→ He said he had arrived **a month before**.

Attention : Quand la personne s'est exprimée en utilisant les modaux, certains d'entre eux subissent des modifications.

Discours direct	Discours indirect
"I **can** come."	She said she **could** come.
"I **will** go there."	I said I **would** go there.
"You **must** see Toronto." (obligation)	She said I **must** / **had to** see Toronto.
"He **must** be late." (quasi-certitude)	They said he **must** be late.
"You **may** find him there." (éventualité)	She said I **might** find him there.
"What **would** you prefer?	He asked me what I **would** prefer.

1. Tu as rencontré un Canadien près de chez toi. Il t'a raconté son histoire. Essaie de te souvenir de ses paroles exactes.

a. He told you he had arrived the month before.
b. He added he had not visited Paris yet.
c. He said he had found a job two days before.
d. He told you he had already found a nice house to live in.
e. He told you he had been pleased to meet you.

2. Rapporte à ton (ta) meilleur(e) ami(e) la conversation que tu as eue avec ta mère hier soir à propos de tes prochaines vacances.

You: "Mum, I would like to go to Aunt Maggie's for the holidays."
Your mum: "I'm afraid you can't. You must go and see your grandparents."
You: "Ok! I'll go to my grandparents' first, and then I'll spend a few days with my cousins."
Your mum: "I won't see you a lot then!"

3. Voici une conversation que tu as eue avec un(e) de tes ami(e)s. Rapporte vos propos à tes parents.

"Have you ever been to Canada?"
"Yes, I visited Toronto three years ago. The festival is great!"
"Can you give me any information about it?"
"You'll find all the information you need on their website. I'll give you the address."
"What are your plans for the next holiday?"
"I may go to Australia."

Plus d'exercices sur ton CD audio-rom

2 Je sais rapporter les ordres ou les suggestions de quelqu'un. → Mémento p. 148

Quand une personne donne un ordre, un conseil, ou fait une suggestion à **l'impératif**, ses propos sont rapportés à l'aide de ***to* + base verbale**.

Le verbe introducteur précise la notion exprimée. La personne peut ordonner *(order, command)*, conseiller *(advise)* ou demander *(ask, tell)* :

- de faire quelque chose.
"**Take** your time."
→ He advised me **to take** my time.

- de ne pas faire quelque chose.
"**Don't wait** for me."
→ He told me **not to wait** for him.

4. Tu vas bientôt partir en voyage. Raconte à tes parents ce que t'a recommandé l'organisateur du séjour.

He told me ... / He advised me ...

a. "Change money before you leave."
b. "Don't be rude to the host family."
c. "Take warm clothes with you."
d. "Don't be late at the airport."
e. "Phone the host family a few days before your stay."

STEP 3 Remember and practise

1 Je sais exprimer un souhait. → Mémento p. 145

On utilise le verbe ***wish*** pour exprimer le souhait que la situation envisagée soit **différente** de la réalité.

• Dans ce cas, ***wish*** est souvent suivi du prétérit ***could*** **+ BV**. Ce prétérit modal n'exprime pas un passé, mais un **souhait** ou un **regret** qui porte sur la situation présente.

I **wish** I **could** get better marks.
J'aimerais avoir de meilleures notes.
(Mes notes ne sont pas aussi bonnes que je le souhaite.)

Do you **wish** you **could** ski?
Souhaiterais-tu savoir skier ? (Ce n'est pas le cas.)

• L'expression ***If only*** est également souvent suivie de ***could*** **+ BV**.

If only we could phone now!
Si seulement nous pouvions téléphoner maintenant !

Remarque : ***wish*** permet d'exprimer ce que l'on souhaite de façon courtoise. Compare ces deux exemples.

I wish you could come home at the weekend.
(Je le souhaite, mais je ne sais pas si c'est réalisable.)

I want you to come home at the weekend.
(C'est ma volonté, que ce soit réalisable ou non ne m'intéresse pas.)

1. Julia quitte le lycée ce soir. Écris ses souhaits en utilisant les éléments proposés. Tu peux employer les verbes ci-dessous.

organize • tell • spend • leave • say

a. wish / goodbye / friends / leaving.
b. wish / party / friends.
c. wish / my friends / miss them.
d. If only / one more day / here.
e. my sister / wish / high school too / but / too young.

2. C'est ton dernier jour au collège. Dis à ton ami que :

a. tu souhaites avoir un emploi cet été.
b. tu souhaites qu'il puisse partir en vacances avec toi.
c. tu souhaites parler l'anglais couramment *(fluently)*.
d. tu souhaites pouvoir organiser une fête pour la fin d'année.

Demande-lui si :

e. il souhaiterait aussi avoir un emploi.
f. son père souhaite qu'il étudie une troisième langue au lycée.
g. ses amis souhaitent partir un an à l'étranger *(abroad)*.

2 Je sais insister sur la réalité de ce que j'affirme. → Mémento p. 149

La **forme emphatique**, ou **forme d'insistance**, sert à **mettre en valeur** ce que l'on affirme.

• Dans les phrases **affirmatives** sans auxiliaire (présent et prétérit simples), on ajoute ***do*** ou ***does*** au présent et ***did*** au prétérit devant la base verbale pour insister sur ce que l'on affirme.
On **accentue** fortement : ***do***, ***does*** ou ***did***, à l'oral.

He **does like** this book. *Il aime vraiment beaucoup ce livre.*
She **did say** that. *Elle l'a vraiment dit.*

Remarques :
On peut employer la forme emphatique avec le verbe *do*.
He **did do** the job perfectly.
(Je vous assure qu') il a fait ce travail à la perfection.

On n'emploie pas la forme emphatique :
- quand ***be*** est utilisé en tant que **verbe** :
We **were** sick, Miss Jones, honestly! (Il faut nous croire !)
- quand la forme verbale présente **déjà** un auxiliaire :
I **was listening** but I didn't hear.
Dans ce cas, on doit accentuer fortement *was* à l'oral :
I **was** listening but I didn't hear.
ou souligner l'auxiliaire à l'écrit :
I **was** listening but I didn't hear.

3. Tu racontes à ton ami(e) la fête de fin d'année de la veille. Utilise la forme emphatique pour mettre en valeur ce que tu affirmes, quand c'est possible.

"We had our school-leaving party yesterday."
"Did you really?"
"Actually, I **told** you, don't you remember? We played basketball and our team beat the teachers' team!"
"Even with Mr Watson, the gym teacher, in the team?"
"Yes, we certainly **won**, and by 15 points! And I think Mr Watson **was** quite angry to lose. And after that, there was a barbecue!"
"Don't tell me you cooked the burgers!"
"No, I didn't cook, but I **helped** with the salads. Then the teachers sang a farewell song with us."
"I can't imagine you singing in public!"
"Sorry, I **sang** with my friends! It was really fun!"
"Did the teachers enjoy themselves?"
"Well, they **said** they were going to practise their basketball!"

PR1JECT

Create your yearbook.

A. Plan out the pages.

- Constituez cinq ou six groupes dans la classe.
Chaque groupe crée son *yearbook*.
- Décidez des rubriques de votre *yearbook* (l'équipe éducative, la photo de classe, les sorties et les activités, les événements sportifs, les cours, les meilleurs moments, la page d'autographes et de messages...).

Attention : pensez à demander à vos camarades leur autorisation pour la diffusion de leurs photos.

B. Layout ideas.

- Réfléchissez à la mise en pages de vos illustrations et commentaires.
- Pensez à varier vos commentaires, à exprimer des regrets sur certains moments, des surprises, des joies...
I wish we could ... again ... / If only ...
- Rappelez-vous les propos de vos professeurs et camarades au moment où les photos ont été prises, afin de les légender.
In this photo, the teacher asked us to ... *X told Y to ...*

C. Make your yearbook!

Mettez en pages votre *yearbook* et présentez-le.

Yearbooks are very important in the United States and the United Kingdom. They commemorate the end of the school year.

PR2JECT

Make a TV review.

Vous avez interviewé des jeunes américains pour savoir comment ils fêtent la fin de leur année scolaire. Imaginez ce qu'ils vous ont dit sur l'ambiance de leur fête, son déroulement, leur bilan de cette année écoulée, leurs regrets et leurs souhaits...

A. Prepare your review.

- Expliquez aux téléspectateurs le sujet général.
- Listez ce que vous avez demandé à ces jeunes et ce qu'ils vous ont expliqué.
We asked some American teenagers if / what ...
Some told us ... / Others explained they ...

B. Show time.

Les reportages sont présentés à la classe à la façon de chroniqueurs sur un plateau télé.
Expliquez en quoi consiste cette fête et rapportez les témoignages des personnes que vous avez interviewées.
Répartissez-vous le temps de parole!

C. Elect the best review.

La classe vote pour les reportages les plus intéressants.

PROJET FINAL :

- Rassemblez les reportages qui ont été sélectionnés dans les *Projects 2* des *Units 4* à *6* et installez les chroniqueurs et les acteurs autour d'une table.
- Choisissez un animateur qui présentera l'émission, annoncera les sujets et qui pourra, à sa guise, les commenter.
- Faites votre émission de télé ! Vous pouvez la filmer ou simplement la présenter devant la classe.

Words

1 **Find the odd one out and give a title to each series.**

a. hot-air balloon • diversion • float • ski-doo • truck
b. beef • rice • chicken • goat • duck
c. pumpkin • stall • peas • potato • rice

2 **Find the correct definition for the following words or expressions.**

a. a bank holiday: a public holiday • a free day to go to the bank
b. an exit: a way out • a way in
c. a citizen: a car • a person who can vote
d. attend (v): wait • be present at
e. be over (v): be finished • start

3 **Which word cannot be associated with "graduation"?**

degree • formal • prom • map • school • gown

4 **Solve the following riddles.**

a. You use me to eat when you don't want to eat with your fingers!
b. You use me to wipe your mouth when you have finished eating.

5 PLAY WITH WORDS!

a. Observe la phrase suivante.
*I got my Canadian **citizenship**.*

b. Réfléchis.
• Quelle est la classe grammaticale de *citizenship* (adj, n, adv, v) ?
• Décompose-le en indiquant la racine et le suffixe.
• Que signifie la racine de ce mot ? Quelle est sa classe grammaticale? Propose une traduction pour *citizenship*.

c. À ton tour !
• Propose une traduction pour le mot en gras dans la phrase suivante.
***Partnership** is important in a team.*
• Observe le mot en gras.
*Bad **leadership** creates tension.*
Décompose-le et indique sa racine. Déduis-en le sens et propose une traduction.
• Comment traduirais-tu en anglais le mot « amitié » ?

CHECKPOINT

Listen to Otis's incredible success story and do the following activities.

a. Find out who Otis Scerbo, Mr Iannuzzi and Mr Murphy are.
b. Say how Otis behaved before fourth grade: was he well-behaved? violent? respectful? ...
c. Explain what changes happened when Otis met Mr Iannuzzi.
d. Find out what Mr Iannuzzi told Otis before his graduation.

Comment on this school report.

a. Say what the teachers think of Edwin's work.
b. Imagine what his parents told him, and what they said he should do.

EDUCATION COMMITTEE

SECONDARY SCHOOL

NAME . Edwin Ferguson . . . . FORM . Year 10. . . . .
Times absent . 3. . . . .
Conduct Grade
A = Excellent (B = Good) C = Fair D = Poor F = Consistenly Unacceptable

SUBJECT	Marks	EFFORT		REMARKS
		Classwork	Homework	
English	A	A	B	Work has been satisfactory. Should read more.
Maths	B+	B	A	Has made good progress.
History	B	B	C	Is passing the course but will have to work hard to improve his marks next term.
French	C+	B	C	Frequently does not complete the assigned homework.
PE	B	B	/	Could do better.

Write a letter to apply for a summer course in England.

a. Sum up your school report. What did your teachers say about you and your work?
b. Say what you wish.
c. Show how enthusiastic you are.

Read the text.

This is an extract from a document published by the US Department of State, about current US foreign policy and American life and culture.

US Independence Day: a Civic and Social Event

On July 4th, 1776, the United States claimed its independence from England. Americans celebrate this anniversary each year on July 4th, a day of patriotic celebration and family events throughout the country.

In the words of John Adams (the second President of the USA), the holiday would be "the great anniversary festival (…) to be solemnized with pomp and parade, with shows, games, sports, guns, bells, bonfires and illuminations, from one end of this continent to the other, from this time forward forever more."

Independence Day is not among the legal holidays fixed on a Monday or Friday, but many employees use vacation time to create an extended weekend. They have picnics or barbecues with food like hot dogs, hamburgers, potato salad ... Parades, concerts, baseball games and fireworks are organized. In New York City, Macy's department store has sponsored the nation's largest fireworks display for 31 years. In 2008 the 30-minute show featured 35,000 shells* launched in the East River and in New York Harbour. Macy's estimated that more than 3,000,000 watched it in person.

www.america.gov

***shell** (n) : *cartouche (de feu d'artifice).*

Fireworks in front of the Capitol, Washington, D.C.

Now do the following activities.

a. What do people celebrate on 4 July? Where does it happen?
b. Give two examples of activities done or food eaten on this day.
c. Say if the following statements are true or false. Justify by quoting from the text.
- John Adams said Independence Day should be greatly celebrated in the country.
- He thought this celebration would not last.
- Most Americans work on 4 July.
- Fireworks are very popular on this day.

d. Explain the title of this article.

Pairwork.

Your best friend is moving to Liverpool during the summer because his/her father has found a new job there. Act out this telephone conversation.

Pupil A

Réponds au téléphone.

Réponds. Explique que tes parents t'ont dit qu'ils allaient visiter une nouvelle maison ce week-end.

Réponds que c'est une bonne idée. Dis que tu souhaiterais pouvoir rester et que ton père puisse trouver du travail ici.

Dis que tu vas demander à ta mère si tu peux et que tu rappelleras tout à l'heure.

Pupil B

Présente-toi et prends des nouvelles de A.

Dis que tu as demandé à tes parents si tu pouvais l'inviter pour le week-end et qu'ils ont dit qu'ils étaient d'accord.

Dis que tu espères vraiment que A puisse venir pour le week-end.

Réponds et raccroche.

Annexes

Story time

Méthodologie

Lexique

Story time

Dup and Strong

by Jim Sukach

Dr J.L. Quicksolve took the elevator up to the second floor and knocked on the door of apartment number 216. Officer Longshot opened the door and let him in. Bill Dup was tall and broad-shouldered. Les Strong was short and thin and wore thick glasses. Officer Longshot said Bill was working out at his health club and Les was in their apartment at the time of the incident. "I'll let Les tell you the story," he said.

"Actually, I was coming in when I was struck from behind and knocked to the floor," Les said. "There were two strange men. Before I could get up, one grabbed my arms. The other guy taped my mouth shut so I couldn't call for help. I have a cold, and I could barely breathe. They tied me to a chair, took my wallet, and got the money out of it. They opened our wall safe there behind the picture of Bill's girlfriend and took the money. Everything happened so fast, and I was woozy from the hit on the head and the trouble I had breathing. They moved fast and were out of here in about three minutes."

"I got here about twenty minutes ago and I found Les tied up," Bill said as he worked the combination of the wall safe. "I passed two men on the stairs on the way up, but I didn't know them. They must have been the thieves." He turned the dial back and forth and opened the safe as he spoke. "You're right, Les. They took all the money." Turning to Dr Quicksolve, he said, "I had three thousand dollars in here. I was buying a used car, and the guy would only take cash. I was going to pick up the car in the morning."

"I think we are hearing less than the truth here," Dr Quicksolve said.

Why does Quicksolve suspect a lie?

Jim Sukach, *Baffling Whodunit Puzzles: Dr Quicksolve Mini-Mysteries* (1997)

Les couldn't speak with his mouth taped shut, so he didn't tell the robbers the combination of the safe. They couldn't open it in three minutes without the combination. Les is lying! He helped his friends get Bill's money.

Yellowstone Valley and the Great Flood
A Cheyenne Legend

He was an old Indian. His face was weather-beaten, but his eyes were still bright. I never knew what tribe he was from, though I could guess. Yet others from the tribe whom I talked to later had never heard his story. We had been talking of the visions of the young men. He sat for a long time, looking out across the Yellowstone Valley through the pouring rain, before he spoke.

"They are beginning to come back," he said.

"Who is coming back?" I asked.

"The animals," he said. "It has happened before."

"Tell me about it."

He thought for a long while before he lifted his hands and his eyes.

"The Great Spirit smiled on this land when he made it. There were mountains and plains, forests and grasslands. There were animals of many kinds—and men." The old man's hands moved smoothly, telling the story more clearly than his voice. "The Great Spirit told the people, 'These animals are your brothers. Share the land with them. They will give you food and clothing. Live with them and protect them. Protect especially the buffalo, for the buffalo will give you food and shelter. The hide of the buffalo will keep you from the cold, from the heat, and from the rain. As long as you have the buffalo, you will never need to suffer.'

For many winters the people lived at peace with the animals and with the land. When they killed a buffalo, they thanked the Great Spirit, and they used every part of the buffalo. It took care of every need.

Then other people came. They did not think of the animals as brothers. They killed, even when they did not need food. They burned and cut the forests, and the animals died. They shot the buffalo and called it 'sport'. They killed the fish in the streams.

When the Great Spirit looked down, he was sad. He let the smoke of the fires lie in the valleys. The people coughed and choked. But still they burned and they killed. So the Great Spirit sent rains to put out the fires and to destroy the people. The rains fell, and the waters rose. The people moved from the flooded valleys to the higher land.

Spotted Bear, the medicine man, gathered together his people. He said to them, 'The Great Spirit has told us that as long as we have the buffalo we will be safe from heat and cold and rain. But there are no longer any buffalo. Unless we can find buffalo and live at peace with nature, we will all die.'

Still the rains fell, and the waters rose. The people moved from the flooded plains to the hills. The young men went out and hunted for the buffalo. As they went they put out the fires. They made friends with the animals once more. They cleaned out the streams.

Still the rains fell, and the waters rose. The people moved from the flooded hills to the mountains. Two young men came to Spotted Bear. 'We have found the buffalo,' they said. 'There was a cow, a calf, and a great white bull. The cow and the calf climbed up to the safety of the mountains. They should be back when the rain stops. But the bank gave way, and the bull was swept away by the floodwaters. We followed and got him to shore, but he had drowned. We have brought you his hide.' They unfolded a huge white buffalo skin. Spotted Bear took the white buffalo hide. 'Many people have been drowned,' he said. 'Our food has been carried away. But our young people are no longer destroying the world that was created for them. They have found the white buffalo. It will save those who are left.'

Still the rains fell, and the waters rose. The people moved from the flooded mountains to the highest peaks. Spotted Bear spread the white buffalo skin on the ground. He and the other medicine men scraped it and stretched it, and scraped it and stretched it.

Still the rains fell. Like all rawhide, the buffalo skin stretched when it was wet. Spotted Bear stretched it out over the village. All the people who were left crowded under it.

As the rains fell, the medicine men stretched the buffalo skin across the mountains. Each day they stretched it farther. Then Spotted Bear tied one corner to the top of the Big Horn Mountains. That side, he fastened to the Pryors. The next corner he tied to the Bear Tooth Mountains. Crossing the Yellowstone Valley, he tied one corner to the Crazy Mountains, and the other to Signal Butte in the Bull Mountains. The whole Yellowstone Valley was covered by the white buffalo skin.

Though the rains still fell above, it did not fall in the Yellowstone Valley. The waters sank away. Animals from the outside moved into the valley, under the white buffalo skin. The people shared the valley with them.

Still the rains fell above the buffalo skin. The skin stretched and began to sag. Spotted Bear stood on the Bridger Mountains and raised the west end of the buffalo skin to catch the West Wind. The West Wind rushed in and was caught under the buffalo skin. The wind lifted the skin until it formed a great dome over the valley. The Great Spirit saw that the people were living at peace with the earth. The rains stopped, and the sun shone. As the sun shone on the white buffalo skin, it gleamed with colours of red and yellow and blue. As the sun shone on the rawhide, it began to shrink. The ends of the dome shrank away until all that was left was one great arch across the valley."

The old man's voice faded away; but his hands said "Look," and his arms moved toward the valley.

The rain had stopped and a rainbow arched across the Yellowstone Valley. A buffalo calf and its mother grazed beneath it.

www.ilhawaii.net/~stony/lore29.html

Messy Room

by Shel Silverstein

Whosever room this is should be ashamed!
His underwear is hanging on the lamp.
His raincoat is there in the overstuffed chair,
And the chair is becoming quite mucky and damp.
His workbook is wedged in the window,
His sweater's been thrown on the floor.
His scarf and one ski are beneath the TV,
And his pants have been carelessly hung on the door.
His books are all jammed in the closet,
His vest has been left in the hall.
A lizard named Ed is asleep in his bed,
And his smelly old sock has been stuck to the wall.
Whosever room this is should be ashamed!
Donald or Robert or Willie or—
Huh? You say it's mine? Oh, dear,
I knew it looked familiar!

Shel Silverstein, *A Light in the Attic*, "Messy Room" (1981)

Garfield, Large and in Charge

by Jim Davis

Peanuts

by Schulz

Méthodologie

COMPRENDRE

1 Écouter un document audio.

Il est normal de ne pas tout comprendre quand on entend un document audio. Cela arrive aussi dans notre langue maternelle (mots inconnus, volume trop bas, etc.).

- Ainsi, quand tu écoutes un enregistrement, **concentre-toi sur les éléments que tu comprends**, plutôt que sur ceux que tu ne comprends pas.

La première écoute.

- **Ne prends pas de notes dès la première écoute**, car pendant que tu notes ce que tu as compris, tu risques de perdre le fil du document sonore. Il vaut mieux avoir **une connaissance globale du document avant de se lancer dans la prise de notes.**

- Repère **les indices** qui t'aident à saisir **le sens général** du document.

• **Le titre du document** peut te mettre sur la voie. Essaie d'anticiper, de deviner le vocabulaire que tu vas certainement entendre dans le document.

> Si le titre est *Survival in the High Seas*, des mots comme boat, danger, island, lose (lost), rescue pourront s'y trouver.

• **Le type de document** (dialogue, interview, journal radio ou télévisé...) et **le nombre de locuteurs**.

• **Les bruits d'arrière-plan** peuvent te donner une indication sur le contexte (bruits de circulation, *jingle* pour annoncer un programme à la radio, etc.).

• **Le ton de la voix et les émotions** qui se dégagent des voix des locuteurs (enthousiasme, ennui, humour, hésitation...) t'aideront à comprendre les réactions des personnages.

Les écoutes supplémentaires et la prise de notes.

- Lors des écoutes supplémentaires, concentre ton attention sur les mots **accentués** (c'est-à-dire les mots que tu entends le plus distinctement) car ils sont généralement **porteurs de sens** (adjectifs, verbes, noms).

• Si tu dois répondre à des questions, **lis l'ensemble des questions avant** de prendre des notes. Les questions peuvent te guider sur le sens du document, et tu sauras alors plus précisément sur quels points tu dois centrer ton attention.

• S'il s'agit d'une prise de notes libre (c'est-à-dire sans questions), **pense à espacer tes notes**. Utilise ensuite un stylo d'une autre couleur **afin de compléter tes notes** durant les autres écoutes et n'écris **pas de phrases complètes**.

2 Lire un texte.

Tu seras amené(e) à lire de plus en plus fréquemment des textes en anglais. Il est absolument **normal de ne pas tout comprendre à la première lecture** (c'est d'ailleurs le cas parfois quand tu lis des textes en français).

- **Avant de lire le texte**, observe le contexte du document. **L'illustration** qui accompagne le texte (s'il y en a une), **le titre** du document, **son origine** (auteur, époque) et **sa nature** (extrait de roman ou de pièce, article de presse...) te donneront des pistes pour mieux comprendre le texte quand tu le liras.
- **À la première lecture**, ne t'arrête pas aux mots inconnus. Au contraire, concentre ton attention sur les mots qui te sont familiers.
- Une seule lecture n'est jamais suffisante. **Lis à nouveau le texte** en essayant de **répondre mentalement** (ou au brouillon) aux questions suivantes :

Who? Where? When? What?

Si des questions de compréhension accompagnent le texte, **lis l'ensemble des questions**. Puis relis le texte en gardant à l'esprit les informations recherchées.

ASTUCE

Que dois-je faire quand je ne comprends pas une phrase ?

- Prends le temps de l'**analyser** en repérant les verbes, leurs sujets, et les compléments (COD, complément circonstanciel) afin de trouver la structure de la phrase.
- Quand il y a des pronoms personnels sujets (he, they...) ou compléments (her, us, them...) et des pronoms relatifs (who, which...), repère le nom qu'ils remplacent afin d'éviter toute confusion de sens.

ASTUCE

Que dois-je faire quand je ne connais pas le sens d'un mot ?

- Essaie de le déduire grâce au sens des mots qui l'entourent.
- Observe attentivement la composition du mot.
Si un mot se termine par le suffixe -ly, il s'agit certainement d'un adverbe.
Si un mot se termine par -ed, le mot est certainement un verbe régulier au prétérit ou au participe passé.
- Essaie de t'appuyer sur les mots transparents, c'est-à-dire les mots d'origine latine ou française et dont le sens est très proche (ou identique) au français.
Attention aux faux amis : utilise le contexte pour vérifier que tes hypothèses sont cohérentes.

QUELQUES FAUX AMIS FRÉQUENTS

- *actually* (*en fait*)
- *character* (*personnage*)
- *figure* (*nombre ; silhouette*)
- *check* (*contrôle, vérification*)
- *close* (adj) (*proche*)
- *copy* (n) (*exemplaire*)
- *eventually* (*finalement*)
- *habit* (*habitude*)
- *medicine* (*médicament*)
- *petrol* (*essence*)
- *phrase* (*expression*)
- *rude* (*grossier*)
- *sensible* (*raisonnable*)...

3 Comprendre un document vidéo.

Comme pour les documents audio et écrits, il est normal de ne pas tout comprendre. Tu dois saisir le **sens général** de la vidéo.

- Avant le visionnage, aide-toi du **titre** du film ou de l'extrait ainsi que du **type de document** (film, publicité, documentaire...) pour imaginer ce que tu vas voir, le vocabulaire que tu pourrais entendre...
- Pendant le visionnage, observe les **décors**, les **gestes** et **attitudes** des personnages, le **ton** de leur voix... Tous ces éléments t'aideront à comprendre la séquence.
- À mesure que tu (re)découvres la séquence vidéo, repère les **techniques de prise de vues utilisées** par le réalisateur. Elles peuvent t'aider à mieux comprendre certains éléments comme les rapports entre les personnages, les sentiments qu'ils expriment, la situation dans laquelle ils se trouvent, etc. (→ voir **astuce** ci-dessous).

ASTUCE

Les différentes techniques

- **Les plans**

Le gros plan (close-up), permet d'observer un détail, une émotion sur un visage, ou un objet.

Le plan américain (medium shot) couvre environ les deux tiers d'un personnage (de la tête à mi-cuisse).

Le plan général (long shot) montre l'environnement du ou des personnages.

- **Les angles de vue**

Les angles de vue permettent de mettre l'accent sur la situation dans laquelle se trouve le personnage.

Une caméra en plongée (high angle shot) filme le personnage ou l'objet de haut, ce qui le rapetisse, et donne une impression de vulnérabilité ou d'infériorité.

Une caméra en contre-plongée (low angle shot) filme le personnage ou l'objet d'en bas ou du dessous, ce qui l'agrandit et donne une impression de puissance.

- Pour la compréhension orale (dialogue, voix off, commentaire du journaliste, etc.), reporte-toi au **paragraphe 1, Écouter un document audio**, p. 124.

Entraîne-toi à regarder chez toi les séries et les films de langue anglaise en version originale, si possible sous-titrée en anglais. Tu apprendras de nombreuses expressions actuelles qui faciliteront ta prise de parole.

S'EXPRIMER

4 Formuler son opinion.

Quand tu t'exprimes, tu es souvent amené(e) à formuler ton opinion sur différents sujets.

QUELQUES EXPRESSIONS UTILES

- **Pour donner mon avis :**
In my opinion ... / To my mind ... *(Selon moi...)*
I think that...
It seems to me that ... *(Il me semble que...)*
- **Pour marquer mon accord :**
I agree with you. *(Je suis d'accord avec toi.)*
I think you're right. *(Je pense que tu as raison.)*
- **Pour marquer mon désaccord :**
I disagree with you. *(Je ne suis pas d'accord avec toi.)*
I think you're wrong. *(Je pense que tu as tort.)*

→ voir **Expressions utiles**, p. 174.

5 Rendre compte d'un document à l'oral.

La prise de parole est un exercice de communication. Il faut donc que tu captes l'attention de ton auditoire.

- Parle **fort et lentement**. Si tu hésites, tu peux employer des ***gap-fillers***, comme You know / Well / I mean ..., afin de ne pas laisser de blancs trop longs lors de ta présentation.
- Si possible, **ne lis pas tes notes**. Écris les idées les plus importantes sur une fiche afin de ne rien oublier. Et n'oublie pas de regarder ton auditoire.
- Pense à structurer ta présentation : commence par une introduction, utilise des mots de liaison pour montrer qu'il y a un enchaînement logique dans ta présentation, et n'oublie pas de faire une conclusion.

Tu peux également écrire au tableau les mots les plus importants ou difficiles pour la classe.

QUELQUES EXPRESSIONS POUR STRUCTURER MA PRÉSENTATION

- **Introduction :**
I'm going to talk about ...
The document is an extract from ...
(Ce document est un extrait de...)
It is a text /a painting/ a film still ...
It deals with ... *(Le document parle de... / traite de...)*
- **Enchaînement des idées :**
first / then / finally / so / that's why / although ...
- **Conclusion :**
To conclude. /To make it short.

6 Parler au téléphone.

- Il est important de bien distinguer le **niveau de langue standard** (quand tu appelles un adulte que tu ne connais pas, une entreprise ou une administration) du **niveau de langue informel** (amis, camarades de classe, famille...).

Niveau standard :

Alex speaking.
Good morning! / Good afternoon! / Good evening!
I'm not sure I've understood. Could you repeat that?
Sorry, I must have the wrong number.
Could I speak to ...
Hold on, please.
Could you ask her/him to phone me back?
Good bye!

Niveau informel :

Hi, it's Alex!
I don't get it.
(Je ne comprends pas.)
Ring me back.
(Rappelle-moi.)
Bye! I'll talk to you soon!

Méthodologie

Attention : Pour dicter un numéro de téléphone, donne tous les chiffres individuellement (et non par dizaine comme en français).

QUELQUES MOTS ET EXPRESSIONS UTILES

mobile (UK) / cell phone (US) : téléphone portable
hang up : raccrocher

• Sur un répondeur, tu entendras fréquemment la phrase :
Please leave a message after the tone.
Si tu souhaites rappeler la personne plus tard :
I'll get back to you later.
Si tu laisses un message et que tu souhaites qu'on te rappelle :
Please, get back to me when you get the message!

7 Commenter un document iconographique (une image, une photo...).

- Présente d'abord le **type de document**.
- **Décris-le** aussi précisément que possible (objets, personnes, couleurs).

QUELQUES MOTS INDISPENSABLES

This document is a picture / a painting / a film still / a photo / the cover of ... / the front page of ... / a portrait / a poster / an ad ...

In the background (À l'arrière-plan)
At the top (Au-dessus de)
In the top right-hand corner (En haut à droite)
In the middle (Au milieu)
In the foreground (Au premier plan)
In the bottom left-hand corner (En bas à gauche)
At the bottom (En bas)

David Hockney (born in 1937), *Mr and Mrs Clark and Percy* (1970-71), acrylic on canvas, 214 x 305 cm (Tate Gallery, London).

- **Commente** le document.

- Émets quelques **hypothèses sur le lieu, l'époque**.
Perhaps/Maybe the photo was taken in ... / It looks like ... / It could/might represent/be ...
- Explique ce que tu trouves intéressant dans ce document.
This document is interesting because it shows/represents/illustrates/symbolizes ...
This document reminds me of / makes me think of... *(Ce document me rappelle...)*
- N'oublie pas de mentionner **les intentions de l'artiste**.
The author wants to show/convince/make people realize/think about ...

- **Conclus.**

In conclusion / To conclude ...
Tu peux dire si le document te plaît mais **justifie** systématiquement ton opinion :
I think it's great/unusual/representative of ... / It reflects ...
This picture doesn't appeal to me because ...
(Je n'aime pas tellement cette image parce que...)

8 Se préparer à une production écrite.

- Commence par **analyser le sujet**. Repère :

- ce qu'on te demande en soulignant les **mots-clés** du sujet pour mieux le cerner ;
- la **forme de la production** attendue (lettre, récit, dialogue...).

ASTUCE

Réutilise **les structures ou le vocabulaire vus en classe** qui se prêtent au sujet, et ajoute **des apports personnels**.

Si la production écrite est un récit, il faudra employer le **prétérit simple**.

Prépare un brouillon.

- Il n'est pas nécessaire de rédiger des phrases complètes au brouillon. Ne note que **quelques idées importantes** ou **quelques mots-clés**.
- **Réfléchis à l'enchaînement des idées <u>avant</u> de passer à la rédaction.** Prévois de créer **un paragraphe par idée ou par argument**.

Rédige avec soin.

- Lorsque tu rédiges au propre, **organise tes phrases en paragraphes**, ce qui rendra ta production plus aérée et agréable à lire.
Marque la fin de l'introduction et le début de la conclusion en allant à la ligne.
- Utilise des **mots de liaison** pour organiser tes idées (first, then, after that, finally, so, that's why, moreover *(de plus)*, in fact) ; ils te permettront de structurer tes idées et d'éviter une simple succession de phrases sans lien apparent.
- Efforce-toi d'avoir **une expression écrite riche et variée** (→ voir **paragraphe 11**, p. 132)
- **Relis-toi attentivement** en veillant plus particulièrement aux points suivants :
  - les accords sujet / verbe (-s de la 3e personne du singulier, accords au singulier ou au pluriel) ;
  - les déterminants possessifs (his/her/their ...) ;
  - l'utilisation des déterminants a, the ou Ø ;
  - le choix des temps ;
  - la place des adjectifs (avant le nom qu'ils qualifient) ;
  - évite de séparer le verbe de son COD.

9 Écrire un dialogue.

Il faut suivre des règles bien précises pour rédiger un dialogue en anglais.

La ponctuation.

- Pour introduire une phrase au discours direct, utilise des **guillemets** *(inverted commas)*, soit "..." soit '...' au début et à la fin de chaque phrase de dialogue.

Attention : Les signes « ... » et les tirets ne s'emploient pas dans les dialogues en anglais.

- Afin de rendre le dialogue plus clair, va **à la ligne** à chaque nouvelle réplique.

The policeman sat down next to me and asked, "So, what's the problem, young man?"
I answered, "I've lost my dog."
"Oh really?" he said.

Introduction du discours direct.

- En général, les phrases d'un dialogue sont suivies ou précédées d'un **verbe introducteur au prétérit**.

Attention : contrairement au français, **on n'inverse pas le sujet et le verbe**.

> "What do you want to do?" Paul asked.
> "Let's watch a DVD." Peter answered.

- Pense à varier le choix des verbes et à ne pas employer uniquement le verbe say afin d'enrichir ton dialogue.

QUELQUES VERBES ET LEURS ÉQUIVALENTS FRANÇAIS

Anglais (base verbale puis prétérit)	Français
say (said)	*dire*
answer (answered) reply (replied)	*répondre*
shout (shouted)	*crier*
ask (asked)	*demander*
whisper (whispered)	*murmurer*
add (added)	*ajouter*

10 Écrire une lettre ou un e-mail.

La lettre.

- Commence par **dater la lettre** et **précise l'endroit** d'où elle est écrite.
- Utilise les **formules d'introduction et de conclusion** appropriées pour la personne à laquelle tu écris.

Destinataire	Formule de début	Formule(s) de fin (plusieurs possibilités)
Ami	Dear + prénom	Take care! *(Prends soin de toi.)* (Lots of) love (UK) / Hugs and kisses (US) That's all for now. *(C'est tout pour aujourd'hui.)* We'll be in touch soon. *(On se recontacte bientôt.)*
Proche parent	Dear Dad / Dear Mum	Love Lots of love
Contexte semi-formel	Dear Mr Jones Dear Mrs Jones Dear Ms* Jones	Best regards Yours Yours sincerely
Contexte formel	Dear Madam Dear Sir	Yours faithfully

*Ms s'emploie quand on ignore si la destinataire d'une lettre est mariée ou célibataire.

Si tu écris à une personne dont tu es très proche, tu peux ajouter xxx après ton nom (équivalent des « bises » en français).

- Rends ta lettre plus claire et agréable à lire en l'aérant et en sautant des lignes.
- Enfin, n'oublie pas de **signer ta lettre**.

Méthodologie

Observe attentivement l'extrait de lettre ci-dessous et la façon dont elle est présentée.

Bordeaux
16 February 2010

Dear Judy,

Sorry I didn't write sooner, but I'm very lazy, you know...

....

....

....

Well, that's all for now, I have to start my homework before having dinner!

Lots of love,

Jay

Le courrier électronique.

- La rédaction d'un courrier électronique *(e-mail)* n'est pas très différente de celle d'une lettre. Le courrier électronique est en général un peu moins formel que le courrier postal.

- L'adresse de ton destinataire peut parfois te fournir une indication sur son origine géographique.

.fr	est employé pour les adresses françaises
.co.uk	pour le Royaume-Uni
.ie	pour l'Irlande
.com	dans un contexte commercial
.edu	dans le domaine éducatif
.org	pour des associations, etc.

- Quelques rappels sur la présentation des e-mails :

From *(de)*	Ligne où apparaît le nom ou l'adresse électronique de l'expéditeur.
To *(à)*	Adresse du destinataire.
CC	Adresse d'un destinataire secondaire (en copie).
Subject *(objet)*	Dans cette ligne, tu dois noter en quelques mots le thème ou le sujet de ton e-mail, par exemple *News from France.*

Méthodologie

POUR ALLER PLUS LOIN...

11 Enrichir son expression écrite.

- Tu peux enrichir ta production en utilisant un **lexique** varié et précis : essaie de réemployer **les mots que tu as appris**.

> Des verbes comme have, do et des adjectifs comme good, bad, nice et beautiful ont un sens trop général et ne te permettront pas d'exprimer tes idées précisément.

ASTUCE

Tu peux te constituer **un carnet** dans lequel tu noteras les nouveaux mots et expressions que tu rencontres au fil des leçons, dans des chansons, ou des films... Relis ce carnet régulièrement pour ne pas oublier ce vocabulaire.

- Tu peux enrichir ta production par la **syntaxe** que tu utilises.
Essaie de lier tes idées en utilisant des conjonctions de coordination ou des propositions relatives quand c'est possible. Veille à limiter les répétitions.

> Paul lives in Brighton. He's one of my best friends. peut devenir : Paul, who lives in Brighton, is one of my best friends.

- Tu peux enrichir ta production en **donnant des exemples** pour illustrer tes idées avec for example ou for instance.

12 Faire une recherche dans le dictionnaire.

Le dictionnaire est un outil essentiel mais il faut l'utiliser avec prudence.

- Avant d'utiliser le dictionnaire, essaie de toujours **deviner le sens du mot** en fonction du contexte.

Si le contexte ne te permet pas d'en deviner le sens, suis les étapes suivantes :
- **Retrouve la « base » du mot**, c'est-à-dire le mot sans terminaison (pour un verbe) ou sans -s pour un pluriel.
- **Identifie la classe grammaticale** du mot recherché (nom, adverbe, adjectif, etc.) pour ensuite regarder la **bonne entrée dans le dictionnaire**.
- **Lis l'ensemble de l'article relatif au mot**. De nombreux mots ont plusieurs sens, et il est important de lire toutes les possibilités afin d'identifier le mot recherché (tout particulièrement dans le sens français → anglais).
- **Appuie-toi sur les exemples pour vérifier** que le mot a bien le sens que tu recherches et pour voir son emploi en contexte.

> Ainsi, « avocat » désigne aussi bien un fruit qu'une profession. En anglais, on distinguera avocado de lawyer.

- Prends le temps de lire la transcription phonétique du mot afin de le prononcer correctement, surtout si tu dois employer le mot recherché dans un contexte oral.

ASTUCE

Dans le cas des **mots composés** ou des **expressions**, tu trouveras en général la traduction en te reportant au terme le plus significatif.

> Pour trouver l'expression « tirer à la courte paille », réfère-toi à l'entrée du mot « paille ». Tu trouveras alors que l'expression se traduit par draw lots.

Mémento grammatical

Mémento

1. Les nombres

■ Les **nombres cardinaux** sont souvent utilisés comme déterminants pour exprimer une quantité précise (pour compter). Ils se trouvent au bas des pages de ton manuel (de 1 à 176).

Remarques : Il y a différentes façons de dire « zéro » :
• **zero** dans les nombres avant ou après le point de la décimale.
0.50 → **zero** point five **zero**
• **zero** dans les différentes mesures (température, capacité, longueur…)
0° → **zero** degrees
• **o**, comme la lettre, dans les numéros de téléphone ou les dates.
081 230 5400 → **o** eight one two three **o** five four **double o**
Attention : On utilise le pluriel après zéro.
0 m → **zero** metres

● **Les nombres composés de trois chiffres et plus.**

100	a hundred *(une centaine)* one hundred *(cent précisément)*
1,000	a thousand / one thousand
400	four hundred
668	six hundred and sixty-eight
7,520	seven thousand five hundred and twenty
600,000	six hundred thousand
5,500,000	five and a half million ou five million five hundred thousand
2,000,000,000	two thousand million (GB) two billion (US)

● **Les adjectifs numéraux sont invariables.**
two **hundred** • four **thousand**
Attention : Lorsque hundred, thousand, million sont des noms, ils sont suivis de **of**, et se mettent au pluriel.
thousand**s** **of** people • hundred**s** **of** books

● En anglais, les **virgules** sont utilisées pour séparer les **chiffres par groupe de trois**.
1,783,427,569

● Les **décimales** (c'est-à-dire les chiffres après la virgule en français) **sont toujours précédées d'un point**. Elles se prononcent **chiffre par chiffre**.
34.125 → thirty four **point** one two five

● On ajoute **and** après hundred s'il est suivi de dizaines ou d'unités.
458 → four hundred **and** fifty-eight
103 → one hundred **and** three

■ Les **nombres ordinaux** servent à indiquer un rang, un ordre. On ajoute **-th** à la fin du nombre cardinal.
four → the four**th** *le quatrième*

Exceptions

1st → the first	9th → the ninth
2nd → the second	12th → the twelfth
3rd → the third	20th → the twentieth 30th / … → the thirtieth / …
5th → the fifth	

● Les **nombres composés** prennent un trait d'union.
Attention : Seul le deuxième chiffre est un ordinal !
21st → the twenty-**first** • 34th → the thirty-**fourth**

● Les nombres ordinaux servent à dire des fractions.
1/5 → a **fifth** ou one **fifth** • 2/3 → two **thirds**
Exceptions: 1/2 → a/one **half** • 1/4 → a/one **quarter**

Écris les chiffres en toutes lettres.
52 • 849 • 9,148 • 5,430 • 24,101 • 6,400,250 • 3/4 • 3/5

2. Dire l'heure

3:20 It's three twenty.	 It's three **o'clock**.
6:30 It's six thirty.	 It's half **past** six.
4:50 It's four fifty.	 It's ten **to** five.
(heures + minutes)	(minutes + to/past + heures)

Attention à la différence entre l'heure (It's three **o'clock**.) et la durée (I waited for one **hour**.).

Remarque : Pour les heures de l'après-midi et du soir, on utilise les chiffres de 1 à 12. Lorsqu'il s'agit des heures avant midi on utilise a.m. (7:05 a.m.) et on utilise p.m. pour les heures après midi (3:10 p.m.). On peut aussi utiliser les expressions in the morning/afternoon/evening.

Dis les heures suivantes en anglais.
3:45 • 8:30 • 12:25 • 15:15

3. Dire la date

■ Les années se disent généralement par tranches de deux chiffres :
1998 → nineteen ninety-eight
sauf celles dont le chiffre des dizaines est un zéro :
1908 → nineteen hundred and eight ou nineteen o eight

Exceptions :
- 16**00** → sixteen hundred • 18**00** → eighteen hundred
- **Avant 1000 :** 916 → nine hundred and sixteen
- **Après 2000 :** 2009 → two thousand and nine
- « **dans les années** 20 » : in the twenties (20s ou 1920s)

■ Les **nombres ordinaux** sont utilisés pour les dates.
I was born **on** May 4 ou **4th** ("on May **the fourth**").
I was born **on** 4 ou **4th** May ("on **the fourth** of May").

● Il existe différents formats de dates.

Britannique	Américain
4th May 2010	May 4th 2010
4 May 2010	May 4 2010
04/05/2010	05/04/2010

Remarques :
• Les jours sont précédés de **on** :
on Monday the first
• Les mois et les années sont précédés de **in** :
in December • **in** 2008

Dis les dates en anglais puis écris-les.
en mai 1946 • le 4 mars 520 • dans les années 90

Dis les dates suivantes à haute voix.
05/07/89 (US) • 02/01/92 (GB)

4. Les pronoms personnels sujets et compléments

■ Ils remplacent un **nom sujet ou complément**.
I am here! Listen to **me**!
He is funny! Look at **him**!
She's lost. Help **her**!
We aren't tired. Look at **us**!
They are nice. Speak to **them**!

● **You** et **it** ont la **même forme** sujet et complément.

Remplace ou complète par le pronom personnel qui convient.
a. *(Cathy)* ... is my best friend, I like ... very much.
b. I don't know *(Tom)* ... very well, ... is very shy.
c. *(My brother and I)* ... went out last night. Our parents saw ..., ... were very angry.

5. Les pronoms réfléchis

■ Les formes au singulier se terminent en **-self** et les formes plurielles en **-selves**.
myself / yourself / himself / herself / itself
ourselves / yourselves / themselves

● Ils renvoient à une personne ou à une chose.
I enjoyed **myself**. • The door closed by **itself**.

● Ils servent parfois à insister sur le sujet.
They did it **themselves**. *Ils l'ont fait eux-mêmes.*

● Associés à **by**, ils signifient « tout seul ».
She stayed **by herself**.

Complète par le pronom réfléchi qui convient.
a. We went there by ...
b. He did his exercise ...
c. It speaks for ...

6. Les déterminants et les pronoms possessifs

■ Les **déterminants possessifs** sont **my** legs / **your** legs / **his**, **her**, **its** legs / **our** legs / **your** legs / **their** legs.

● En anglais, on choisit le déterminant possessif en fonction de **la personne à qui appartient l'objet**.
Her mobile. → ***Son*** *portable (à **elle**).*
His mobile. → ***Son*** *portable (à **lui**).*

■ Les **pronoms possessifs** remplacent un nom et dépendent du possesseur. Ils ne s'accordent ni en genre ni en nombre.
I've got **mine** / **yours** / **his** / **hers** / **its** / **ours** / **yours** / **theirs**.
J'ai le mien / le tien / le sien ...

Complète à l'aide d'un déterminant possessif puis reformule avec un pronom possessif.

... notebook
It's ...

... house
It's ...

... toy
It's ...

Complète à l'aide du déterminant ou du pronom qui convient.
a. I haven't got ... mobile, can I use ..., please?
b. He gave ... sister ... old bike because ... was broken.
c. The pupils wrote ... names on the list but Sue didn't write ...

Mémento

7. Le génitif

■ Le **génitif** s'emploie pour marquer un **lien de possession**. Il s'applique aux êtres vivants, aux groupes, aux institutions ou aux repères temporels.
Alan's brother /z/ • Matt's book /s/ • Joyce's dolls /ɪz/ • The government's priority /s/ • Today's paper /z/

● En anglais, on place l'élément auquel s'applique le lien de possession en premier.

Mary's jacket → *la veste **de** Mary*
Teddy and Ally's parents → *les parents **de** Teddy et Ally*

Remarques :
• Lorsque le génitif porte sur un mot pluriel se terminant par un **-s**, on n'ajoute que l'apostrophe.
My friends' house.
• Si un nom singulier se termine par -s on ajoute 's.
Thomas's pen /ɪz/.
• Si le possesseur est un pluriel irrégulier, on ajoute **'s**.
The children's bags.
• Parfois le deuxième terme n'est pas mentionné, soit parce qu'il est évident soit pour éviter une répétition.
I'm going to John's. (Le mot *house* est évident.)
My house is old, Karen's is new. (Il y aurait répétition.)

■ Le double génitif

● Cette forme sous-entend souvent une idée de choix (parmi ceux de…). Elle se construit avec le **nom** suivi de of puis d'un **pronom possessif**.
A friend **of mine**. → *Un(e) de mes ami(e)s.*

Remarque : Cette construction est aussi possible avec le génitif.
A sister **of Tom's**. *Une des sœurs de Tom.*

Dis en anglais.
a. Où sont les clés de ta sœur ?
b. La chambre de mon frère est grande, celle de ma sœur est petite.
c. La voiture de mes parents est neuve.
d. Les chaussures de Max et de Thomas sont dans le hall.

8. Les articles *a (an)*, *the* et *Ø*

■ **A(n)** est un article indéfini qui sert à désigner un **élément indéterminé**.
Take **a** biscuit! (N'importe lequel.)

Remarques :
• Devant un son voyelle ou un *h* muet, on utilise **an** pour permettre la liaison.
an apple • **an** hour • **an** umbrella mais **a** university
• Les noms de métiers sont précédés de **a** ou **an**.
She is **a** nurse. • She is **an** artist.
• Certaines expressions s'utilisent avec **a** ou **an**.
once **a** day • half **an** hour

■ The désigne quelque chose ou quelqu'un de **précis**.
Give me **the** keys.
(La personne sait de quelles clés je parle.)

■ **Ø** (absence d'article) désigne des personnes, objets, animaux ou notions **en général** sans préciser de quantité.
Chris loves **Ø** sport and **Ø** war films.

Remarque : On ne met généralement pas d'article devant les noms propres, les jours de la semaine, les expressions de temps ou les institutions.
Ø Princess Ann • **Ø** Sunday • **Ø** last week/month • in **Ø** hospital

Complète avec *the*, *a*, *an* ou *Ø*.
a. On … Sunday I went to … hospital because I often have … headaches.
b. I don't like … soccer, I prefer … baseball.
c. Give me … salt on … table and … glass from … cupboard.
d. His mother is … actress and his father is … surgeon.
e. I bought … trainers yesterday.
f. … trainers I bought are terrific!

9. Les démonstratifs *this* et *that*

■ **This** et **that** sont des **démonstratifs** : ils servent à montrer une chose ou une personne.

● Pour montrer quelque chose qui est **proche** (en termes de lieu, de temps ou de sentiment), on utilise **this** ou son pluriel **these**.
This singer is great. • I like **these** shoes.

● Pour montrer quelque chose qui est **éloigné** (en termes de lieu, de temps ou de sentiment), on utilise **that** ou son pluriel **those**.
I hate **those** paintings.
I was ill on **that** day. *J'étais malade ce jour-là.*

■ Les démonstratifs peuvent être des **adjectifs** ou des **pronoms**.
I like **this** colour. (adjectif)
I don't like **those**! (pronom)

Complète à l'aide d'un démonstratif.
a. … girls are really beautiful!
b. I'm not going to wear … ugly hat!
c. Look, I've just bought … great CD.
d. It's so sad, people were so poor in … days.
e. Look at … kittens over there, they're so small!

10. Les noms dénombrables et indénombrables

■ Les noms **dénombrables** font référence à des choses que l'on **peut compter** (donc que l'on peut mettre au singulier ou au pluriel).

■ Les noms **indénombrables** font référence à des choses que l'on **<u>ne</u> peut <u>pas</u> compter** (on ne peut pas les faire précéder de a(n) ou de two ...)
bread • fruit • news *(des nouvelles)* • luggage *(des bagages)*...

● Pour pouvoir les compter, on utilise :
- **a piece of** *(un morceau de...)* : **a piece of** bread/fruit ...
- **a glass of** *(un verre de...)* : **a glass of** water/milk ...
- **a cup of** *(une tasse de...)* : **a cup of** coffee/tea ...

Ajoute une légende aux dessins suivants.

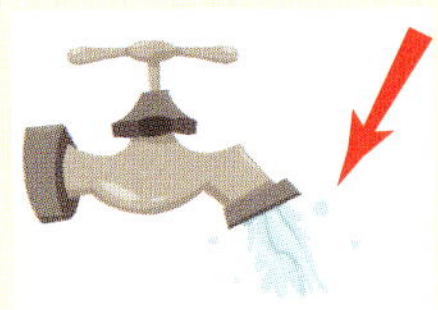

a. .... b. ....

c. .... d. ....

11. *Some, any* et *no*

■ Some et any sont des déterminants qui expriment une **quantité indéfinie**.

● Some s'emploie dans une **phrase affirmative** ou dans une **question** par laquelle on offre quelque chose ou à laquelle la **réponse attendue** est **positive**.
I'd like **some** tea, please.
Would you like **some** milk? (J'en propose.)

● Any s'emploie dans une **phrase négative** ou dans une question pour une **demande de renseignement**.
I don't need **any** friends.
Have you got **any** stamps?
(Je demande un renseignement.)

Remarque : Some et any peuvent être des **pronoms**.
"I'd like an apple."
"Sorry, I haven't got **any**. But I've got biscuits, do you want **some**?"

● No indique l'**absence** de quelque chose ou de quelqu'un et s'emploie dans une phrase affirmative.
We have **no** time. • He's got **no** friend.

■ Les **composés** de some, any et no suivent les mêmes règles.
Did you see **anyone**? *(quelqu'un)*
No, I didn't see **anyone**. *(personne)*
Can I have **something** to eat? *(quelque chose)*
There is **nothing** to eat. *(rien)*
I saw him **somewhere**. *(quelque part)*

● **Anybody**, **somebody**, **nobody** peuvent remplacer anyone, someone, no one (en deux mots).

Complète avec *some, any, no* ou un composé.
a. Can you give me ... water, please?
b. I don't know ... in this room!
c. He's sad because ... called him for his birthday.
d. I'd like ... peas. And have you got ... beans, please?
e. I have ... to tell you, I don't know ... about this story!

12. L'expression de la quantité

	Avec un nom dénombrable	Avec un nom indénombrable
Quantité indéfinie	**Some** / **any** pens	**Some** / **any** water
Tous / toutes	**All the** boys	**All the** luggage
Beaucoup	**Many** / **a lot of** / **lots of** books	**Much** / **a lot of** / **lots of** money
Peu / un peu	**Few** / **a few** cars	**Little** / **a little** time
Aucun / aucune	**No** / **not any** girls	**No** / **not any** fruit
La plupart	**Most** pages / **Most of** the men	**Most** news
Les deux	**Both** men	

Remarque : most n'est pas suivi de **of** lorsque le nom qui suit a un sens général.

Dis en anglais.
a. Il n'a pas beaucoup de temps.
b. J'ai lu la plupart de ses livres.
c. Il a beaucoup d'amis.
d. Il n'y a pas d'eau et peu de pain.
e. Les deux livres sont chers.

13. Comparer

■ **Le comparatif**
Le comparatif sert à comparer **<u>deux</u> choses**.

● **Le comparatif d'égalité** (« aussi... que... »)
Tom is <u>as clever as</u> Sally. (**as** + adj. + **as**)

Remarque : À la forme négative, il établit une **inégalité**.
You aren't <u>as tall as</u> John. = John is taller.

● **Le comparatif de supériorité** (« plus... que... »)
Adjectif long : **more** + adj. + **than**
The book is <u>more interesting than</u> the film.
Adjectif court : adj. + **-er** + **than**
You are <u>younger than</u> my brother.

Remarques :
• Les **adjectifs courts** contiennent une seule syllabe, ou deux syllabes se terminant par **-y**, **-ow** ou **-er** (pretty, narrow, clever...).
• Les **adjectifs longs** contiennent plus de deux syllabes ou deux syllabes ne se terminant pas par **-y**, **-ow** ou **-er** (boring...).

Attention aux exceptions :
- Les adjectifs se terminant en **-y** : le **y** se transforme en **i** (happy → happier).
- Les adjectifs d'une syllabe se terminant par une seule voyelle suivie d'une seule consonne doublent cette dernière consonne (hot → hotter)
- Adjectifs irréguliers : well / good → **better** • bad → **worse** • far → **farther** (en distance) / **further** (en degré, en temps ou en distance).

● **Le comparatif d'infériorité** (« moins... que... »)
- Adjectif long : **less** + adj. + **than**
The book is **less** interesting **than** the film.
- On n'utilise généralement pas **less** avec un adjectif court. On ne dira pas :
He is ~~less tall than~~ me. mais : He is **smaller than** me.

■ Le double comparatif

● « de plus en plus... » :
- Adjectif court : adj. + **-er and** adj. + **-er**
He's getting tall**er and** tall**er**.
- Adjectif long : **more and more** + adj.
She's **more and more** romantic.

● « de moins en moins... » : **less and less** + adj. long.
It's **less and less** comfortable.

Remarque : Le double comparatif peut également être associé à un nom.
We have **more and more** work and **more and more** problems! (indénombrable/dénombrable)
There are **fewer and fewer** French songs on the radio. (dénombrable)
People have **less and less** time for hobbies. (indénombrable)

Dis en anglais.
a. Il est plus grand et de plus en plus beau !
b. Je ne suis pas aussi riche mais je suis plus drôle.
c. Ce livre n'est pas meilleur mais il est moins cher.

■ Le superlatif

● On utilise le superlatif pour **comparer un élément avec les autres de sa catégorie** (« le/la/les plus... », « le/la/les moins... »).

● **Le superlatif de supériorité**
- Adjectif long : **the most** + adj.
This is **the most** expensive car **in** the world.
- Adjectif court : **the** + adj. + **-est**
I've got **the** small**est** part.

Remarques :
• **in** introduit un lieu, dans les autres cas on utilise **of**.
He's **the best** player **in** the world.
Those were **the best** years **of** my life.
• **Le superlatif** est souvent associé au ***present perfect*** avec **ever** pour souligner un caractère exceptionnel.
It's **the** funni**est** thing **I've ever done**.
C'est la chose la plus drôle que j'aie jamais faite.

● **Le superlatif d'infériorité** ne se construit qu'avec un adjectif long.
It's **the least** important point.

Attention aux exceptions :
well / good → **the best** • bad → **the worst** • far → **the farthest** (distance) / **the furthest** (en degré, en temps ou en distance)

Complète avec un adjectif au comparatif ou au superlatif.
a. My Dad is ... than my Mum. *(old)*
b. He is ... actor I've ever seen. *(bad)*
c. His car is ... mine. *(comfortable)*
d. It was ... day of the year. *(hot)*
e. These are ... burgers in town! *(good)*

14. Les adjectifs composés

■ Les **adjectifs composés** se forment en associant **deux mots**, généralement reliés par un trait d'union.
Le 1er élément qualifie le 2nd. Ce 2nd élément peut être :
- un **adjectif** : light-**green** • navy-**blue**
- un **verbe en -ing** : good-look**ing** • hard-work**ing**
- un **participe passé** : home-**made** • well-**dressed**
- un **nom** + **-ed** : dark-hair**ed** • left-hand**ed**

Complète avec un adjectif composé.
a. Someone who writes with his right hand is ...
b. A tee-shirt that has the same blue as the sky is ...
c. He behaves well, he is ...
d. A story that breaks your heart is ...

15. Le gérondif

■ Le **gérondif** est un verbe auquel on ajoute **-ing** et qui s'emploie comme un nom.

● Il peut avoir la fonction de :
- **sujet** : **Singing** is what I love!
- **complément** (très souvent après les verbes de goût) :
I enjoy **skating**. • I practise **swimming**.

● Il peut être employé après :
- **certaines prépositions** :
I'm good at **dancing**. • He left after **eating**.
- **certains verbes** comme start, stop, suggest, regret, admit, consider...
It stopped **raining**.

16. Les mots interrogatifs et les expressions interrogatives

■ Placés au début d'une question, ils servent à obtenir une information sur :
- l'**identité** d'une personne :
Who's that girl? *Qui... ?*
- la **nature** d'une chose, d'une activité :
What do you want? *Que... ?*
- un **moment** :
When are you coming? *Quand... ?*
- un **lieu** :
Where is your school? *Où... ?*
- une **raison** :
Why are you here? *Pourquoi...?*
- un **possesseur** :
Whose dog is it? *À qui appartient... ?*
- une **manière** :
How did you do? *Comment... ?*
- une **heure** :
What time did she phone? *À quelle heure... ?*
- une **couleur** :
What colour are your eyes? *De quelle couleur... ?*
- un **but** :
What are you doing that **for**? *Pour quelle raison... ?*
- une **origine** :
Where are your parents **from**? *D'où... ?*
- un **âge** :
How old is your dad? *Quel âge... ?*
- une **quantité** (indénombrable), un **prix** :
How much water did you drink? *Combien... ?*
How much did you pay for your cap?
- un **nombre** :
How many pets has he got? *Combien... ?*
- une **fréquence** :
How often do you do sport? *À quelle fréquence... ?*
How many times a day do you call him? *Combien de fois par... ?*
- une **taille** :
How tall is your dad? *Combien mesure... ?*
- une **hauteur** :
How high is Big Ben? *Combien mesure...?*

Retrouve les questions portant sur les éléments manquants.
a. I am from ... .
b. I am leaving at ... tomorrow.
c. She's absent because ... .
d. It's ...'s MP3 player.
e. There are ... books in this library.

17. Les questions

■ Les questions **fermées** (ou ***Yes/No questions***) commencent par un auxiliaire. On y répond par **Yes**, ... ou **No**, ...
"**Do** you like tea?"
"**Yes**, I do." / "**No**, I don't."
"**Will** they come tomorrow?"
"**Yes**, they will." / "**No**, they won't."

■ Les questions **ouvertes** (ou ***Wh- questions***) commencent par un mot ou une expression interrogative. On **ne peut pas** répondre par **Yes**, ... ou **No**, ...
What sport do you practise?
Why are you late?

■ L'auxiliaire dans une question se place avant le sujet.
Are you going to the cinema?
Which colour **do you prefer**?
Cependant, lorsque le **mot interrogatif** est **sujet** du verbe, l'auxiliaire n'apparaît pas.

Sujet	Complément
Who **wants** a drink?	Who **do you prefer**?
What **happened**?	What **did you do**?

Remarque : Dans une question, il ne faut pas confondre :
• le **verbe like** (« aimer », « apprécier »).
Did you **like** the film?
• la **préposition like**, qui se construit avec le verbe **be** ou **look**.
What **is** he **like**? *Quel est son caractère ?*
Does he **look like** you? *Est-ce qu'il te ressemble ?*

Retrouve les questions.
a. Yes, I do. Fish and chips is my favourite dish.
b. My sister looks like my mother.
c. No, I'm not interested in classical music.
d. He went to New York last year.

18. Les propositions relatives

■ Elles apportent des **précisions sur un groupe nominal**, voire une **proposition**.

● Le choix du pronom relatif dépend de :
- la **nature de son antécédent** (mot placé avant le pronom) : une personne, une chose ou un animal ;
- sa **fonction** dans la proposition relative : sujet, complément d'objet ou complément du nom.

Fonction	Antécédent humain	Antécédent non humain
Sujet	who • that	which • that
Complément d'objet	Ø • that* • who	Ø • that* • which
Complément du nom	whose	

*Uniquement dans les relatives restrictives.

● On utilise également les pronoms relatifs :
- **when** lorsque l'antécédent désigne un moment ;
I remember the day **when** I first met him.
- **where** lorsque l'antécédent désigne un lieu.
This is the place **where** Shakespeare was born.

■ Il existe deux types de propositions relatives.

● Les **propositions relatives restrictives** apportent une information essentielle pour identifier l'antécédent.
This is the girl **who** is in my class.
Voici la fille qui est dans ma classe.
Tennis is a sport **Ø** I like very much.
Le tennis est un sport que j'aime beaucoup.

Remarque : Quand un verbe est suivi d'une préposition, celle-ci reste à côté de lui dans la proposition relative.
The man I chatted **with** is interesting.
L'homme avec lequel j'ai discuté est intéressant.

● Les **propositions relatives descriptives** ajoutent une information supplémentaire, sans être indispensables. Les pronoms relatifs sont la plupart du temps précédés d'une virgule.
Lucy, **who** works hard, often has good marks.
Ils ne peuvent pas être remplacés par **Ø**, ni par **that**.

Remarque : which est aussi utilisé pour remplacer une proposition entière.
My parents sent me to bed early last night, **which** I didn't appreciate.

Complète avec un pronom relatif.
a. The photos ... he showed me were amazing.
b. I saw them yesterday in town, ... surprised me.
c. Here is the man ... house was burnt last week.
d. Here is the book ... I loved so much!
e. John, ... you met yesterday, is my best friend.

19. Les mots de liaison

■ Pour marquer une **opposition** ou un **contraste**, on utilise **whereas** (« alors que » / « tandis que »).
He lives in Sydney **whereas** I live in Melbourne.

■ Pour exprimer la **concession**, on utilise soit **however** (« cependant ») en début de proposition, en général suivi d'une virgule, soit **although** (« bien que ») dans une subordonnée.
She doesn't live far. **However**, we don't see her very often.
Although she doesn't live far, we don't see her very often.

■ Pour exprimer une **conséquence**, on utilise **so** (« donc ») ou **that's why** (« c'est pourquoi »).
I live near the school, **so** / **that's why** I cycle to school.

Complète les phrases suivantes avec un mot de liaison.
a. ... it's cold, they're playing outdoors.
b. I want to have a good mark ... I'm learning my lesson well.
c. I'm good at Maths ... Daisy is good at English.
d. I'm tired. ..., I can't sleep.

20. L'expression du but

■ Pour exprimer le but en anglais on utilise **to + BV**.
I want a new bike **to go** to school. *Je veux un nouveau vélo **pour aller** à l'école.*

Attention : Il ne faut pas confondre **to** avec **for**, qui se traduit aussi par « pour » en français. On utilise **for** pour :
- la cause ou le motif.
He's famous **for** his novels.
- une destination ou un destinataire.
I'm leaving **for** Paris.
It's a present **for** you.

■ La question qui porte sur le but sera : **What ... for?**
What did you do this **for?** *Dans quel but... ?*

Attention : Il ne faut pas confondre **What ... for?** avec **Why** qui amène une réponse en **because**.
Why did you do that? *Pourquoi as-tu fait cela ?*

Dis les phrases suivantes en anglais.
a. Ils sont venus pour nous aider.
b. J'ai pris un train pour être à l'heure.
c. Ce gâteau n'est pas pour elle.

21. L'expression du moyen

■ Pour exprimer le **moyen d'obtenir un résultat**, on utilise l'expression **by** + BV**-ing**.
You will have good marks **by** work**ing** hard.
Tu auras de bonnes notes en travaillant dur.

■ La question correspondante commence par **How**.
How can you communicate? *Comment... ?*

Traduis les phrases suivantes.
a. Comment as-tu gagné cet argent ?
b. J'ai pu arriver à l'heure en partant très tôt.
c. J'ai gagné en m'entraînant tous les jours.

22. *So* et *neither*

■ On utilise **so** ou **neither** pour exprimer un **point commun** entre deux personnes (« ... aussi » ou « ... non plus »).

● Pour réagir à une phrase affirmative : **so** + aux. + sujet.
I am French, **so is Tom**.

● Pour réagir à une phrase négative : **neither** + aux. + sujet.
I don't like tea, **neither does my friend**.

Remarques :
• Le choix de l'auxiliaire dépend du temps de la phrase de départ.
She bought this book and **so did I**.
• L'auxiliaire est toujours à la forme affirmative.
I can't come, **neither can they**.

Complète en utilisant l'information entre parenthèses.
a. I ate at home. *(Dad)*
b. She wasn't at home. *(her brother)*
c. She didn't call me. *(you)*
d. He's angry. *(I)*

23. *Be*

■ Le verbe **be** correspond au verbe « **être** » en français.
We **are** at school.
Mais ce n'est **pas toujours** le cas.
I **am** 14. *J'ai 14 ans.*
He **is** afraid of spiders. *Il a peur des araignées.*
Are you thirsty? *As-tu soif ?*

● L'auxiliaire **be** est utilisé dans :
- les **formes en BV + -ing** (pp. 142-144).
I **am** danc**ing**.
- la **voix passive** (p. 149).
Obama **was** elected in 2008.
- l'expression **there + be** (« il y a »), qui peut être conjuguée à **tous les temps** et **accompagnée d'auxiliaires modaux**.
There is a dog. (singulier) / **There are** dogs. (pluriel)
There were two libraries here before.
There can't be two solutions.

■ **Formation**
Présent

Affirmation	I **am**/**'m**. You **are**/**'re**. He/She/It **is**/**'s**. We/You/They **are**/**'re**.
Négation	I **am not**/ **'m not**. You **are not**/ **aren't**. He/She/It **is not**/ **isn't**. We/You/They **are not**/ **aren't**.
Interrogation	**Am** I? **Are** you? **Is** he/she/it? **Are** we/you/they?

Prétérit

Affirmation	I **was**. You **were**. He/She/It **was**. We/You/They **were**.
Négation	I **was not** / **wasn't**. You **were not** / **weren't**. He/She/It **was not** /**wasn't**. We/You/They **were not** /**weren't**.
Interrogation	**Was** I? **Were** you? **Was** he/she/it? **Were** we/you/they?

Complète à l'aide de *be* à la personne et au temps qui conviennent.
a. Mrs Jones ... reading at the moment.
b. ... you hungry or thirsty?
c. There ... a lot of people at the party yesterday.
d. How old ... you? When ... you born?
e. *Death on the Nile* ... written by Agatha Christie.

24. *Have*

■ Il ne faut pas confondre le **verbe have** et l'**auxiliaire have**.

● Le **verbe have**.
I **have** English at 5. *J'ai cours d'anglais à 5 heures.*
I **have** my breakfast at 7. *Je prends mon petit-déjeuner à 7 heures.*
Did you have a party yesterday? *Est-ce que tu as organisé une fête hier ?*

● L'**auxiliaire have**.
- Il est utilisé dans l'expression **have got** (pour exprimer la possession).
Have you **got** a sister?
Plus généralement, il sert à former le *present perfect* (p. 143) et le *past perfect* (p. 144).
He **has** visited Canada.

Remarque : Have to est utilisé pour exprimer une obligation (p. 146).

Dis en anglais.
a. Nous avons un chien.
b. Je prends mon déjeuner à l'école.
c. Nous n'avons jamais visité Londres.
d. Je dois ranger ma chambre.
e. Nous ne sommes pas obligés de porter un uniforme en France.

25. Le présent simple

■ Le **présent simple** s'emploie pour exprimer des **habitudes** ou des **généralités**.
The sun **rises** in the east.
I **live** in France.
He **does** sport regularly / three times a week.

● Il est aussi utilisé avec les verbes de **pensée** (think, agree, know, remember...) ou de goût (like, hate).
I **love** tennis. • He **thinks** you're right.

Mémento

Formation

Affirmation	I **play**. You **play**. He/She/It **plays**. We/You/They **play**.
Négation	I **don't play**. You **don't play**. He/She/It **doesn't play**. We/You/They **don't play**.
Interrogation	**Do** I **play**? **Do** you **play**? **Does** he/she/it **play**? **Do** we/you/they **play**?

Remarques : À la **troisième personne du singulier** :
• il faut ajouter un **-s** au verbe (**-es** lorsque le verbe se termine par -y, -s, -x, -sh, -ch ou par -o).
She work**s**. • She watch**es** TV. /ɪz/
• aux **formes négative et interrogative**, l'auxiliaire **do** devient **does**.
Does she work? She **doesn't** work.

Complète avec un verbe au présent simple.
a. Julie ... tennis on Wednesdays.
b. I sometimes ... TV after dinner.
c. How often ... you ... your grandparents?
d. ... he ... you an e-mail regularly?
e. I'm sorry but I ... this film.

26. Le présent en *be* + BV-*ing*

Il est utilisé pour parler d'une **action en train de se dérouler**.
She **is running**. (L'action se fait en ce moment.)

• Il ne s'utilise pas avec les verbes dont on n'envisage pas le déroulement, comme les verbes de goût (like, love, hate...) et les verbes de pensée (know, remember, understand...).

Il permet d'exprimer un **projet dans un futur proche**. Dans ce cas, il est généralement accompagné d'un marqueur temporel du futur (p. 144).
I'm leaving tomorrow. *Je pars demain.*

Formation

Affirmation	I **am** going. You **are** going. He/She/It **is** going. We/You/They **are** going.
Négation	I **am not** going. You **are not** going. He/She/It **is not** going. We/You/They **are not** going.
Interrogation	**Am** I going? **Are** you going? **Is** he/she/it going? **Are** we/you/they going?

Conjugue ces phrases au présent simple ou en *be* + BV-*ing*.
a. We ... *(go)* on holiday tomorrow.
b. I ... *(like)* eating chocolate.
c. What ... she ... *(do)*? ... she ... *(cook)*?
d. We ... *(go)* to the cinema this afternoon.
e. What ... you ... *(want)* to do tonight?

27. Le prétérit simple

Le **prétérit simple** est utilisé pour des **événements passés terminés**. Il est souvent accompagné d'un marqueur temporel du passé (**in** 1900, **when** I was 10, **yesterday**, **last** year ...).

Formation

• À la **forme affirmative**, on ajoute **-ed** à la base verbale (**-d** si le verbe se termine par un **-e**) pour les verbes réguliers.

La terminaison **-ed** se prononce :
/ɪd/ après les sons /t/ ou /d/ (started) ;
/t/ après les sons /f/, /k/, /p/, /s/, /θ/, /ʃ/ (watched) ;
/d/ dans les autres cas (phoned).

Attention : Les verbes irréguliers ont une forme spécifique à apprendre par cœur (pp. 172-173).
I **sang**. • He **threw** it across the room.

• Aux **formes négative et interrogative**, on utilise l'auxiliaire **did** et le verbe est à la base verbale.

Affirmation	I play**ed**. You play**ed**. He/She/It play**ed**. We/You/They play**ed**.
Négation	I **didn't** play. You **didn't** play. He/She/It **didn't** play. We/You/They **didn't** play.
Interrogation	**Did** I play? **Did** you play? **Did** he/she/it play? **Did** we/you/they play?

Dis en anglais.
a. L'année dernière, nous sommes allés au Canada.
b. Quand lui as-tu téléphoné ?
c. Ils n'ont pas joué de guitare hier.
d. Nous sommes restés à la maison mardi dernier.

28. Le prétérit en *be* + BV-*ing*

■ Le **prétérit en** be + **BV**-ing est utilisé pour dire ce qui **était en train de se produire à un moment du passé**. Comme un arrêt sur image, il sert à poser le cadre d'une action dans le passé. Il permet de mettre en valeur une action dans son déroulement.
She **was** prepar**ing** dinner.
Elle était en train de préparer le dîner.

■ **Formation**

Affirmation	I **was** play**ing**. You **were** play**ing**. He/She/It **was** play**ing**. We/You/They **were** play**ing**.
Négation	I **wasn't** play**ing**. You **weren't** play**ing**. He/She/It **wasn't** play**ing**. We/You/They **weren't** play**ing**.
Interrogation	**Was** I play**ing**? **Were** you play**ing**? **Was** he/she/it play**ing**? **Were** we/you/they play**ing**?

Remarque : While (« pendant que ») associé au prétérit en **be** + BV-**ing** marque la simultanéité entre deux actions : une action étant déjà en train de se dérouler au moment où l'autre action s'est produite.
Quand le sujet est identique dans les propositions principale et subordonnée, on peut utiliser while + BV-ing.
While (they **were**) hav**ing** dinner they received a call.
Pendant qu'ils dînaient, ils ont reçu un appel.

Conjugue ces verbes au prétérit simple ou au prétérit en *be* + BV-*ing*.
a. What ... you ... *(do)* yesterday at 5?
b. ... they *(visit)* New Zealand last year?
c. When we ... *(come)* in, she ... *(play)* cards.
d. I ... *(listen)* to music all day long.

29. Le *present perfect*

■ Le ***present perfect*** établit un **lien entre le présent et le passé**.

■ Il sert à parler **d'expériences**.
We **have been** to Canada. *Nous sommes allés au Canada.*
I **have** never **taken** the plane. *Je n'ai jamais pris l'avion.*

● Pour dire « **déjà** », on utilise **ever** dans une **phrase interrogative** et **already** dans une **phrase affirmative**, et on les place **devant le participe passé du verbe**.
"**Have** you ever **seen** this man?" *As-tu déjà vu cet homme?*
"Yes, I **have** already **seen** him." *Oui, je l'ai déjà vu.*

● Les **adverbes de fréquence** (often, sometimes, never) se placent **devant le participe passé** du verbe.
I **have** often **seen** him.

● Les **locutions exprimant le nombre de fois** que l'action a eu lieu se placent en **fin de proposition**.
I**'ve seen** him once / twice / three times ...
Je l'ai vu une fois / deux fois / trois fois...

■ Le *present perfect* sert à faire un **constat**, un **bilan** ou à exprimer les **conséquences présentes d'une action passée**.
He **has travelled** a lot.
Il a beaucoup voyagé.
They **haven't seen** it yet.
Ils ne l'ont pas encore vu.

■ Le *present perfect* est utilisé pour des actions qui ont **commencé dans le passé** et qui **continuent dans le présent**.
How long **have** they **lived** here?
Depuis combien de temps habitent-ils ici ?
They**'ve lived** here for some years / since 2004.
Ils habitent ici depuis quelques années / depuis 2004.

■ **Formation :** Le ***present perfect*** se forme avec **have** conjugué au **présent** suivi du **participe passé** du verbe.

Affirmation	I **have taken**. You **have taken**. He/She/It **has taken**. We/You/They **have taken**.
Négation	I **haven't taken**. You **haven't taken**. He/She/It **hasn't taken**. We/You/They **haven't taken**.
Interrogation	**Have** I **taken**? **Have** you **taken**? **Has** he/she/it **taken**? **Have** we/you/they **taken**?

Dis en anglais.
a. Je n'ai jamais pris l'avion.
b. Nous avons cassé un vase.
c. Il a vu ce film trois fois.
d. Elle est dans le magasin depuis 20 minutes.
e. As-tu déjà vu un crocodile ?

30. Le *present perfect* en be + BV-*ing*

■ Le ***present perfect* en** be + **BV**-ing permet de mettre en valeur l'activité qui est celle **du sujet depuis un certain temps**.

■ On l'emploie pour des actions qui ont **commencé dans le passé** et qui **continuent dans le présent**.
I've **been playing** for 10 minutes / since I arrived.
Je joue depuis 10 minutes / depuis que je suis arrivée. (Je joue encore.)
How long **have you been reading**?
Depuis combien de temps lis-tu? (La personne lit encore.)

● On l'emploie pour des activités qui **viennent de se terminer** et dont on constate les effets présents sur le sujet.
He's **been fighting**.
Il s'est battu. (On voit les traces sur le sujet.)

● On l'emploie pour faire des **reproches**.
You've **been fighting** again!
Tu t'es encore battu !

● Il ne peut pas être utilisé avec des verbes dont on n'envisage pas le déroulement (love, like, know, be...) ni avec un complément indiquant une quantité précise.
I've **sent** two e-mails.
J'ai envoyé deux e-mails.

■ **Formation :** Il se forme avec **have** conjugué au présent suivi de **been** et d'un verbe en BV**-ing**.

Affirmation	I **have been** working. You **have been** working. He/She/It **has been** working. We/You/They **have been** working.
Négation	I **have not been** working. You **have not been** working. He/She/It **has not been** working. We/You/They **have not been** working.
Interrogation	**Have** I **been** working? **Have** you **been** working? **Has** he/she/it **been** working? **Have** we/you/they **been** working?

Conjugue les verbes suivants au *present perfect* simple ou au *present perfect* en be + BV-*ing*.
a. The dog is wet. He ... *(run)* in the rain.
b. He ... *(buy)* two cars in one month!
c. I ... *(do)* my homework since 10 a.m.
d. You look tired. What ... you ... *(do)*?
e. I ... always ... *(love)* comics.

31. Le *past perfect*

■ **Le *past perfect* simple**

● Il est utilisé pour parler d'**actions** qui **s'étaient déjà produites avant un autre moment du passé**.
When he phoned, I **had** already **left** home.
Quand il a appelé, j'étais déjà partie de chez moi.
When the bell rang, I **had** just **finished** my essay.
Quand la sonnerie a retenti, je venais juste de finir mon devoir.

● Il est souvent utilisé avec des repères comme **by** (**by** September), **before** (**before** 2008) ou **when** + prétérit (**when** I arrived ...).

■ **Formation :** Il se construit avec l'auxiliaire **had** + **participe passé**.

Affirmation	I **had** worked. You **had** worked. He/She/It **had** worked. We/You/They **had** worked.
Négation	I **had not** worked. You **had not** worked. He/She/It **had not** worked. We/You/They **had not** worked.
Interrogation	**Had** I worked? **Had** you worked? **Had** he/she/it worked? **Had** we/you/they worked?

■ **Le *past perfect* en be +BV-ing**

● Il est utilisé pour indiquer que l'**action**, déjà **commencée au passé**, était **toujours en cours à un autre moment du passé**.
When they arrived, he **had been phoning** for 30 minutes.
Quand ils sont arrivés, cela faisait 30 minutes qu'il téléphonait.

● Il est souvent utilisé avec **for** (suivi de la durée de l'action) ou **since** (suivi du point de départ de l'action).

● Il ne peut pas être utilisé avec une quantité précise.
When we arrived, he had written two letters.
Quand nous sommes arrivés, il avait écrit deux lettres.

Conjugue les verbes suivants au *past perfect* ou au prétérit.
a. He ... *(realize)* he ... *(lose)* his keys.
b. When I ... *(arrive)*, they ... *(already eat)*.
c. I ... already ... *(write)* 10 e-mails by 10 o'clock.
d. He ... *(not see)* her before.

32. Le futur

■ Il existe plusieurs structures pour exprimer le futur.

● **will + BV** sert à parler de ce qui est **prévu** ou **planifié**.
I **will**/'**ll come** tomorrow.
Je viendrai demain.
They **will not**/**won't take** their car.
Ils ne prendront pas leur voiture.

Remarque : **will** ne peut pas être suivi d'un auxiliaire modal. Pour exprimer une obligation, une capacité ou une permission future, on utilise donc les équivalents des modaux (p. 146).
I'll **be able to go** to John's birthday party.
Je pourrai aller à l'anniversaire de John.

● **be going to** + **BV** sert à exprimer des **intentions** (ce qu'on va faire), des **déductions** ou des **prédictions** (ce qui va arriver).
I'm **going to learn** English.
Je vais apprendre l'anglais.
It's cold and cloudy. It's **going to snow**.
Il fait froid et il y a des nuages. Il va neiger.

● **be** + **BV-ing** avec un marqueur temporel du futur sert à exprimer un **projet dans un futur proche**.
They**'re leaving** on Friday, they**'re travelling** by train.
Ils partent vendredi, ils prennent le train.

■ Contrairement au français, les **subordonnées de temps** (introduites par when, as soon as, while ...) sont **au présent** même si la proposition principale est au futur.
As soon as I arrive, I'll call you.
Dès que j'arriverai, je t'appellerai.

■ Le futur est souvent utilisé avec des marqueurs temporels tels que :
tomorrow → *demain*
next Monday/weekend/month/year → *lundi / le week-end / le mois / l'année prochain(e)*
in 3 months (durée) → *dans 3 mois*
in 2030 (date) → en 2030
when I am older → *quand je serai grand*

Justifie l'emploi des formes verbales.
a. As soon as I arrive, I'll swim in the ocean.
b. It's going to rain.
c. Phone her, she'll be happy.
d. We won't tell him the truth.
e. He's repairing my car this afternoon.

33. Le prétérit modal

■ Quand le prétérit ne renvoie pas au passé mais à une **situation imaginaire**, on parle de **prétérit modal**.

Il se forme comme le prétérit temporel (ou prétérit simple).
If I **won** the lottery ...

Attention : Le verbe **be** est conjugué avec **were** à toutes les formes (I were, you were, he were...).

Remarque : was remplace de plus en plus **were**, notamment quand la situation n'est pas impossible.
If there **was** a storm, I would be careful.
S'il y avait un orage, je ferais attention.

34. Le conditionnel

■ Il est utilisé pour exprimer les **conséquences possibles d'une situation imaginaire**.

● L'**hypothèse** (la situation imaginaire) est **introduite par if** et le verbe est conjugué au prétérit modal.

● Pour évoquer les **conséquences possibles** de cette hypothèse, on utilise l'auxiliaire **would** + BV.
If I **went** to Australia, I **would/'d visit** Sydney.
Si j'allais en Australie, je visiterais Sydney.

■ **Formation**

Affirmation	I **would work**. You **would work**. He/She/It **would work**. We/You/They **would work**.
Négation	I **would not work**. You **would not work**. He/She/It **would not work**. We/You/They **would not work**.
Interrogation	**Would** I **work**? **Would** you **work**? **Would** he/she/it **work**? **Would** we/you/they **work**?

Complète les phrases suivantes en conjugant les verbes au prétérit et au conditionnel.
a. If I ... *(can)*, I ... *(buy)* myself a big house.
b. ... she ... *(be)* afraid if she ... *(see)* a spider?
c. If I ... *(be)* you, I ... *(not take)* the train.

35. Le souhait ou le regret

■ Pour exprimer le souhait que la situation soit différente de la situation réelle, on utilise l'expression **I wish** ou **if only**.

● Ces deux expressions peuvent être suivies d'un prétérit modal mais sont aussi souvent suivies d'une subordonnée avec **could** + BV.
I **wish** I **could be** rich.
J'aimerais être riche.
I **wish** you **could come** with me.
J'aimerais que tu puisses venir avec moi.
If only I **could talk** to him!
Si seulement je pouvais lui parler !

Traduis les phrases suivantes.
a. Si seulement tu pouvais arriver tôt !
b. J'aimerais être là.
c. J'aimerais que tu puisses me comprendre.

36. *Used to, not any more, no longer*

■ **Used to**

● L'expression **used to** + **BV** marque un **contraste fort entre le passé et le présent**. Elle est utilisée pour des actions ou des situations qui étaient vraies dans le passé mais qui ne le sont plus à présent. Il peut s'agir :
- d'**habitudes passées** ;
He **used to sing**.
Il chantait. (Il chantait souvent mais il ne chante plus.)

- de **faits passés**.
There **used to be** a park here.
Il y avait un parc ici. (Mais il n'y est plus.)

● **Used to** fonctionne comme un verbe au prétérit.
He **didn't use** to sing.
Il ne chantait pas.
Did he **use to** swim?
Nageait-il ?

■ **Not any more, no longer, not any longer**
On peut aussi marquer la rupture entre le passé et le présent en utilisant **not any more** / **not any longer** à la fin d'une phrase négative ou **no longer** devant un verbe ou après un auxiliaire.
I don't see him **any more**/ **any longer**. / I **no longer** see him.
Je ne le vois plus.

Traduis les phrases suivantes.
a. Il me lisait des histoires avant.
b. J'habitais à Sydney à ce moment-là.
c. Il n'y avait pas de supermarché ici avant.
d. Je ne fais plus de sport.

37. La modalité

■ On utilise un **auxiliaire modal** pour exprimer des notions telles que la **possibilité**, la **permission**, la **capacité**, l'**interdiction**...

● Ils sont suivis d'une base verbale.
I must **obey**.

● Ils ne prennent pas la terminaison **-s** à la troisième personne du singulier au présent.
He **can** phone.

● Ils n'ont pas besoin d'un autre auxiliaire aux formes interrogative et négative.
Can you dance ? • I **can't** sing.

● Ils ne peuvent se placer **ni après** to, **ni après un autre auxiliaire modal**. Ils sont donc remplacés par une **tournure équivalente**, notamment à l'**infinitif**, au **futur** ou au **conditionnel**.
I **will have to** work.

■ **Can** / **can't**

● **Can** est utilisé pour exprimer la **permission** (I **can** go out.), la **capacité** (I **can** ski well.) ou la **possibilité** (You **can** take a taxi.).

● **Can't** exprime l'**absence de permission** (You **can't** take photos.), l'**incapacité** (Babies **can't** walk.) ou l'**impossibilité** (I **can't** come.).

● L'équivalent de **can** / **can't** est **be allowed to** dans le cas d'une **permission**, **be able to** dans les **autres cas**.
I **was/wasn't allowed to** take photos.
I **will be able to** ski.

● Le prétérit **could** est utilisé pour une **situation générale** tandis que **was**/**were able to** s'utilise pour une **situation particulière**.
People **couldn't** phone before 1876.
I **was able to** see him on that day.

■ Au présent, **must** exprime l'**obligation**.
I **must** obey my parents. *Je dois obéir à mes parents.*

Remarque : Au présent, contrairement à **must**, **have to** exprime une obligation indépendante de la personne qui parle.
You **must** tell her. (Je te l'impose.)
You **have to** tell her. (C'est le règlement.)

● Aux autres temps, on emploie l'équivalent **have to**.
I **had to** tell him.
J'ai dû / j'ai été obligé de le lui dire.
I **will have to** tell him.
Je devrai / je serai obligé de le lui dire.

Remarque : Have to est utilisé à la forme négative pour exprimer l'absence d'obligation.
I **didn't have to** show my driving licence.
Je n'étais pas obligée de montrer mon permis de conduire.

■ **Mustn't** est utilisé pour une **interdiction**.
You **mustn't** be late. *Tu ne dois pas être en retard.*

● Son équivalent est **be forbidden to** ou **not be allowed to**.
It **was forbidden to** / **wasn't allowed to** take photos.

■ **Should** / **shouldn't**

● **Should** et **shouldn't** expriment un **conseil** ou un **reproche**.
You **should** come.
Tu devrais venir.
You **shouldn't** speak so loud.
Tu ne devrais pas parler aussi fort.

Dis en anglais.
a. Il ne pourra pas rester tard.
b. Je n'aurai pas le droit de lui téléphoner.
c. Nous devrions être à l'heure.
d. Elle n'a pas eu à se lever tôt.
e. Vous ne pourrez pas conduire.

■ Les auxiliaires modaux sont aussi utilisés pour exprimer le **degré de certitude** d'un événement.

● Ils peuvent exprimer une **forte probabilité** ou **quasi-certitude** (**must**), une **probabilité** (**may**), une **faible probabilité** (**might**) ou une **impossibilité** (**can't**).
He **must** be ill.
Il doit être malade.
He **may** / **might** come tomorrow.
Il se peut / Il se pourrait qu'il vienne demain.
It **can't** be him.
Ce ne peut pas être lui.

Remarque : On peut aussi évaluer la probabilité qu'un événement se soit produit dans le passé. Dans ce cas, l'auxiliaire modal est suivi de **have** + **participe passé**.
He **may have phoned** you.
Il t'a peut-être téléphoné.
He **can't have forgotten** me.
Il n'a pas pu m'oublier.

Traduis en anglais.
a. Il se peut qu'il ait cassé ses lunettes.
b. Il doit être au lit à présent.
c. Elle ne peut pas le connaître.
d. Il se pourrait qu'il devienne médecin.

38. *Had better*

■ **Had better** est utilisé pour **conseiller vivement** à quelqu'un de faire ou de ne pas faire quelque chose.
Si la personne ne suit pas ces conseils, elle s'expose à des **conséquences négatives**. C'est pourquoi **had better** a parfois une valeur de **menace**.
You **had**/**'d better** tell him.
Tu ferais mieux de le lui dire.

● **Had better** est suivi d'une base verbale ou de **not** + base verbale.
You **had**/**'d better** not leave now.
Tu ferais mieux de ne pas partir maintenant.

Traduis les phrases suivantes.
a. Tu ferais mieux d'apprendre tes leçons.
b. Il ferait mieux de ne pas sortir sans blouson.
c. Nous ferions mieux de nous entraîner davantage.

39. La suggestion

■ Pour faire une suggestion, on peut utiliser différentes formes.

● Suggestion aimable ou neutre :
- **What about** / **How about** + BV**-ing**?
What about / **How about eating** out tonight?
- **Why not** + BV?
Why not listen to music?
- **Could** + BV?
We **could** invite them?

● Suggestion plus insistante :
- **Why don't** + sujet + BV?
Why don't we rent a DVD?
- **Let's** + BV!
Let's order a pizza!

Remarque : Avec **Let's**, celui qui parle s'inclut dans la proposition.

Dis en anglais.
a. Et si tu rangeais ta chambre ?
b. Regardons un film !
c. Pourquoi n'achète-t-elle pas ce livre ?
d. Pourquoi ne pas aller au cinéma ?

40. La volonté, la contrainte, la permission

■ La volonté

● **want to** + **BV** exprime **ce que l'on veut faire**.
would like to + **BV** exprime **ce que l'on voudrait faire**.

Ce que je veux / voudrais faire.
I **want to** go home.
She **doesn't want to** go.
I **would like to** eat.
I **wouldn't like to** sleep here.

● Pour exprimer ce que l'on veut ou voudrait que **quelqu'un d'autre fasse**, on ajoute le nom ou le pronom personnel complément entre **want** / **would like** et **to** + BV.

Ce que je veux / voudrais que quelqu'un fasse.
I **want** you to go home. *Je veux que tu rentres.*
She **doesn't want** us **to go**. *Elle ne veut pas que nous partions.*
She **would like** Tom (him) **to eat**. *Elle aimerait que Tom (qu'il) mange.*
I **wouldn't like** the children (them) **to sleep** here. *Je ne voudrais pas que les enfants (qu'ils) dorment ici.*

Attention : « **que** » ne se traduit pas dans ces phrases.
Remarque : Cette structure s'utilise aussi avec des verbes comme ask, tell, expect, teach, offer…
I **expect** him **to** call.

■ La contrainte

● Pour exprimer une contrainte, on utilise **make** + **nom ou pronom complément** + **BV**.
I **made** my brother (him) **wash** the dishes.
J'ai fait laver la vaisselle à mon frère.

■ La permission

● Pour exprimer une **permission**, on utilise **let** + **nom ou pronom complément** + **BV**.
I **let** Sonia (her) **do** it.
J'ai laissé Sonia le faire.
Avec **let**, la personne laisse faire sans forcément approuver.

Reformule les phrases suivantes en expliquant ce que ces personnes veulent. Utilise des pronoms personnels sujets et compléments.
a. Sally: "Sandra, you can use my computer."
b. Dad is very strict: we had to tidy our room all afternoon.
c. Mum: "Don't touch this, Kyle!"
d. Teacher: "Look at the board!"

41. Le discours indirect

■ Le **discours indirect** est utilisé pour **rapporter les paroles** de quelqu'un.
Les verbes introducteurs sont variés et peuvent exprimer des nuances : ask (« demander »), answer (« répondre »), shout (« crier »), whisper (« murmurer »)...

● Lorsqu'on rapporte les paroles de quelqu'un d'autre avec un **verbe introducteur au présent**, il existe des **changements de pronoms personnels et de déterminants possessifs**.
"I called **my** mother yesterday."
→ He says **he** called **his** mother yesterday.
« J'ai appelé ma mère hier. »
→ *Il dit qu'il a appelé sa mère hier.*

● Lorsqu'on rapporte les paroles de quelqu'un **au passé**, les **temps** aussi sont modifiés.

Discours direct	Discours indirect He said ... *Il a dit qu'...*
"I **am** a good driver." *« Je suis un bon conducteur. »*	... he **was** a good driver. *...il était un bon conducteur.*
"I **am going** to drive." *« Je vais conduire. »*	... he **was going to** drive. *...il allait conduire.*
"I **drive** well." *« Je conduis bien. »*	... he **drove** well. *...il conduisait bien.*
"I **drove**." *« J'ai conduit. »*	... he **had driven**. *...il avait conduit.*
"I **have** never **driven**." *« Je n'ai jamais conduit. »*	... he **had** never **driven**. *...il n'avait jamais conduit.*
"I **can** drive." *« Je sais conduire. »*	... he **could** drive. *...il savait conduire.*
"I **will** drive." *« Je conduirai. »*	... he **would** drive. *...il conduirait.*
"I **must** drive." *« Je dois conduire. »*	... he **must** / **had to** drive. *...il devait conduire.*
"I **may** drive." *« Il se peut que je conduise. »*	... he **might** drive. *...il se pourrait qu'il conduise.*

Pour aller plus loin : Le prétérit n'est pas modifié :
- lorsqu'il s'agit d'un verbe d'état ;
"I **was** ill." → He said he **was** ill.
- lorsque le verbe exprime une habitude ;
"I often **played** the drums."
→ She said she often **played** the drums.
- dans les subordonnées de temps.
"We visited Ottawa when we **went** to Canada."
→ They said they visited Ottawa when they **went** to Canada.

● Les **marqueurs spatio-temporels** subissent aussi des modifications lorsque les propos ne sont pas rapportés dans le même temps de référence.
"I am leaving tomorrow."
→ He said he was leaving **tomorrow**.
(Les paroles sont rapportées le même jour.)
→ He said he was leaving **the next day**.
(Les paroles sont rapportées un autre jour.)

today / now / this afternoon ...
→ **that day** / **then** / **that** afternoon ...
tomorrow / next year ...
→ **the next day** / **the following** year ...
yesterday / last month / two years ago
→ **the day before** / **the** month **before** / two years **before** ...

here → **there**
this / that → **these** / **those**

Remarques :
• Pour rapporter une **question** au style indirect, on rétablit la **forme affirmative**.
- Une ***Yes/No question*** est introduite par **if**.
"Is he disappointed?"
→ I wondered **if** he was disappointed.
« Est-il déçu ? »
→ *Je me demandais s'il était déçu.*
- Pour les ***Wh- questions***, le mot interrogatif est inchangé.
"**When did** you **arrive**?"
→ I asked him **when** he had **arrived**.
« Quand es-tu arrivé ? »
→ Je lui ai demandé quand il était arrivé.

• Pour rapporter des **ordres** ou des **suggestions**, on utilise **to + BV**.
"Phone me."
→ He asked me **to** phone him.
« Téléphone-moi. »
→ *Il m'a demandé de lui téléphoner.*
"Don't cry."
→ He told her **not to** cry.
« Ne pleure pas. »
→ *Il lui a dit de ne pas pleurer.*

Rapporte les paroles suivantes au style indirect.
a. "I arrived yesterday." → He said ...
b. "When will you start?" → They asked her ...
c. "Tell me the truth." → He ordered them ...
d. "I'm leaving this afternoon." → She told him ...

42. La voix passive

■ Cette forme est utilisée lorsque l'**on ne connaît pas** ou qu'**on ne s'intéresse pas** à l'auteur de l'action. La voix passive est plus fréquente en anglais qu'en français.

● Le complément d'agent est introduit par **by**.
We **were invited** by Clara to her birthday party.

■ **Formation :** sujet + auxiliaire **be** au temps voulu + participe passé du verbe
My mobile **was stolen**.

● **Présent simple**

Affirmation	This office **is cleaned** every day.
Négation	This office **isn't cleaned** every day.
Interrogation	**Is** this office **cleaned** every day?

● **Prétérit simple**

Affirmation	This computer **was bought** here.
Négation	This computer **wasn't bought** here.
Interrogation	**Was** this computer **bought** here?

■ **Cas particuliers**
Lorsque le verbe a deux compléments, on peut choisir celui que l'on mettra en valeur, c'est-à-dire en position sujet.
She **was given** a prize.
(C'est à elle qu'on l'a donné.)
A prize **was given** to her.
(C'est un prix et pas autre chose qu'on lui a donné.)

■ **Traduction du « on »**

● Quand le sujet « on » ne renvoie à personne de précis, on le traduit en général par la voix passive en anglais. Dans ce cas, on ne mentionne pas le complément d'agent.
English **is spoken** in Australia.
On parle anglais en Australie.
I **was told** you were here.
On m'a dit que tu étais là.

Mets les phrases suivantes à la voix passive.
a. They're building a new road.
b. She gave me a present. *(2 solutions)*
c. I can't open that door!

Dis en anglais.
a. On nous a envoyé une lettre.
b. On m'a demandé de m'asseoir.

43. La forme emphatique

■ Pour insister sur la réalité de ce que l'on affirme, on emploie la **forme emphatique**.
Elle s'utilise au présent et au prétérit. On ajoute l'auxiliaire **do/does** ou **did** devant la base verbale du verbe dans la phrase affirmative.
I **did** tell him!
Je le lui ai vraiment dit !
She **does** play soccer!
Mais si, elle joue au football !
I **do** like tea.
J'aime vraiment le thé.

Remarques :
• La forme emphatique est possible avec le verbe **do**.
I **did** do my homework!
Je vous assure que j'ai fait mes devoirs !
• Elle existe également à l'impératif.
Do come in! *Entrez donc !*

■ On n'emploie pas la forme emphatique **quand be est utilisé en tant que verbe** ou **quand il y a déjà un auxiliaire**.
Dans ce cas, on souligne l'auxiliaire à l'écrit et on l'accentue à l'oral.
We were at home! • Of course she had slept!

Transforme les phrases suivantes en ajoutant une forme emphatique quand c'est possible.
a. I went to bed early.
b. He's sorry.
c. She lives in my street.
d. Take a seat!

Lexique

Lexique

Anglais ➔ Français

Abréviations utilisées

GB : anglais britannique	**US** : anglais américain
n : nom	**adj** : adjectif
v : verbe	**prep** : préposition
pl. : pluriel	
sb : *somebody*	**sth** : *something*

Les verbes en rouge sont irréguliers.

A

aboard	à bord
accommodation	logement
according to	selon
across	au travers ; de l'autre côté de
actually	en fait
adaptor	adaptateur
add	ajouter
advertisement	publicité
advice (a piece ~ of)	conseil
advise (v)	conseiller
aerial	antenne
afraid (be ~)	avoir peur
again	encore
against	contre
agree	être d'accord
AIDS	sida
alien	extraterrestre
ally	allié
allow	autoriser
almost	presque
alone	seul
also	aussi
although	bien que
amazement	stupéfaction
among	parmi
angry	en colère
another	un(e) autre
answer	répondre
anyway	de toute façon
apologize	s'excuser
apply (for)	formuler une demande
appropriately	de façon appropriée, convenablement
area	région, quartier
argue	affirmer ; se disputer
around	autour
as soon as	dès que
asleep	endormi
at least	au moins
attempt (v)	essayer
attend	assister à
attractive	attrayant
author	auteur
available	disponible
avoid	éviter
award (v)	attribuer
award (n)	récompense
away (run ~)	s'enfuir
awful	affreux

B

back	arrière ; derrière
background	milieu socio-culturel
ballooning (go ~)	faire du ballon dirigeable
ban	interdire, exclure
bank holiday	jour férié
banknote	billet de banque
bark (v)	aboyer
barracks	caserne
basement	sous-sol
beach	plage
bead	perle
bear (can't ~)	ne pas supporter
beat	battre (qqn)
beat-up (adj)	déglingué
become	devenir
beehive	ruche
behave	se comporter
behaviour	comportement
behind	derrière
believe	croire
bell	cloche
belong (to)	appartenir (à)
below	ci-dessous
bench	banc
between	entre
beyond	au-delà de
birth	naissance
bit (a ~)	un peu
blanket	couverture
blood	sang
blouse	chemisier
blush	rougir
boarding-school	internat
boil	bouillir
bonfire	feu de joie
book (v)	réserver
booklet	brochure
boost	hausser, faire monter
both	les deux
bow (n)	arc

bow (v)	baisser (la tête)
brand-new	flambant neuf
break out of	sortir de, s'échapper de
breakdown	panne
breath	respiration, souffle
bring	apporter
~ up	élever
Brittany	Bretagne
build	construire
bullet	balle
bully (v)	persécuter, brutaliser
bunch	groupe
burglary	cambriolage
burgle	cambrioler
burglar	cambrioleur
burn	brûler
butterfly	papillon
buttonhole	boutonnière
by the way	au fait

C

caber tossing	*(jeu écossais)* lancer de troncs
calf	veau
claim	réclamer, prétendre
call	appeler
camera	appareil photo
campaign (for/against)	faire campagne (pour/contre)
can (n)	canette, bombe aérosol
care (n)	soin
care (v)	se soucier de
career	carrière
careful	prudent
be ~	faire attention
carpenter	charpentier
carry	transporter
cast	lancer, jeter
~ a spell	jeter un sort
~ a vote	voter
castle	château
cattle	bétail
cave	grotte
celebrate	célébrer
cell phone	téléphone portable
century	siècle
character	personnage
chat (v)	bavarder
cheap	bon marché
check	vérifier
check-in	*(avion)* enregistrement
checkers (US), draughts (GB)	jeu de dames
chicken	poulet
child	enfant
choice	choix
choose	choisir
chores	tâches ménagères, corvées
church	église
citizen	citoyen
citizenship	citoyenneté
claw	griffe
clear (v)	débarrasser, nettoyer ; innocenter
clever	intelligent
clothes, clothing	vêtements
clue	indice
coach (v)	faire répéter, entraîner
cold (n)	rhume
collect	ramasser, collectionner
comic strip	bande dessinée
commercial (n)	spot publicitaire
Commonwealth	le Commonwealth
composure	sang froid, calme
contest	concours, compétition
convict (v)	déclarer coupable
cook (n)	cuisinier
cope (with)	surmonter
corn (US)	maïs
corpse	cadavre
cost (n)	coût
cost (v)	coûter
cosy	confortable
couch	canapé
counter	comptoir
country	pays
county	conté
cover	couverture
crazy	fou
creak (v)	grincer, craquer
creepy	qui donne la chair de poule
cross	traverser
crosswords	mots croisés
crowd	foule
cruise	croisière
cry (n)	cri
cry (v)	pleurer ; crier
culprit (n)	coupable
currency	monnaie (d'un pays)
curried	au curry
custom	coutume
customer	client

D

dandy (n)	élégant (n)
date	rendez-vous galant
day off	jour de congé
deal (a great ~ of)	beaucoup de
death	mort

Lexique

decade	décennie
defeat (n)	défaite
defeat (v)	vaincre
degree	diplôme
deliver	livrer
department store	grand magasin
depend (on)	dépendre (de)
deserve	mériter
desk	bureau
desolate	désert, dévasté
despair	désespoir
device	appareil
diary	agenda, journal intime
die	mourir
director	réalisateur (de film)
disable	mettre hors d'état
disagree	ne pas être d'accord
disappointed	déçu
discover	découvrir
discovery	découverte
disease	maladie
disgusting	dégoûtant
disorientating	déroutant
display	montrer
district	quartier
doll	poupée
doubtful	peu convaincu
draw	dessiner
drawbacks	inconvénients, désavantages
dream	rêver
driving	conduite
~ licence	permis de conduire
drum	tambour
dry	sec
dust (v)	dépoussiérer

E

each	chaque
early	tôt
easy-going	facile à vivre
eery	sinistre
effect	effet
efficient	compétent, efficace
endure	subir
enjoy	profiter de
~ oneself	s'amuser
enough	assez
entail	entraîner
erratic	irrégulier, fantasque
escape	s'échapper
especially	particulièrement
estate	lotissement
even (adj)	moyen
even if	même si
event	événement
everyone	tout le monde
everything	tout
everywhere	partout
evidence	preuve
evil (adj)	malveillant
evil (n)	forces du mal
exhibition	exposition
expel	exclure, renvoyer

F

face (v)	rencontrer, faire face à
facilities	installations
fact	fait
fail	échouer
fame	gloire
famous	célèbre
faraway	loin, lointain
farewell	adieu
fast	rapide
fear (n)	peur
feature (v)	faire figurer
features	traits, caractéristiques
fed up with (be ~)	en avoir assez de
feel	ressentir, se sentir
fellow (n)	semblable
few (a ~)	(un) peu de
fiddle (v)	tripoter, jouer avec qqch
field	terrain, champs
fight (v)	se battre
figure	nombre ; silhouette
file	fichier
find (out)	trouver, découvrir
fingerprint	empreinte digitale
fireworks	feu d'artifice
fish (n)	poisson
fish (v)	pêcher
fist	poing
fit	aller bien *(vêtements, chaussures)*
flag	drapeau
flat	appartement
flight	*(avion)* vol
flip-flops	tongs
floor	étage
focus on	se concentrer sur
fold (one's arms)	croiser (les bras)
fond of (be ~)	apprécier
food	nourriture
foot (*pl.* feet)	pied
footstep	pas
foreign	étranger *(pays)*

forensic scientist	médecin légiste
forensics	médecine légale
forever	pour toujours
formally (to be dressed ~)	en tenue de soirée
former	ancien, précédent
forward (look ~ to)	attendre avec impatience
foster (adj)	nourricier, adoptif
found (v)	fonder
free	libre ; gratuit
freedom	liberté
frighten	effrayer
front (in ~ of)	devant
frost	givre
fry	frire
funny	drôle, amusant
fur	fourrure
furniture	mobilier
further information	plus d'information

G

game	jeu ; gibier
gardener	jardinier
gardening	jardinage
gate	portail
gather	(se) rassembler
gesture	geste
get	obtenir, recevoir
~ off	descendre *(bus, train)*
~ rid of	se débarrasser de
gift	don
give	donner
~ off	libérer, laisser échapper
~ up	abandonner
glamour (n)	attrait
gloves	gants
go	aller
~ off	sonner *(alarme)*
god	dieu
gold	or
gown	toge
grab	saisir, s'emparer de
graduation	remise des diplômes
grazing	pâturage
greasy	gras
grow (up)	grandir
guess	deviner
guidebook	guide
guilty (adj)	coupable
gun	pistolet

H

habit	habitude
hairstyle	coiffure
half	moitié
hammer	marteau
hand (on the other ~)	d'un autre côté
handsome	beau
hang out (with friends)	traîner (avec des copains)
hanker (for/after)	rêver de
happen	arriver
hard-working	travailleur
harmless	inoffensif
head	tête
headline	une de journal
health	santé
hear	entendre
heart	cœur
heaven	le ciel
heavy	lourd
helmet	casque
hide	cacher
high	haut, élevé
high school	lycée
hike (v)	faire de la randonnée
hiking	randonnée
hire	engager
hit	frapper
hoax (n)	canular
hold	tenir
homemade	fait maison
hope	espoir
host (v)	accueillir
host family	famille d'accueil
hostel	auberge de jeunesse
hour	heure *(durée)*
housemaid	bonne (n)
housework	ménage
however	cependant
human being	être vivant
hungry	affamé
hunt	chasser
hurry	se précipiter
hurt	blesser, faire (du) mal
husband	mari
hut	hutte, cabane

I

idea	idée
improve	améliorer
inefficient	incompétent, inefficace
infamous	infâme
inflame	enflammer

Lexique

inhabitant	habitant
investigate	enquêter
investigation	enquête
involve	impliquer
iron	repasser

J

jacket	manteau, veste
join	rejoindre
joke	plaisanterie
journey	voyage
juggling	jonglerie
jump	sauter

K

keen on (be ~)	apprécier
keep	garder
~ on doing sth	continuer à faire qqch
~ an eye on sth	garder un œil sur qqch
kid (n)	gosse
kind (adj)	gentil
knight	chevalier
knit	tricoter
knock	frapper (à une porte)
knot	nœud
knowledge	connaissance

L

lab	laboratoire
lake	lac
land	terre
landing	atterrissage
landscape	paysage
last	durer
late	en retard
laugh (v)	rire
launch	lancer (une campagne)
launder	laver (le linge)
law	la loi, le droit
leaflet	dépliant
learn	apprendre
leather	cuir
leave	partir, quitter
lecture	cours, conférence
ledger	grand livre (de comptes)
lend	prêter
less	moins
let	laisser
library	bibliothèque
licence (GB), license (US)	permis
driving ~	permis de conduire
lie	être allongé
lift	ascenseur
link	lien
literate	instruit
living being	être vivant
located	situé
lonely	isolé, seul
look	regarder
~ after	s'occuper de
~ for	chercher
~ forward to	attendre avec impatience
lose	perdre
loud	fort, bruyant
lovable	adorable
lucky	chanceux
lunch	repas du midi

M

mail	courrier
manner	manière
map	carte
marvellous	merveilleux
match (v)	associer
maybe	peut-être
mean	vouloir dire
meaning	signification, sens
means	moyen
meet	rencontrer
meeting	réunion
mess	désordre, pagaille
midnight	minuit
mind	esprit
I don't ~	Cela ne me dérange pas.
minor	mineur
miserable	malheureux
misery	souffrance
miss	manquer
mistake	erreur
mix	mélanger
monitor	contrôler
month	mois
moreover	de plus
most (of)	la plupart de
mostly	surtout
motto	devise
moving (adj)	émouvant
mummy	momie

N

nearby	tout près, à proximité
need	avoir besoin de
neighbour	voisin
neighbourhood	quartier, voisinage
network	réseau
newcomer	nouvel arrivant
news (n. sg.)	des nouvelles
newspaper	journal *(presse)*
next	prochain, suivant
nice	agréable
nightmare	cauchemar
Nobel Peace Prize	Prix Nobel de la paix
noisy	bruyant
north	nord
northern	du nord
novel	roman
nowadays	de nos jours
numerous	nombreux
nursing	soins
nutshell **in a ~**	coquille de noix en un mot

O

obviously	évidemment
octopus	pieuvre
once	une fois
opposite	en face de
order	commander
orphan	orphelin
other	autre
outcast (n)	exclu, pariah, banni
outside	à l'extérieur
oven	four
over	au-dessus de
overcoat	pardessus
overwhelming	écrasant
own **my/your/his ~**	posséder mon/ton/son propre

P

pain	douleur
parade	défilé
pass (v) a test	réussir un test
path	chemin
pea	petit pois
penguin	pingouin
perhaps	peut-être
petrol	essence
pick sb up	aller chercher qqn
pigtail	queue de cheval
pinch	pincer
pioneer	pionnier
bagpipe	cornemuse
plan (v)	projeter
play (n)	pièce de théâtre
pleased	content, ravi
plug	prise de courant
pocket money	argent de poche
policy	une politique
polish (v)	polir, cirer
pond	étang
post	poteau
pound	livre (≈ 500 gr)
poverty	pauvreté
power	pouvoir
powerful	puissant
practise	s'entraîner
price	prix
Prime Minister	Premier Ministre
producer	producteur *(film)*, metteur en scène *(théâtre)*
promote	promouvoir
prop	accessoire
proud	fier
provide	fournir
pull	tirer
pumpkin	potiron, citrouille
push **~ off/away**	pousser repousser
put **~ forward (a watch)** **~ on** **~ out**	poser avancer (une montre) mettre, enfiler *(vêtement)* sortir (qqch)

Q

queen	reine
quiet	calme
quote (n)	citation
quote (v)	citer

R

race	course
railway	chemin de fer
raincoat	imperméable
raise	lever
reach	atteindre
real estate agent	agent immobilier
really	vraiment
recall	se souvenir
receipt	reçu
record (v)	enregistrer

Lexique

registration	inscription
rehearse	répéter
relationship	relation
remember	se rappeler, se souvenir
remove	enlever
rent	louer
repair	réparer
report (n)	rapport, compte rendu
research	recherche
reservation	réserve (indienne) ; réservation *(restaurant)*
retired	à la retraite
review (n)	revue, critique, compte rendu
rice	riz
right	un droit
be ~	avoir raison
ring (n)	anneau, bague
road	route, rue
rob	voler, dévaliser
robbery	vol
role-playing game (RPG)	jeu de rôle
root	racine
rope (v)	attacher avec une corde
rope	corde
rough	rude ; brusque
rude	impoli
rule	règlement
run	courir
~ out of	être à court de
run-down (adj)	délabré, vétuste
rush (v)	se précipiter

S

safe (adj)	sûre, prudent
safe (n)	coffre-fort
safety	sécurité
saffron	safran
sailing	navigation , la voile
same (the ~)	même (le ~)
sample	échantillon
scared	effrayé
scattered	dispersé
scream	crier, hurler
screenplay	scénario
scrub	récurer, laver à la brosse
seat	siège, place
seatbelt	ceinture de sécurité
seed	graine
sell	vendre
seller	vendeur
send	envoyer
set	poser, placer, régler
~ off	tirer *(feu d'artifice)*
settle	s'installer, s'établir
settler	colon
several	plusieurs
share	partager
sharp	aiguisé, pointu
sheep	mouton
shelter (n)	abri
short	court
~-lived	de courte durée
~ story	nouvelle
shoulder	épaule
show	montrer
show (n)	spectacle
shower	douche
shy	timide
side by side	côte à côte
sign	panneau
significant	significatif
silver	argent
single room	chambre pour une personne
size	taille
skating rink	patinoire
skill	habileté, compétence
skin	peau
skirt	jupe
skull	crâne
slam	claquer (une porte)
slaughter	massacrer
slave	esclave
slavery	esclavage
sleeve	manche
soap opera	feuilleton
soft	mou
solve	résoudre
son	fils
sort	trier
sound	son
soundproof	insonoriser
south	sud
southern	du sud
space	espace
spaceship	vaisseau spatial
spacesuit	combinaison spatiale
speech	discours
spell (n)	sort
spend	passer du temps ; dépenser
spick-and-span	impeccable
spicy	épicé
spiky	en épi
spoil	abîmer, gâcher, gâter
spot (v)	repérer
spray	vaporiser, pulvériser
spread	répandre
square	carré
staff (n)	personnel

stage manager	régisseur
stagecoach	diligence
stall	étal
stand (make a ~)	prendre position
stand (can't ~)	ne pas supporter
stare	fixer du regard
starvation	famine
starving	affamé, qui meurt de faim
statement	propos, déclaration
stay	rester, séjourner
steal	voler, dérober
stencil (n)	pochoir
stencil (v)	peindre au pochoir
step up	monter sur une marche
still (n)	photo (d'un film)
still (adv)	toujours, encore
store (department ~)	grand magasin
storytelling	lecture (d'histoire)
strain (v)	mettre à rude épreuve, s'efforcer
stranger	étranger, inconnu
strength	force
striking	saisissant, frappant
strong	fort
study (v)	étudier
stuff	affaires
submarine	sous-marin
suburb	banlieue
successful	couronné de succès
suddenly	soudainement
suffer (from)	souffrir (de)
suit	costume
suitable	convenable
suitcase	valise
summer	été
sunrise	lever de soleil
sunset	coucher de soleil
survey	enquête
suspend	exclure, renvoyer qqn
sweat (n)	transpiration
sweep	balayer
sword	épée

T

tackle	s'attaquer à
talkative	bavard
tasteless	insipide, sans goût
tear (n)	larme
teddy bear	ours en peluche
tell	dire
text (v)	envoyer des sms
text message	SMS, texto
that's why	c'est pourquoi
thief (*pl.* thieves)	voleur
thousand	mille
threatening	menaçant
thrilling	palpitant, excitant
through	à travers
throughout	partout dans
throw	lancer
ticket	billet
tidy	ranger
tie	cravate
till	jusqu'à
tinker	bricoler
toil	avancer péniblement
tour	voyage, périple
tow	remorquer
town	ville
trade (v)	faire le commerce
trail	piste
trailer	remorque
train (v)	(s') entraîner
trainee	stagiaire
travel agency	agence de voyage
treasure	trésor
tribe	tribu
trick	ruse, astuce, tour
trolley (US)	tramway
trust (in) (v)	faire confiance (à)
truth	vérité
try	essayer
tube	le métro (de Londres)
turn (in ~)	chacun son tour
turn	tourner
~ off	éteindre
~ on	allumer
tuxedo (US)	smoking
TV aerial	antenne de télévision
twice	deux fois
typewriter	machine à écrire

U

ugly	laid
unemployment	chômage
until	jusqu'à
untruth	contre-vérité, mensonge
update (v)	mettre à jour
upper class	classe supérieure
upright	à la verticale
utterly	complètement

V

vacation (US)	vacances
vacuum (v)	passer l'aspirateur

van	camionnette
veggies / vegetables	légumes

W

wake up	se réveiller
wand	baguette
war	guerre
warden	gardien
warrior	guerrier
waterproof (adj)	imperméable
wave (v)	agiter, faire signe
weak	faible
wealthy	riche
weapon	arme
wear	porter *(vêtement)*
weary	épuisé, très fatigué
wedding	marriage
weigh	peser
weight	poids
well-behaved	bien élevé
well-known	connu
wheel	roue
whenever	chaque fois que
whereas	tandis que
wherever	partout où
whether	si
while	pendant que
widely	largement
wild	sauvage
wilderness	étendue déserte, région déserte
windsurfing	planche à voile
wipe	essuyer
~ out	anéantir
~ off	effacer
wish (v)	souhaiter
witch	sorcière
within	*(espace)* à l'intérieur de ; *(durée)* en
witness (n)	témoin
witness (v)	être témoin
wonder (v)	se demander
wonder (n)	émerveillement
wonderful	merveilleux
workshop	atelier
worried	inquiet
worse	pire
wrap	emballer, envelopper

Y

youngsters	des jeunes

Français ➔ Anglais

Abréviations utilisées

GB : anglais britannique	**US :** anglais américain
n : nom	**adj :** adjectif
v : verbe	***pl.*** **:** pluriel
sb : *somebody*	**sth :** *something*

Les verbes en rouge sont irréguliers.

A

à l'étranger	abroad
à part	apart
à peine	hardly
à plein temps	full-time
abandonner	give up, quit
abîmer	damage
abolir	abolish
aborigène (adj)	Aboriginal
aborigène (n)	Aborigine
absent	absent, missing
absolument	absolutely, definitely
accepter	accept
accord (être d'~)	agree
accueillir	welcome
accuser	accuse
achat	purchase
acheter	buy, purchase
activité *(passe-temps)*	hobby
actuel	current
actuellement	nowadays
adapter (s'~)	adapt
adolescent	teenager, teen
adoptif	adoptive, foster
adulte	grown-up, adult
adversaire	contestant, opponent
affaire (criminelle)	case
affaires *(choses)*	stuff
affamé	hungry, starving
affirmer	claim, maintain
affronter	face
afin de	to (+ BV)
agence (de voyage)	(travel) agency
agréable	pleasant
aider	help
aimer, apprécier	like, enjoy
ajouter	add
alentours	surroundings
alibi	alibi
aller chercher qqn	pick sb up
aller	go
allié	ally
allumer	turn on, switch on
ambiance	atmosphere
amélioration	improvement
améliorer	improve
américain	American
amitié	friendship
amulette	amulet
ancien	former
anglais	English
année	year
anniversaire	birthday
annoncer	announce
antenne	aerial
antenne parabolique	satellite dish
Antilles	Caribbean Islands, the West Indies
apparaître	appear
appareil	device
~ photo	camera
appartement	flat (GB), apartment (US)
appartenir (à)	belong (to)
appeler	call
applaudir	applaud, clap
apporter	bring
apprendre	learn
après Jésus-Christ	A.D. (= Anno Domini)
arme	weapon
armure	armour
arrivant (nouvel ~)	newcomer
arrivée	arrival
arriver	arrive, come ; *(survenir)* happen
~ à, se débrouiller	manage
article *(objet)*	item
assassiner	assassinate
assez	enough
assister à	attend
attaque	attack
atteindre	achieve, reach
attendre	wait for
s'~ à	expect
~ avec impatience	look forward to (+ BV-ing)
atterrir	land
attraper	catch
~ brusquement	grab
au lieu de	instead of (+ BV-ing)
au loin	in the distance
aussi	also, too
aussitôt	immediately
australien	Australian
auteur	author
autoriser	allow
autre	other
un ~	another
avant Jésus-Christ	B.C. (= Before Christ)
aventureux	adventurous
avion	plane
avocat *(métier)*	lawyer

Lexique

avoir l'air	*(vue)* look ; *(ouïe)* sound
avoir lieu, se situer	be set

B

bagages	luggage
baguette	wand
balle	bullet
bandes dessinées	comic strip, comics
bateau	ship, boat
battre (se ~)	fight
bavard	talkative
bavarder	chat
beaucoup	a lot of
~ plus	much more
bénéficier (de)	benefit (from)
besoin (avoir ~)	need
bétail	cattle
bibliothèque	library
bien que	although
bientôt	soon
bijou	jewel
billet	*(argent)* banknote ; *(transport)* ticket
biographie	biography
bizarre	weird
boire	drink
boisson	drink
~ sans alcool	soft drink
Bon appétit !	Enjoy your meal!
bon marché	cheap
bouger	move
bricoler	tinker
brochure	booklet
bruit	noise
brutaliser, harceler	bully
brutalité, harcèlement	bullying
bruyant	noisy
but	aim

C

cadeau	gift, present
camarade	schoolmate, classmate
cambriolage	burglary
cambrioler	burgle
cambrioleur	burglar
canadien	Canadian
carrière	career
carte	map, card
~ d'identité	identity card
~ postale	postcard
cas (au ~ où)	just in case
casque	helmet
CDI	school library
célèbre	famous
célébrer	celebrate
cependant	however
chaîne *(TV)*	channel
chair de poule (qui donne la ~)	spooky, creepy
chanceux	lucky
chanson	song
chaque	every, each
~ fois que	whenever, each time
charger	load
chasser	hunt
château	castle
chaud	hot
chemin de fer	railway (GB), railroad (US)
cher *(coût)*	expensive
chercheur d'or	gold digger
chevalier	knight
cheville	ankle
choisir	choose, pick
chômage	unemployment
circulation	traffic
citer	quote
citoyen	citizen
citoyenneté	citizenship
classe	form (GB) ; grade (US)
clavier	keyboard
client	customer
climat	climate
coiffer (se ~)	do one's hair
coiffure	hairstyle
colère	anger
en ~	angry
colon	settler
colonie (de vacances)	summer camp, holiday camp
combinaison spatiale	spacesuit
commander	order
comme	as, like
commencer	begin, start
commerçant	trader, shopkeeper
commerce	trade
commun	common
communiquer	communicate
compagnie aérienne	airline company
comparé à	compared to/with
compléter	fill in
comportement	behaviour
comporter (se ~)	behave
compris (y ~)	including
concours	contest, competition
confiance (avoir ~)	be confident
connaître	know
connu	well-known
conseil	advice
conseiller	advise

considérable	significant
construire	build
content, ravi	happy, thrilled
continuer (à)	keep (on)
contraire (au ~)	contrary (on the ~)
contrairement (à)	unlike
contrarié	upset
contre	against
convenir	suit
convertir	convert
corps	body
corvées	chores
costume	suit *(vêtements)* ; costume *(déguisement)*
coton	cotton
coup de feu	gunshot
coupable (adj)	guilty
coupable (n)	culprit
courageux	courageous, brave
couramment	fluently
courrier	mail
cours	class
coutume	custom
cracher (du feu)	belch out
crainte	fear
créer	create, design
crème glacée	ice cream
crêpe	pancake
crier	cry, shout, scream
crime	crime
critiquer	criticise
croire	believe
croisière	cruise
croyance	belief
cru	raw
cuisinier	cook

D

dangereux	dangerous
débarrasser (la table)	clear (the table)
débarrasser (se ~ de)	get rid of
débarquer	land
débrouiller (se ~ avec)	cope with
début	beginning
décalage horaire	time change, jet lag
décennie	decade
décoller	take off
décontracté	casual
découverte	discovery
découvrir	discover, find out
déçu	disappointed
défaire ses valises	unpack
défilé	parade
dégoûtant	disgusting
déjà	already, ever
demain	tomorrow
demander	ask
se ~	wonder
déménager	move
départ	departure
dépaysé (être ~)	feel lost, feel like a fish out of water
dépêcher (se ~)	hurry
dépendre de	depend on
dépenser	spend
dépenses	expenses
déplacer (se ~)	get around, move
dépliant	leaflet
depuis	for (+ durée), since (+ date)
dernier	last
déroutant	disorientating, puzzling
dès que	as soon as
descendre *(moyen de transport)*	get off
désespéré	desperate
désordonné	messy
détruire	destroy
devenir	become
deviner	guess
devoirs (faire ses ~)	homework (do one's ~)
diplôme	degree, diploma, certificate
direct (en ~)	live (adj)
discours	speech
disparaître	disappear
disparu	extinct
disponible	available
disputer (se ~)	argue, quarrel
distribuer	deliver
divers	miscellaneous
douane	customs
douche	shower
douloureux	painful
drapeau	flag
droit	right
drôle	funny
dur, difficile	hard, tough, difficult
durer	last

E

eau	water
échantillon	sample
échapper (s'~)	escape
échouer	fail
économiser	save
écossais	Scottish
écran	screen
écraser (s'~)	crash

Lexique

écrire	write
écrivain	writer
éducatif	educational
effacer	wipe off, remove
effrayant	frightening, scary
effrayé	frightened, scared
effrayer	frighten, scare
effroyable	horrible, frightful
égal	equal
Ça m'est ~.	I don't mind.
égalité	equality
égoïste	selfish
élevé (mal ~)	rude
élever	bring up
éliminer	eliminate
embarrassé	confused
embaucher	hire, employ
émeute	riot
émigrer	emigrate
émission	TV programme
empêcher de	prevent from (+ BV-ing)
empreinte digitale	fingerprint
~ de main	handprint
~ de pied	footprint
emprunter	borrow
encore	*(toujours)* still, *(à nouveau)* again
pas ~	not ... yet
encourager	encourage
endroit	place
enfreindre le règlement	break the rule
enlever	take off, remove
ennuyé	bored
ennuyer (s'~)	get bored
ennuyeux	boring
enquête	*(sondage)* survey ; *(police)* investigation
enquêter	investigate
ensemble	together
ensuite	then, afterwards
entendre	hear
s'~ avec	get on with
entier	whole
entraîner (s'~)	train
entraîneur	coach
environ	about, around
envoyer	send
~ des SMS	text, send text messages
éparpillé	scattered
épée	sword
épicé	spicy
épices	spices
équitation	horse-riding
érable	maple tree
erreur	mistake
esclavage	slavery
esclave	slave
espérer	hope
espoir	hope
plein d'~	hopeful
essence	petrol (GB), gas (US)
est (de l'~)	eastern (adj)
étage	floor
état	state
éteindre	turn off, switch off
étonné	puzzled, surprised
étrange	strange
étranger (adj)	foreign
étranger (n)	foreigner
à l'~	abroad
être sur le point de	be about to
être humain	human being
études	studies
étudier	study
événement	event
évidemment	obviously
éviter	avoid
excitant, passionnant	exciting
excursion	tour
excuser (s'~)	apologize
exemplaire	copy
exemple	example
par ~	for example, for instance
explorateur	explorer
exporter	export
exposition	exhibition
expression	phrase, expression
exprimer (s'~)	express oneself
extrait	extract
extraordinaire	extraordinary
extraterrestre	alien
extrêmement	extremely

F

façon	way
faible	weak
faim	hunger
avoir ~	be hungry
faire confiance	trust
~ du tourisme	go sightseeing
~ la lessive	do the washing
~ mal	hurt
~ une randonnée	hike
fait (en ~)	actually
famille d'accueil	host family
famine	starvation
fascinant	fascinating
fatigué	tired
férié (jour ~)	public holiday, bank holiday
fermer à clé	lock
fermier	farmer
fêter	celebrate

feu	fire
~ d'artifice	fireworks, firework display
~ de circulation	traffic light
feuille	leaf (*pl.* leaves)
feuilleton	soap opera
fiche d'inscription	registration form
fier	proud
fin	end
finalement	finally, eventually
finir	end
fois	time
une ~	once
deux ~	twice
trois ~	three times
fonder	found
forme (en ~)	fit
formé, qualifié	trained
formulaire, fiche	form
fort	*(force physique)* strong ; *(volume sonore)* loud
foule	crowd
fourrure	fur
frapper	hit, knock
frère	brother
frontière	border
fuir	run away
fusée	rocket

G

gagnant	winner
gagner	*(jeu)* win ; *(argent)* earn
~ sa vie	earn a living
garder	keep
gens du pays	native
gouverner	rule, govern
grâce à	thanks to
grandeur nature	full-size
grandir	grow up
gratte-ciel	skyscraper
grève (en ~)	strike (on ~)
griffe	claw
grimper	climb up
guerre	war
Guerre de Sécession	Civil War

H

habillé *(élégant)*	formal
habiller (s'~)	get dressed
habitant	inhabitant
habité	inhabited
habiter	live
habitude	habit
habituellement	usually
harcèlement	harassment, bullying
harceler	harass, bully
haut (n)	top
hauteur	height
hériter	inherit
hésiter	hesitate
heure de cours	period
histoire	story
faire des ~	make a fuss
horriblement	awfully, horribly
hôte	host
humain	human
humeur	mood
de bonne ~	in a good mood
de mauvaise ~	in a bad mood, cross

I

identifier	identify
identité	identity
île	island
image de synthèse	computer-generated image
immense	huge
immobile	motionless, still
impeccable	*(propreté)* spick-and-span, *(perfection)* perfect
impoli	rude, impolite
important	significant
impressionnant	impressive
impressionner	impress
imprimer	print
inclure	include
inconnu	unknown
inconvénients	drawbacks
incroyable	incredible
indice	clue
indien	Indian
infirmerie	infirmary
infirmière	nurse
ingénieur	engineer
inhabituel	unusual
inoffensif	harmless
inondé	flooded
inquiet	worried
inquiéter (s'~ de)	worry (about)
inscription	registration, enrolment
inscrire (s'~)	sign up, register, enrol
installations	facilities
installer (s'~)	settle
instruire	educate
interdire	forbid
interdit	forbidden
internat	boarding-school
introduire	introduce

Lexique

inutile	useless
inventer	invent
irlandais	Irish
isolé	lonely, remote

J

jamais	never ; ever *(dans une négation)*
jeter	throw
~ un sort	cast a spell
jeu	game
jeune	young
jeunesse	youth
joindre	join
jouer *(film, théâtre)*	act
jour de congé	day off
~ férié	bank holiday
journal	newspaper
~ de bord, ~ intime	diary
jours (de nos ~)	nowadays
jusqu'à	until
jusqu'ici, jusqu'à présent	so far, until now
justifier	justify

L

lac	lake
lâcher, laisser tomber	drop
laisser	leave
~ tranquille	leave alone
langue	language
large	big, large
leçon de conduite	driving lesson
lecteur MP3	MP3 player
légume	vegetable, veggie
lessive (faire la ~)	washing (do the ~)
liberté	freedom
libre	free
lien	tie, link
lieu	place
~ touristique	tourist site
au ~ de	instead of (+ BV-ing)
limiter	limit, restrict
lire	read
lit	bed
livrer	deliver
logement	accommodation
loi	law
loin	far
lorsque	when
louer	rent, hire
lumière	light
lutte	struggle
lutter (contre/pour)	fight (against/for)
luxueux	luxurious

M

magasin	shop, store
magnifique	wonderful
maigre	thin
maillot de bain	bathing suit
maïs	maize (GB), corn (US)
mal *(douleur)*	pain
~ à la tête	headache
les forces du ~	evil
malade	ill, sick
maladie	disease, illness
maladroit	clumsy, awkward
malheureusement	unfortunately
malheureux	miserable, unhappy
manger	eat
manifestation	demonstration
manifester	demonstrate
manquer	miss
marcher	walk
mariage	wedding, marriage
mauvais pour la santé	unhealthy
méchant	mean, nasty
médecin légiste	forensic scientist
médecine légale	forensics, forensic science
même	same
en ~ temps	at the same time
même si	even though, even if
menaçant	threatening
menace	threat
menacer	threaten
ménage	housework
mentir	lie
méprisant	contemptuous, scornful
métier	job, occupation
métro	tube, underground (GB) ; subway (US)
mettre	put
~ la table	set the table, lay the table
meurtre	murder
meurtrier	murderer
mille	thousand
milliers (de)	thousands (of)
mince	slim
minuit	midnight
mobilier	furniture
mode de vie	way of life
moins	less
à ~ que	unless
mois	month
moitié	half
momie	mummy

monde	world
monnaie (d'un pays)	currency
montagne	mountain
montant	amount
monter ***(vélo, cheval)***	ride
montrer	show
morceau	piece
mort (adj)	dead
mort (n)	death
mortel	deadly
mouillé	wet
mourir	die
moyen (adj)	average
moyen (n) **~ de transport** **avoir les ~s**	means means of transport can afford
musée	museum
mystérieux	mysterious

N

nager	swim
naissance	birth
naviguer	sail
négligence	carelessness
neige	snow
neigeux	snowy
néo-zélandais	New Zealander
nettoyer	clean
nombreux	numerous
nommer	name
nord (du ~)	northern (adj)
nostalgique	homesick, nostalgic
nourrir	feed
nourriture	food
nouvel arrivant	newcomer
nouvelle (n)	short story
nuageux	cloudy
nuisible	harmful
nulle part	not anywhere, nowhere

O

objets de valeur	valuables
obligatoire	compulsory
obscurité **dans l'~**	darkness in the dark
occasion	opportunity
occupé	busy
occuper (s'~ de)	take care of, look after, deal with
optimiste	optimistic
ordinateur	computer
organiser	organize
orphelin	orphan
oser	dare
oublier	forget
ouest (de l' ~)	western (adj)
ouvrier	worker
ouvrir	open

P

paisible	peaceful
palpitant	thrilling, exciting
panier repas	packed lunch
panne d'électricité	power cut, power failure
panneau de signalisation **~ publicitaire**	road sign billboard
paraître	*(vue)* look like, *(ouïe)* sound like
par-dessus tout	above all
parfois	sometimes
parmi	among
paroles de chansons	lyrics
part (à ~)	apart
partager	share
particulièrement	especially
partout dans	everywhere (in), throughout
partout où	wherever
pas ... encore **~ du tout** **~ étonnant !**	not ... yet not at all No wonder!
passé (dans le ~)	in the past
passer (se ~) **~ du temps**	happen, take place spend one's time (+ BV-ing)
passe-temps	hobby, pastime
pauvre	poor
pauvreté	poverty
pays	country
paysage	landscape, scenery
peau	skin
pêcher	fish
peindre	paint
peine (à ~)	hardly
peinture	painting
pendant **~ que**	during, for while
pensif	thoughtful
permis (adj)	allowed, permitted
permis de conduire	driving licence (UK), driving license (US)
personnage	character
personnel (n)	staff
petit-déjeuner	breakfast
pétrole	oil
peu convaincu **un ~ plus**	doubtful a little more
peuplé	populated
peur	fear

Lexique

peut-être	maybe, perhaps
photo	picture, photo
~ de film	still
photographe	photographer
pièce de théatre	play
pied (à ~)	foot (on ~)
pire	worse
pistolet	gun, pistol
plage	beach
plaindre (se ~)	complain
plainte (déposer ~)	press charges
planifier	plan
plateau de tournage	set
plein de	a lot of, lots of, plenty of
plein temps (à ~)	full-time
pleurer	cry
plus (non ~)	not any more, no longer
plusieurs	several
plutôt	rather
poignarder	stab
point (être sur le ~ de)	be about to
pointu	sharp, pointed
poison	poison
politique	policy
port	harbour, port
porter	carry ; *(vêtements)* wear
poser	put
~ sa candidature	apply
posséder	own
pour toujours	forever
pourquoi	why
c'est ~	that's why
préféré	favourite
préjugé	prejudice
premièrement	first
prendre	take
~ soin de	take care of
préoccupé	concerned
être ~ par	be ~ about
présentateur	newsreader, presenter
présenter	introduce
se ~	introduce oneself
presque	almost, nearly
~ jamais	hardly ever
prêter	lend
preuve	evidence
prévisions météorologiques	weather forecast
principalement	mainly, mostly
prise de vue	shot
~ électrique	plug
privé	private
privilégié (adj)	exclusive, privileged
prix	*(argent)* price ; *(distinction)* prize
Prix Nobel	Nobel Prize
probablement	probably
problème	trouble, problem
prochain	next
produire	produce
se ~ en spectacle	perform
projeter	plan
propos	statement
proposer	suggest, propose
propre	clean
propriétaire	owner
prospectus	flyer
protégé	protected
protéger (se ~)	take cover, protect oneself
protestation	protest
prudent	careful
publicité	advertisement
puissance	power
puissant	powerful

Q

quand	when
quant à	as for
quartier	district, neighbourhood, area
quitter	leave
quotidien (n)	daily

R

raconter	tell
raison	reason
avoir ~	be right
ramasser	pick up
randonnée	hiking
faire de la ~	hike
ranger	tidy
rappeler (se ~)	remember
rappeler (qqch à qqn)	remind (sb of sth)
rapport *(compte rendu)*	report
rarement	rarely
rassembler	collect, assemble
se ~	gather
ravi	thrilled
réagir	react
réalisateur	director
rebeller (se ~ contre)	rebel (against)
recevoir	receive
rechercher	search (for)
récompense	prize, award
rédaction *(devoir)*	essay
regarder la télévision	watch TV
règle	*(règlement)* rule ; *(objet)* ruler
règlement	rule
relation	relationship
remarquable	outstanding, noteworthy, remarkable
remarquer	notice

remplir	fill in
rencontrer	meet
rendez-vous	appointment, date
rendre visite	visit
renseigner (se ~)	make enquiries
repas	meal
repassage	ironing
repasser	iron
repère	landmark, reference point
répondre	reply, answer
reportage	report
reposer (se ~)	rest, relax
reproche	reproach
reprocher (qch à qn)	reproach (sb with sth)
réserve (indienne)	reservation
réserver	book, reserve
résoudre	solve
respect	respect
respecter	respect
respectueux	respectful
ressembler à	look like
ressentir	feel
rester	remain, stay
résultat	result
retard (en ~)	late
retarder	delay
retirer	remove
retour	comeback, return
réussir	achieve, succeed, manage ; *(examen)* pass
réveiller (se ~)	wake up
révéler	reveal
revenir	come back
revolver	gun, revolver
rhume	cold
rire	laugh
robe (du soir)	(evening) dress
rôle	part
jeu de ~	role-playing game (RPG)
roman	novel
romancier	novelist
ruée vers l'or	gold rush

S

sable	sand
sac à dos	backpack
saison	season
salaire	wage
sale	dirty
salle de cours	classroom
sang	blood
sans	without
sans-abri	homeless
santé	health
sauf	except
~ si	unless
sauvage	wild
sauver	save
savoir (n)	knowledge
savoir (v)	know
scandaleux	outrageous, scandalous
scénario	screenplay
scène (d'un théâtre)	stage
scolarisation	school attendance, schooling
sec	dry
secourir	rescue
séjour	trip, stay
sel	salt
selon	according to
semaine	week
sembler	seem, look
sensible	sensitive
sentier	trail, path, track
sentiment	feeling
série TV	TV series
sérieux *(réfléchi)*	thoughtful
serviable	helpful
seuil de pauvreté	poverty level
seul	alone, single
si	if
sida	AIDS
siècle	century
siège	seat
signifier	mean
situer	locate
slogan	motto
smoking	tuxedo (US), dinner jacket (GB)
SMS	text message
sœur	sister
soin	care
sol	ground
soldat	soldier
solitaire	lonely
sombre	dark
son (n)	sound
sondage	survey
sonner	ring
sorcellerie	witchcraft
sorcier	wizard
sorcière	witch
sort	spell
sortie *(film, disque)*	release
sortir	go out
soucier de qqn (se ~)	care for someone
soucieux de (être ~)	be concerned about
souffrance	suffering
souhait	wish
souhaiter	wish

soulagement	relief
soulager	relieve
souligner	underline
sourd	deaf
soutenir	support
souvenir	*(cadeau, objet)* souvenir ; *(pensée)* memory
souvenir (se ~ de)	remember
souvent	often
spacieux	roomy, spacious
spectacle	show
spectaculaire	spectacular
spot publicitaire	commercial
stade	stadium
station de tourisme	resort
stressant	stressful
stressé	tense, stressed out
succès	success
qui a du ~	successful
sud (du ~)	southern (adj)
suivant	following
suivre	follow
sujet de discussion	topic
sûr, sans danger	safe
surnom	nickname
surprenant	amazing, surprising
suspense	suspense
sympathique	friendly, nice

T

tabac	tobacco
tâches ménagères	chores
taille	size
tandis que	whereas
tard	late
taux	rate
taxi	taxi (GB) ; taxi, cab (US)
tel que	such as
télécommande	remote control
téléphone portable	mobile phone (GB) ; cell phone (US)
téléphoner	phone, call, ring
témoigner	testify
témoin	witness
être ~	witness
temps	time; *(météo)* weather
de ~ en ~	now and then
en ce ~ -là	in those days
en même ~	at the same time
~ libre	leisure, spare time
bon vieux ~	the good old days
passer son ~ à	spend one's time (+ BV-ing)
tendance (avoir ~ à)	tend to
tenir	hold
se ~ debout	stand
tentative	attempt
terminer (se ~)	come to an end, finish
terrain	field, ground
terre	land ; *(planète)* Earth
terrifié	terrified
texto, SMS	text message
thé	tea
timide	shy
tirer	pull ; *(arme)* shoot ; *(feu d'artifice)* set off
toge	gown
toit	roof
tomber	fall
tort (avoir ~)	be wrong
tôt	early
toujours	always, *(encore)* still
tour *(carte, magie)*	trick
tourisme (faire du ~)	go on a sightseeing tour, go sightseeing
tournage *(film)*	shooting
tourner *(film)*	shoot
tournoi	tornament
tout à coup	suddenly
toute l'année	all year long
traces	traces
traduire	translate
traîner avec des copains	hang out with friends
traiter	treat
~ de qqch	deal with
tranquillement	quietly, peacefully
transport (moyen de ~)	means of transport
travailler	work
travailleur (adj)	hardworking
travers (à ~)	through
traverser	cross
trésor	treasure
tribu	tribe
tribunal	court
tricher	cheat
triste	sad
trottoir	pavement (GB) ; sidewalk (US)
tuer	kill ; *(arme à feu)* shoot
tueur	killer

U

une de journal	headline
un peu plus	a little more
urgence	emergency
usine	factory
utile	useful
utiliser	use

V

vacances	holidays (GB) ; vacation (US)
vaincre	conquer
vaisseau spatial	spaceship
vaisselle	dishes
faire la ~	do the washing-up , wash up
valise	suitcase
faire une ~	pack
variété	variety
grande ~	wide range
végétarien	vegetarian
vendeur	seller, salesman
vendre	sell
venir	come
vente	sale
ventre (mal de ~)	stomach ache
vérifier	check
vérité	truth
verre	glass
vers, dans la direction de	towards
vertigineux	dizzy
vestiges	remains
vêtements	clothes, clothing
viande	meat
victime	victim
vide	empty
vie	life
ville	town, city
visage	face
visite guidée	guided tour
visiter	visit, tour
vitesse	speed
vivant	alive
voile (faire de la ~)	sail
voisin	neighbour (GB) ; neighbor (US)
voisinage *(quartier)*	neighbourhood
vol *(délit)*	robbery
vol *(avion)*	flight
voler *(dévaliser)*	rob, steal
voler *(avion, oiseau)*	fly
voleur	thief (*pl.* thieves), robber
volontaire (n)	volunteer
voter	vote, cast a vote
vouloir	want
~ dire	mean
voyage	trip ; journey
~ d'affaires	business trip
voyager	travel
vrai	true
vraiment	really, definitely
vue	view

Y Z

y compris	including
zone	area

Verbes irréguliers

	Infinitif	Prétérit	Participe passé	Traduction
B	be	was/were	been	*être*
	beat /iː/	beat	beaten	*battre*
	bet	bet	bet	*parier*
	become	became	become	*devenir*
	begin	began	begun	*commencer*
	bite /aɪ/	bit /ɪ/	bitten /ɪ/	*mordre*
	blow /əʊ/	blew /uː/	blown /əʊ/	*souffler*
	break	broke	broken	*casser*
	bring	brought	brought	*apporter*
	build /ɪ/	built /ɪ/	built /ɪ/	*construire*
	burn	burnt	burnt	*brûler*
	buy /aɪ/	bought /ɔː/	bought /ɔː/	*acheter*
C	cast	cast	cast	*jeter, lancer*
	catch	caught /ɔː/	caught /ɔː/	*attraper*
	choose	chose /əʊ/	chosen /əʊ/	*choisir*
	come	came /eɪ/	come	*venir*
	cost	cost	cost	*coûter*
	cut /ʌ/	cut /ʌ/	cut /ʌ/	*couper*
D	deal /iː/	dealt /e/	dealt /e/	*distribuer* ; (~ with) *traiter de*
	do	did	done	*faire*
	draw /ɔː/	drew /uː/	drawn /ɔː/	*dessiner*
	dream /iː/	dreamt /e/	dreamt /e/	*rêver*
	drink	drank	drunk	*boire*
	drive /aɪ/	drove /əʊ/	driven /ɪ/	*conduire*
E	eat /iː/	ate /eɪ/	eaten /iː/	*manger*
F	fall /ɔː/	fell /e/	fallen	*tomber*
	feed /iː/	fed /e/	fed /e/	*nourrir*
	feel /iː/	felt	felt	*sentir, ressentir*
	fight /aɪ/	fought /ɔː/	fought /ɔː/	*combattre, se battre*
	find /aɪ/	found /aʊ/	found /aʊ/	*trouver*
	fly /aɪ/	flew /uː/	flown /əʊ/	*voler (dans l'air)*
	forbid /ɪ/	forbade /eɪ/	forbidden	*interdire*
	forget	forgot	forgotten	*oublier*
	forgive	forgave /eɪ/	forgiven	*pardonner*
	freeze /iː/	froze /əʊ/	frozen /əʊ/	*geler*
G	get	got	got	*obtenir ; devenir*
	give	gave /eɪ/	given	*donner*
	go	went	gone	*aller*
	grow /əʊ/	grew /uː/	grown /əʊ/	*grandir, faire pousser*
H	have	had	had	*avoir*
	hear /ɪə/	heard /ɜː/	heard /ɜː/	*entendre*
	hide /aɪ/	hid /ɪ/	hidden /ɪ/	*(se) cacher*
	hit	hit	hit	*frapper*
	hold	held	held	*tenir*
	hurt /ɜː/	hurt /ɜː/	hurt /ɜː/	*(se) faire mal, (se) blesser*
K	keep /iː/	kept /e/	kept /e/	*garder*
	know /əʊ/	knew /juː/	known /əʊ/	*connaître, savoir*

Verbes irréguliers

L	lead /iː/	led /e/	led /e/	*mener, conduire*
	learn /ɜː/	learnt /ɜː/	learnt /ɜː/	*apprendre*
	leave /iː/	left	left	*quitter, partir*
	lend	lent	lent	*prêter*
	let	let	let	*laisser*
	lose /uː/	lost	lost	*perdre*
M	make /eɪ/	made /eɪ/	made /eɪ/	*faire, fabriquer*
	mean /iː/	meant /e/	meant /e/	*signifier, vouloir dire*
	meet /iː/	met /e/	met /e/	*rencontrer*
P	pay /eɪ/	paid /eɪ/	paid /eɪ/	*payer*
	put /ʊ/	put /ʊ/	put /ʊ/	*mettre, poser*
R	read /iː/	read /e/	read /e/	*lire*
	ride /aɪ/	rode /əʊ/	ridden /ɪ/	*faire du cheval, du vélo*
	rise /aɪ/	rose /əʊ/	risen /ɪ/	*se lever*
	ring	rang	rung	*sonner*
	run	ran	run	*courir*
S	say /eɪ/	said /e/	said /e/	*dire*
	see	saw /ɔː/	seen	*voir*
	sell	sold /əʊ/	sold /əʊ/	*vendre*
	send	sent	sent	*envoyer*
	set	set	set	*mettre, poser*
	shake /eɪ/	shook /ʊ/	shaken /eɪ/	*secouer*
	shine	shone	shone	*briller*
	show /əʊ/	showed	shown	*montrer*
	shoot /uː/	shot /ɒ/	shot /ɒ/	*tirer (arme à feu)*
	shut /ʌ/	shut	shut	*fermer*
	sing	sang	sung	*chanter*
	sit	sat	sat	*être assis*
	sleep /iː/	slept /e/	slept /e/	*dormir*
	smell	smelt	smelt	*sentir (odeur)*
	speak /iː/	spoke /əʊ/	spoken /əʊ/	*parler*
	spell	spelt	spelt	*épeler*
	spend	spent	spent	*passer du temps ; dépenser*
	spoil	spoilt	spoilt	*gâter, gâcher*
	spread /e/	spread /e/	spread /e/	*étendre ; répandre*
	stand	stood	stood	*être debout*
	steal /iː/	stole /əʊ/	stolen /əʊ/	*voler (dérober)*
	stick	stuck /ʌ/	stuck /ʌ/	*coller*
	strike /aɪ/	struck /ʌ/	struck /ʌ/	*frapper*
	sweep /iː/	swept /e/	swept /e/	*balayer*
	swim	swam	swum	*nager*
T	take /eɪ/	took /ʊ/	taken /eɪ/	*prendre*
	teach /iː/	taught /ɔː/	taught /ɔː/	*enseigner*
	tell	told /əʊ/	told /əʊ/	*dire, raconter*
	think	thought /ɔː/	thought /ɔː/	*penser*
	throw /əʊ/	threw /uː/	thrown /əʊ/	*jeter*
U	understand	understood	understood	*comprendre*
W	wake up	woke up /əʊ/	woken up /əʊ/	*(se) réveiller*
	wear	wore /ɔː/	worn /ɔː/	*porter (un vêtement)*
	win	won /ʌ/	won /ʌ/	*gagner*
	write /aɪ/	wrote /əʊ/	written /ɪ/	*écrire*

Révise les verbes irréguliers en t'amusant. CD Rom : Verbes irréguliers

Expressions utiles

Encouraging someone.

I'm sure you can do it.	*Je suis sûr(e) que tu peux le faire.*
Well done!	*Bien !*
Have a try / a go!	*Essaie !*
Try again!	*Essaie encore !*
Let's hope for the best!	*Espérons que tout se passe au mieux !*
Do your best.	*Fais de ton mieux.*
Trust me!	*Fais-moi confiance !*

Giving your opinion.

What a brilliant idea!	*Quelle bonne idée !*
It's obvious!	*C'est évident !*
It's all right with me.	*C'est d'accord.*
I agree with you.	*Je suis d'accord avec toi.*
I don't agree with you.	*Je ne suis pas d'accord avec toi.*
I doubt it!	*J'en doute !*
I haven't got a clue / the faintest idea!	*Je n'en ai pas la moindre idée !*
What a shame!	*Quel dommage !*

Using your senses.

That sounds great!	*Ça a l'air bien/super !*
It smells nice!	*Ça sent bon !*
It tastes bitter.	*Ça a un goût amer.*
It feels like silk.	*Ça ressemble à de la soie. (au toucher)*
It looks good!	*Ça a l'air bon !*
Let me have a look!	*Fais voir !*
I'd like to see you try!	*Je voudrais t'y voir !*
We'll see soon enough.	*Nous allons bien voir.*

Expressing feelings.

I'm fed up.	*J'en ai assez.*
Not too soon!	*C'est pas trop tôt !*
Don't lose your temper.	*Ne t'énerve pas.*
I had a good time!	*Je me suis bien amusé(e) !*
I'm longing to see him again.	*Il me tarde de le revoir.*

Checking for understanding.

Do you understand what I mean?	*Tu comprends ce que je veux dire ?*
Does that make sense?	*Est-ce que ça te paraît logique ?*
I see what you mean.	*Je vois ce que tu veux dire.*
I'm not sure I get your point.	*Je ne suis pas sûr(e) de te comprendre.*
I don't get it.	*Je ne vois pas.*

Découvre d'autres expressions! CD Rom : Expressions utiles

Phonétique

Vowels

/ɪ/ swim

/iː/ sleep

/ɒ/ jog

/ɔː/ walk

/æ/ catch

/ɑː/ garden

/ʌ/ run

/ɜː/ turn

/ʊ/ cook

/uː/ move

/e/ rest

/ə/ listen

Diphthongs

/aʊ/ frown

/ɔɪ/ boil

/əʊ/ close

/eə/ repair

/ɪə/ fear

/eɪ/ skate

/aɪ/ climb

Consonants

/θ/ throw

/ð/ bathe

/ʃ/ shave

/tʃ/ teach

/ʒ/ measure

/dʒ/ jump

/ŋ/ sing

/j/ yawn

TABLE DES ILLUSTRATIONS

12 h Famille pakistanaise / ph © Fly Fernandez / Zefa / Corbis • 12 b Aéroport d'Heathrow, Londres. / ph © Felix Clay / Financial Times / REA • 13 h Brick Lane. / ph © Janine Wiedel Photolibrary / Alamy / Photo12 • 13 hd Brick Lane. / ph © Alex Segre / Alamy / Photo12 • 13 b Curry restaurant, Bric Lane. / ph © Jiri Rezac / REA • 14 g Maison, Vermont, États-Unis. / ph © Christophe Boisvieux / Hoa-Qui / Eyedea • 14 d Immeuble à Brick Lane. / p © Geogphotos / Alamy / Photo12 • 15 Elèves de collège. / ph © Kelly Redinger / Design Pics Inc. / Alamy / Photo12 • 16 Oyster card. / ph © Davi Pearson / Alamy / Photo12 • 17 h, bg ph © Brian Lawrence / Imagestate / GHFP / Eyedea • 17 bm ph © Travelshots.com / Alamy / Photo12 • 17 bd p © David Jones / Alamy / Photo12 • 18 hg Las Vegas. / ph © Japack / Sunset • 18 hd Les Experts. / ph © Rue des Archives • 18 bg Sherlock Holmes. ph © H. Armstrong Roberts / Corbis • 18 bd Herbert Menzies Marshall (1841-191), Matin à Parliament Square, 1889, aquarelle sur papier, collectio privée. / ph © Chris Beetles, London, U.K. / The Bridgeman Art Library • 20 g ph © Bettmann / Corbis • 20 d Jaquette vidéo du coffret Megaset. / p © D.R. • 21 Le Crime de l'Orient-Express, film réalisé par Sidney Lumet, 1974, avec Albert Finney dans le rôle d'Hercule Poirot. / Coll. Christophe L • 2 h1 Balles. / ph © Rick Barrentine / Corbis • 22 h2 ph © William Whitehurst / Corbis • 22 h3 ph © Roger-Viollet • 22 h4 ph © Jean-Claude Moschetti REA • 22 h5 ph © D.R. • 22 h6 ph © Mehau Kulyk / Science Photo Library / Cosmos • 22 bg Scène de crime, recherche d'indices. / ph © Ashley Coo per / Corbis • 22 bd Cours magistral, Académie du FBI. / ph © Anna Clopet / Corbis • 23 h Frances Glessner Lee construisant un diorama. / ph © Th Glessner House Museum • 23 b ph © Courtesy of Corinne May Botz • 24 Couverture, A Cry in the Night, Mary Higgins Clark. / ph © D.R. • 25 Couverture, The Collector, John Fowles. / ph © D.R. • 26 hg ph © Joan Street • 26 hd Coll. Christophe L • 26 b Couverture, Predator, Patricia Cornwell. / ph © D.R. • 27 ph © Jessica Kovaks / Sygma / Corbis • 31 Couverture, Postmortem, Patricia Cornwell. / ph © D.R. • 33 Poste de police, Battersea, Londres / ph © Peter Macdiarmid / Getty Images • 34fond de page Reconstitution historique d'un wagon train, Wyoming. / ph © Mike Nelson / AFP / Getty Images • 34 hg Indien chassant un bison, gravure sur bois aquarellée, d'après une peinture de George Catlin, 1840, collection privée. / ph © Akg-Images • 34 hd Biker Navajo, Arizona. / ph © Frilet / Sipa Press • 34 bg Cowboys, Dakota du Sud. / ph © Frilet / Sipa Press • 34 bd L'Ouest sauvage peinture de Harold von Schmidt, vers 1930, collection privée. / ph © Akg-Images • 36 g Jeune homme, Rajasthan. / ph © Dinodia Picture Agence / Sipa Press • 36 d Jeune indienne, Réserve indienne de Hoopa Valley, Californie. / ph © Marilyn Angel Wynn / Nativestock.com / Getty Images • 37 h Jeune Navajo, photographie, vers 1890. / ph © Bettmann / Corbis • 37 b Jeunes Navajos, Utah. / ph © Marilyn Angel Wynn / Nativestock.com / Getty Images / ph © Ronald C. Modra / Sports Imagery / Getty Images • 38 g Chercheurs d'or, Dakota du Sud, photographie de 1889, collection privée. / ph © Bianchetti / Leemage • 38 m Trappeur faisant du troc avec des Indiens, lithographie, 19ème siècle, La Rochelle, Musée du Nouveau Monde. / ph © Photo Josse / Leemage • 38 d Affiche proposant des Terres à vendre, vers 1870. / ph © Bettmann / Corbis • 39 h Cowboys, Oregon. / ph © Frédéric Chehu / Sunset • 39 b Rhinestone cowboy. / ph © Neal Preston / Corbis • 40 Irma Hotel, Cody, Wyoming. / ph © D.R. • 41 g Sitting Bul et Buffalo Bill, photographie de 1886, collection privée. / ph © Selva / Leemage • 41 d Couverture du programme du spectacle de Buffalo Bill The Wild West, vers 1889. / ph © Smithsonian Institution / Corbis • 42-43 Monument Valley, Arizona. / ph © José Fuste Raga / Corbis • 42 h Gravure du 19e siècle, collection privée. / ph © North Wind Pictures / Leemage • 42 b Gouache sur papier, début 20e siècle, collection privée. / ph © Look and Learn / The Bridgeman Art Library • 43 Lithographie, début 20e siècle, collection privée. / ph © Peter Newark American Pictures / The Bridgeman Art Library • 46 Bisons, Parc National de Yellowstone. / ph © Mark Hamblin / Sunset • 47 Totem du Stanley Park, Vancouver, Canada. / ph © Rex Interstock / Sunset • 48 Couverture, Little House on the Prairie, Laura Ingalls Wilder. / ph © D.R. • 49 Reconstitution de la petite maison dans la prairie, d'après les descriptions de Laura Ingalls Wilder, Independence, Kansas./ ph © D.R. • 50 Cabine téléphonique, Londres. / ph © Bruno Perousse / Hoa-Qui / Eyedea• 52 hg Panneau de signalisation, Californie. / ph © André Jenny / Alamy / Photo12 • 52 hm Panneau de signalisation, Idaho. / ph © David R. Frazier Photolibrary Inc. / Alamy / Photo12 • 52 hd Panneau de signalisation, Yorkshire. / ph © Nigel Lloyd / Alamy / Photo12 • 52 m Cycliste, Londres. / ph © Xavier Desmier / Rapho / Eyedea • 52 b Scooter, Londres. / ph © Jensen Ortega / Alamy / Photo12 • 53 Drive Cam, Madison, Wisconsin. / ph © Andy Manis / AP / Sipa Press • 54 hg Campagne de sensibilisation au bullying. / ph © Viennaphoto / Alamy / Photo12 • 54 hm Tentative de vol de portable. / ph © Angela Hampton Picture Library / Alamy / Photo12 • 54 hd Scène de bullying au collège. / ph © Helene Rogers / Alamy / Photo12 • 54 b Ecran d'ordinateur. / ph © Michel Gaillard / REA • 55 Manifestation anti-bullying, Londres. / ph © Janine Wiedel Photolibrary / Alamy / Photo12 • 56 h Tag. / ph © Sébastien Baussais / Alamy / Photo12 • 56 b Nettoyage de tags. / ph © Gisone / Olympia / Sipa Press • 57 h Pochoir. / ph © D.R. • 57 b Pochoir. / ph © James Clarke Images / Alamy / Photo12 • 58 h ph © Jérôme Eagland Conquy / NoManzland / Picturetank • 58 b ph © GAPA • 59 ph © Vanessa Burger / Images of Africa Photobank / Alamy / Photo12 • 63 Trivial Pursuit. / ph © Sylva Villerot / REA • 65 ph © Roadwitch.org.uk • 66 hg Inde, deux frères. / ph © Roland et Sabrina Michaud / Rapho / Eyedea • 66 hd Opéra de Sydney. / ph © Ludovic Maisant / hemis.fr • 66 mg Célébration de la culture aborigène à Saint Michaels School, Palm Island, Queensland, Australie. / ph © Cameron Laird / Rex Features / Sipa Press • 66 md Ségrégation, fontaine à eau, vers 1960. / ph © Bettmann / Corbis • 66 bg Le Club des Présidents, Barack Obama, George W. Bush, Bill Clinton, George H. W. Bush, Jimmy Carter, le 7 janvier 2009. / ph © J. Scott Applewhite / AP / Sipa Press • 66 bd Une femme Dalit, New Delhi. / ph © Mikkel Ostergaard / PANOS-REA • 68 Esclaves noirs récoltant le coton en Géorgie. / ph © Bettmann / Corbis • 69 hg Dessin satirique de Bill Mauldin publié le 15 mai 1962 dans le Saint Louis Post-Dispatch. / ph © D.R. • 69 hd Vote des afro-américains aux Elections Primaires, 4 juillet 1946, Jackson, Mississipi. / ph © Bettmann / Corbis • 69 m Barack Obama. / ph © Emmanuel Dunand / AFP Photo • 69 b ph © John Bazemore / AP / Sipa Press • 70 h © D.R. • 70 b Le navigateur James Cook (1728-1779) arrivant à Tahiti le 13 avril 1769, gravure sur acier de Carl Mayer, vers 1845. / ph © Akg-Images • 71 ph © D.R. • 72 h ph © Johnston Christie / Sipa Press • 72 b ph © Luciano Mortula / Alamy / Photo12 • 73 Bombay. / ph © Bruno Perousse / Hoa-Qui / Eyedea • 74 h ph © AP / Sipa Press • 74 b ph © Bettmann / Corbis • 75 h ph © AP / Sipa Press • 75 b ph © Bettmann / Corbis • 78 Jeunes filles travaillant à la récupération de chiffons, bidonville d'Indore, Inde. / ph © Jean-Claude Coutausse / Rapho / Eyedea • 79 h Militants pour les Droits Civiques défilant entre une rangée de tanks et les Gardes nationaux, baïonnettes aux fusils, Memphis, Tennessee, 1968. / ph © Bettmann / Corbis • 79 b © D.R. • 81 ph © Danny Lyon / Magnum Photos • 82 Fond de page Lever de Terre, Mission Apollo 11, 21 juillet 1969. / ph © NASA / Ciel et Espace • 82 h1 Maldives, Atoll Faafu. / ph © Bertrand Gardel / hemis.fr • 82 h2 Femme au bureau. / ph © Michel Gaillard / REA • 82 h3 Collégienne. / ph © Ian Shaw / Alamy / Photo12 • 82 h4 Second Life. / ph © Jean-Claude Moschetti / REA • 82 bg Père célibataire. / ph © Michel Gaillard / REA • 82 bd Robot ASIMO, Honda, 2008. / ph © Kurita Kaku / Gamma / Eyedea Presse • 85 h1 Billet de banque de Nouvelle-Zélande. / ph © Mob Images / Alamy / Photo12 • 85 h2 Enseigne de magasin. / ph © Dauwe / Planet Reporters – REA • 85 h3 Panneau de signalisation. / ph © David Hancock / Alamy / Photo12 • 85 h4 Panneau de signalisation. / ph © Nick Hanna / Alamy / Photo12 • 85 h5 Panneau de signalisation. / ph © Duncan Snow / Alamy / Photo12 • 85 b Statue Maori, Nouvelle-Zélande. / ph © Picture Finders / Sunset • 86 Jeu video The Lord of the Rings, The return of the King. / © D.R. • 88 Affiche du film Red Planet réalisé par Antony Hoffman avec Val Kilmer, 2000. / Coll. Christophe L • 88 Affiche du film I, robot réalisé par Alex Proyas avec Will Smith, 2004. / Coll. Christophe L • 89 h Scène du film I, robot réalisé par Alex Proyas avec Will Smith et Bridget Moynahan, 2004. / ph © 20th Century Fox / The Kobal Collection • 89 bg Chien robot AIBO ERS-7M3, Sony, 2005. / ph © Yoshikazu Tsuno / AFP Photo • 89 bd Robot humanoïde, NICT, Japon. / ph © Paolo Patrizi / Alamy / Photo12 • 90, 91 h ph © Courtesy of The Museum of New Zealand Te Papa Tongarewa • 91 b Coll. Christophe L • 94 Scène du film Into the Wild réalisé par Sean Penn avec Emile Hirsch, 2007. / ph © River Road / Paramount / The Kobal Collection • 95 h Adolescent. / ph © Michel Gaillard / REA • 95 b ph © Bertrand Gardel / hemis.fr • 96 ph © Robotics & Multibody Mechanics Research Group (R&MM), Bruxelles • 97 ph © Greg Vaughn / Alamy / Photo12 • 98 hg Fête d'anniversaire. / ph © David Young-Wolff / Alamy / Photo12 • 98 hd Saint Patrick, Dublin. / ph © Frilet / Sipa Press • 98 bg Famille américaine. / ph © Jupiterimages / AFP • 98 bd Supporters anglais, Coupe du Monde de Rugby 2007. / ph © Michael Sawyer / AP / Sipa Press • 100 g Parade du Carnaval de Notting Hill, Londres, 2007. / ph © Wenn / Sipa Press • 100 hd Carnaval de Notting Hill, Londres. / ph © Anthony Thorogood / Alamy / Photo12 • 100 bd Vendeuse de beignets, Carnaval de Notting Hill, Londres. / ph © Getty Images / AFP • 101 h Arrêt de bus, Londres. / ph © Eric Nathan / Alamy / Photo12 • 101 b Adolescents. / ph © John Powell Photographer / Alamy / Photo12 • 102 h Adolescents, Ottawa, Ontario. / ph © Garry Black / Alamy / Photo12 • 102 b The Canadian Cowgirls Association, Canada Day. / ph © Jeff McIntosh / AP / Sipa Press • 103 ph © Louise Oligny / Gamma / Hachette Photos Presse • 104 g Lauréate entourée de ses parents. / ph © Bill Bachmann / Alamy / Photo12 • 104 d Graduation Day 2006, Université de Birmingham, West Midlands. / ph © John James / Alamy / Photo12 • 105 h Etudiants, Prom Night 2006. / ph © A. T. Willett / Alamy / Photo12 • 105 b Couple d'étudiants. / ph © Najlah Feanny / Corbis • 106 h ph © Tessa Oksanen / Alamy / Photo12 • 106 b ph © Jason Baxter / Alamy / Photo12 • 107 ph © DGB / Alamy / Photo12 • 111 h Collège, Saint Paul, Minnesota. / ph © Steve Skjold / Alamy / Photo12 • 111 m Roi et Reine de la Prom Night. / ph © Nicole Lacour Young / AP / Sipa Press • 111 b Etudiante et équipe de reporters. / ph © David Stonner / AP / Sipa Press • 113 ph © Jupiterimages / AFP • 122 ph © 2009 by PAWS, Inc. • 123 ph © United Feature Syndicate Inc., 2009 / Gary Groth, 2009 • 128 ph © David Hockney

CRÉDITS DES TEXTES

p. 21 © The Mysterious Affair at Styles by Agatha Christie. D.R. • p. 23 The Forensic Examiner, American College of Forensic Examiners Institute • p. 24 Reprinted with the permission of Pocket Books, a Division of Simon & Schuster, Inc,. from back cover of A Cry in the Night by Mary Higgins Clark (New York: Pocket Books, 2004) • p. 25 © John Fowles, The Collector (1963). Alexander Aitken. D.R. • p. 32 © Jim Sukach, Baffling Whodunit Puzzles: Dr Quicksolve mini mysteries (1997). Sterling Publishing D.R. • p. 37 www.Mondovista.com. Gary Vey / editor/ viewzone.com • p. 49 www.littlehouseontheprairie.com D.R. • p. 53 www.ghsa.org. D.R • p. 55 www.anti-bullyingalliance.org.uk • p. 65 www.oxfordmail.net • p. 69 Los Angeles Times, "A range of emotions as black voters cast ballots in Southern California" by Mitchell L and Sberg, published November 5, 2008. • p. 80 Mulk Raj Anand, Untouchable (1935). Penguin D.R. • p. 84 www.guestnewzealand.com • p. 85 http://www.nzyourway.com • p. 88 « Reason », © 1941 by Street and Smith Publications, Inc., from I ROBOT by Isaac asimov. Used by permission of bantam Books, a division of Random House, Inc. • p. 96 www.we-make-money-not-art.com. D.R. • p. 102 www.brontevillage.net. D.R. • p. 103 www.cic.gc.ca, Minister of Public Works and Government Services Canada, 2009. Adapted and reproduced with the permission of the Minister of Public Works and Government Services Canada, 2009. • p. 117-120 www.ilhawaii.net; D.R. • p. 121 © Shel Silverstein

Copyright CD Elève

Piste 21 © Robert Frenette. D.R. • Piste 27 © Chicago Review Press. D.R. • Piste 30 © Australian Human Rights Commission. • Pistes 32-34 © Mike Dowling. D.R. • Piste 52 www.northbayliteracycouncil.ca • Piste 54 © Chis Gallatin. D.R.

Achevé D'imprimer en Italie par Rotolito Lombarda
Dépôt légal n° 118174 - Avril 2009

UNITED KINGDOM
AND
REPUBLIC OF IRELAND
Shetland Islands
Orkney Islands
Outer Hebrides
Loch Ness
Aberdeen
Braemar
ATLANTIC OCEAN
SCOTLAND
NORTH SEA
Dunoon
Glasgow
Edinburgh
Clyde
Tweed
Tyne
Newcastle-upon-Tyne
NORTHERN IRELAND
Belfast
Isle of Man
Leeds
Galway
DUBLIN
Liverpool
Manchester
Sheffield
Shannon
REPUBLIC OF IRELAND (EIRE)
IRISH SEA
Nottingham
Trent
Limerick
Tamworth
Birmingham
ENGLAND
Warwick
Stratford-upon-Avon
Cambridge
Severn
WALES
Cork
Oxford
LONDON
Thames
Cardiff
Bristol
Canterbury
Channel Tunnel
Dover
Calais
Southampton
Brighton
Exeter
Isle of Wight
English Channel
Guernsey
Jersey
FRANCE
100 miles

THE UNITED STATES OF AMERICA
CANADA
MEXICO
PACIFIC OCEAN
ATLANTIC OCEAN
Gulf of Mexico
THE BAHAMAS
CUBA
Lake Superior
Lake Michigan
Lake Huron
Lake Ontario
Lake Erie
Missouri
Mississippi
Colorado
Rio Grande
WASHINGTON
Olympia
Seattle
OREGON
Salem
CALIFORNIA
Sacramento
San Francisco
Los Angeles
Las Vegas
NEVADA
Carson City
IDAHO
Boise
MONTANA
Helena
WYOMING
Cody
Cheyenne
UTAH
Salt Lake City
ARIZONA
Phoenix
Canyon de Chelly
COLORADO
Denver
NEW MEXICO
Santa Fe
Bosque Redondo
NORTH DAKOTA
Bismarck
SOUTH DAKOTA
Pierre
NEBRASKA
Lincoln
KANSAS
Topeka
OKLAHOMA
Oklahoma City
TEXAS
Austin
Dallas
MINNESOTA
Saint Paul
IOWA
Des Moines
MISSOURI
Jefferson City
Independence
ARKANSAS
Little Rock
LOUISIANA
Baton Rouge
New Orleans
WISCONSIN
Madison
ILLINOIS
Springfield
Chicago
MICHIGAN
Lansing
INDIANA
Indianapolis
OHIO
Columbus
KENTUCKY
Frankfort
TENNESSEE
Nashville
MISSISSIPPI
Jackson
ALABAMA
Montgomery
GEORGIA
Atlanta
FLORIDA
Tallahassee
Miami
SOUTH CAROLINA
Columbia
NORTH CAROLINA
Raleigh
VIRGINIA
Richmond
WEST VIRGINIA
Charleston
Washington D.C.
Annapolis
Dover
PENNSYLVANIA
Harrisburg
NEW YORK
Albany
New York
Trenton
Hartford
Providence
Boston
Harvard
Concord
Montpelier
MAINE
Augusta
1
2
3
4
5
6
7
8
1. VERMONT
2. NEW HAMPSHIRE
3. MASSACHUSETTS
4. RHODE ISLAND
5. CONNECTICUT
6. NEW JERSEY
7. DELAWARE
8. MARYLAND
250 miles
RUSSIA
ALASKA
Anchorage
CANADA
Juneau
250 miles
HAWAII
Honolulu
125 miles